A Daunting Journey

Ndirangu Wachanga
With best wishes
[signature]
10/01/16.

Jeremiah Gitau Kiereini

Edited by
Mutu wa Gethoi

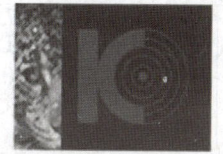

Kenway Publications

Published by
Kenway publications
an imprint of
East African Educational Publishers Ltd.
Brick Court, Mpaka Road/Woodvale Grove
Westlands, P.O. Box 45314
Nairobi – 00100
KENYA.

email: eaep@eastafricanpublishers.com
website: www.eastafricanpublishers.com

East African Educational Publishers Ltd.
C/O Gustro Ltd.
P.O. BOX 9997
Kampala
UGANDA.

Ujuzi Books Ltd.
P.O. Box 38260
Dar es Salaam
TANZANIA.

East African Publishers Rwanda Ltd.
Tabs Plaza, Kimironko Road,
Opposite Kigali Institute of Education
P.O. Box 5151, Kigali
RWANDA.

© Jeremiah Gitau Kiereini 2014

First published 2014
Reprinted 2015

All Rights Reserved.

ISBN 978-9966-25-978-3

Printed in Kenya by
Printwell Industries Ltd.
P.O. Box 5216-0506
Nairobi, Kenya

Contents

Dedication v
Foreword vi
Preface ix
Acknowledgements.. xi
Abbreviations... xii
Maps xiv
Prologue xvii
Chapter 1: The Early Years 1
Chapter 2: Growing up in a Time of Division 9
Chapter 3: School in a Season of War...................... 32
Chapter 4: Makerere and After 49
Chapter 5: Working on the 'Pipeline' 85
Chapter 6: From Rehabilitator to Administrator...... 109
Chapter 7: Taking Over from the Colonialists 121
Chapter 8: The New World of Independence........... 141
Chapter 9: Running the Defence Docket 165
Chapter 10: Fear and Uncertainty............................. 175
Chapter 11: At the Helm of the Civil Service 182
Chapter 12: Crushing the 1982 Coup Attempt......... 191
Chapter 13: Bowing out of Service........................... 210
Chapter 14: Family Life and Community Service... 218
Chapter 15: The World of Business 235
Chapter 16: Reflections.. 246
Annex 254
Index 259

Kenway biographies/autobiographies

1. *A Fly in Amber*, Susan Wood
2. *A Love Affair with the Sun*, Michael Blundell
3. *Facing Mount Kenya*, Jomo Kenyatta
4. *From Simple to Complex: The Journey of a Herdsboy*, Prof Joseph Maina Mungai
5. *Illusion of Power*, GG Kariuki
6. *The Mediator: General Sumbeiywo and the Sudan Peace Process*, Waithaka Waihenya
7. *Madatally Manji: Memoirs of a Biscuit Baron*, Madatally Manji
8. *My Journey Through African Heritage*, Allan Donovan
9. *Nothing but the Truth*, Yusuf K Dawood
10. *Tales from Africa*, Douglas Collins
11. *Theatre Near the Equator*, Annabel Maule
12. *The Southern Sudan: Struggle for Liberty*, Elijah Malok
13. *Wings of the Wind*, Valerie Cuthbert
14. *Tom Mboya: The Man Kenya Wanted to Forget*, David Goldsworthy
15. *Not Yet Uhuru*, Jaramogi Oginga Odinga
16. *Freedom and After*, Tom Mboya
17. *Dreams in a Time of War*, Ngũgĩ wa Thiong'o
18. *Beyond Expectations: From Charcoal to Gold*, Njenga Karume with Mutu wa Gethoi
19. *A Profile of Kenyan Entreprenuers*, Wanjiru Waithaka and Evans Majeni
20. *Running for Black Gold: Fifty Years of African Athletics*, Kevin Lillis
21. *Kiraitu Murungi: An Odyssey in Kenyan Politics*, Peter Kagwanja with Humphrey Ringera
22. *In the House of the Interpreter*, Ngũgĩ wa Thiong'o
23. *Kenyan Student Airlifts to America, 1959-1961: An Educational Odyssey*, Robert F Stephens
24. *A Daunting Journey*, Jeremiah Gitau Kiereini
25. *Dash Before Dusk, A slave descendant's journey in freedom*, Joe Khamisi

Dedication

"Nothing gives greater joy than tackling a daunting challenge and being successful."

These memoirs are dedicated to our son, Mburu, who passed away on 13 August 2010, struck down by Motor Neurone Disease (MND) in the prime of his life. This is my humble appreciation of the joy he gave to Muringo and I, as his parents, to his wife Wambui, his son Gitau, and his siblings, during his tragically shortened life.

It is my hope that, with due humility, my reflections on life will be a fitting tribute to the qualities Mburu exemplified. One of these was his unfathomable courage in the face of great adversity.

As the debilitating illness took its toll and Mburu came to know his destiny, he never complained and often told his wife, Wambui, "I don't understand why people feel sorry for me. I have been and continue to be blessed abundantly."

Mburu had high moral standards and never compromised his principles. He was always committed to excellence, whether at work or in play. This was evident throughout his academic career at St Mary's School in Nairobi, Sherborne School in Dorset, England, and in the London School of Economics (LSE). After he graduated from LSE in 1995 and joined the banking world, he rose to the position of Industry Head of Corporate Banking, Barclays Bank of Kenya.

Mburu loved the outdoors and the sporting life, especially rugby and football. He also had a great sense of humour, often self-deprecating. Furthermore, he loved children and his interactions with them were never patronising. The birth of his son, Gitau, was therefore one of the greatest joys in his life.

My earnest desire in these memoirs is that they become a constant reminder of the ideals and commitments that Mburu held so high.

Foreword

After the lull that followed the immediate post-independence autobiographies published by such pioneers as J.M. Kariuki, Oginga Odinga, and Bildad Kaggia, among others, something wonderful is happening on Kenya's literary scene. The pace at which fresh autobiographies are being released is very commendable. In less than a decade, we have seen more than twenty interesting autobiographies published by Kenyans who have wanted to share their life stories. From renowned artists, writers, scientists and academics to businessmen and politicians, like Muthoni Likimani, Wambui Otieno, Prof. Ngugi wa Thiong'o, Dr Benjamin Kipkorir, Hon. Simeon Nyachae, Hon. G.G. Kariuki, former President Daniel arap Moi, Prof. Wangari Maathai, Dr Martin Oduor-Otieno, Hon. Njenga Karume, Prof. Joseph Mungai, Dr Betty Gikonyo and former Prime Minister Hon. Raila Odinga, the diversity has been impressive. Kenya's story is being told through many colourful voices and perspectives.

Even more fascinating is the number of recent biographies from persons who have served in senior levels of the public service. The list is remarkable: former head of public service and cabinet minister Simeon Nyachae's *Walking Through the Corridors of Service,* former minister for internal security G.G. Kariuki's *Illusions of Power*: *Fifty Years in Kenyan Politics,* former head of civil service and governor of the Central Bank Duncan Ndegwa's *Walking in Kenyatta Struggles,* former Director of Criminal Investigation Department Francis arap Sang's *A Noble But Onerous Duty,* former Prime Minister Raila Odinga's *The Flame of Freedom* and now former head of the public service Jeremiah Kiereini's *A Daunting Journey.*

I was surprised and delighted when I was asked by Jeremiah Kiereini to introduce readers to his autobiography. I was delighted because it took over ten years for him to succumb to unending calls from his peers, his golfing colleagues and friends to document his memoirs. It is a real honour for me to be able to do this for one of my oldest friends.

As a student of Kenya's history, I welcome this addition to the growing body of literature documenting the long struggle to build our nation and its institutions; undoubtedly our annals and archives are much the richer for it. As with all good biographies, this book is more than the story of a man and the times he lived in, it is the story of an epoch and the many people who defined it.

I have known Jeremiah Kiereini for two decades. We have debated – mostly very animatedly – a variety of issues ranging from history and politics to culture, religion and, of course, his beloved schools: Alliance High School and Makerere. He has, without doubt, a deep reservoir of knowledge on our history, our society and our politics; he is one of the last great oral historians – a wonderful storyteller – of our times. I always found his reminiscences of the events that shaped post-independence Kenya, and the role he played in them, very fascinating. On several occasions, I encouraged him to record these experiences for posterity as I felt that his story needed to reach a wider audience.

Indeed, it was fascinating to hear Kiereini berate our mutual friend, Mutu wa Gethoi, for incessantly nudging and prodding him to write his story and let it enter our body of national literature.

We often wondered how a Mau Mau oath-taker, seemingly of two minds – both for and against, loyal and disloyal – would not relate how this came to be.

I was, therefore, very pleasantly surprised to learn that this truly reluctant biographer actually had – without alerting anyone – written this amazing account of his life and times.

I am, therefore, overjoyed to write this *Foreword*.

Kiereini's biography is an amazing story of resilience, perseverance and sheer dogged determination to overcome adversity and to serve his country. He tells the fascinating story of his life in a most lyrical and eloquent manner. Equally, he narrates the story of a fledgling nation and the men and women who shaped its destiny with the awesome insights of an insider.

Some biographies tend to be a monotonous narrative of the personal voyage of the writer's life and a few can be quite self-aggrandising. This is not the case with this wonderful story of a man who has truly lived the Kenyan dream, who tells his story in a manner that is both humbling and inspiring. With this memoir, Kenya is the richer.

Indeed, it is through the gradual but deliberate natural accumulation of annals of a people that a nation documents its past. Those who do not know their past, nor know from whence they came, are to be pitied, and they certainly will not know where or how they fare in comparison. This autobiography ranges from the recollections of a virtually traditional, if deprived, childhood that young *Gitau wa Kiereini* trudged through in 1930s, to the rough exposure of racial discrimination inflicted by the colonial education system and on to the systematic if rushed transition from colonial to an African administration in Kenya at independence. Through the rough and tumble of post independence politics, this story is narrated boldly and incisively. Here is a truly reluctant biographer who has challenged all of us to tell our stories, too.

Prof. Githu Muigai
Attorney General
Republic of Kenya
20 October 2013

Preface

By reaching the decision to document his life experience, Elder Jerry Gitau Kiereini has proved that Kenyans care about their past and their cultural identity. Truly, our people are keen about their past, so much so that in social gatherings and in the social media, individuals passionately debate their recent history.

If we do not tell our own stories, others may write it, but they may distort it out of all recognition. Jerry agrees with me.

Jerry has decided to open up his life history to the public gaze and, because all biographies are personal, he has bravely put himself in the line of fire from an army of readers, not excluding academicians, historians and those dissectors called 'literary critics'.

Even more importantly, Jerry is one of those rare Kenyans who confidently transited Kenya's three governmental regimes as a senior civil servant in the Colonial Administration, under Kenyatta and as the Head of Civil Service and Secretary to the Cabinet in Moi's regime and latterly, at the pinnacle of the captains of industry.

As is clearly demonstrated in the pages that follow, Jerry is a storyteller in his own right and he surely has a unique and fascinating story to tell. For a nationalist who knowingly took the Mau Mau oath of unity, though he had philosophical reservations about violence, there are few who match such a variegated lifespan.

How Kenya's nascent civil service assumed responsibility and transited from the British monarchy-oriented administration into the republican model and highly nationalistic civil administration comes out clearly in his narrative. One need only compare the management of Kenya's economy and governance with what we have witnessed in, for example, former Belgian Congo, Somalia or even Zimbabwe, to appreciate the differences with those who inherited post-independence Kenya.

The best of the colonial legacy was carried forward in the likes of Jerry.

Naturally, some will poke holes in Jerry's narrative and, while that is to be expected, there is a limit to personal or family details. Equally, there is no doubt that there are a few sensitive aspects of the story that Jerry could have enlightened the public on, if it were not for his modesty and his hesitation to hurt colleagues or others who are still alive, or indeed, over some elements touching on national security.

Jerry very much regrets that he did not retain notes or archive documents while he worked in the public service. Good memory pays dividends.

Mutu wa Gethoi
Independent Scholar
mgethoi@yahoo.com
March 2014

Acknowledgements

I would like to thank all those who made the publication of this book possible. Working under Professor Mutu wa Gethoi, the House of History team, that is Dorothea Holi, Loise Gakenia King'ori, together with Joe Mwega Nugi, John Njonjo Kihuria, Wahome Karengo, Neville D. Masika and Emma Malmqvist, have my profound thanks for organising and arranging these recollections and memories into a coherent and readable form. The team's careful attention to detail, their probing questions, research and meticulous translation (wherever this proved necessary) have been woven into a manuscript that covers many of the remarkable and challenging events of my life, which will hopefully provide the reader with insights and thought-provoking stimulus.

I am especially indebted to Mutu for initiating this project. Without his persistence and energy, this project may never have seen the light of day. His passionate interest, searching curiosity and probing analysis of cultural history have created a perceptive and vibrant backdrop to my personal history.

I would also like to thank Prof. Micere Mugo, Mumbi Kiereini and Githae Kiereini for careful reading and thoughtful review of the manuscript, their advice and many suggestions.

Furthermore, I owe thanks to my wife, Eunice Muringo Kiereini, for her moral support and encouragement. My deep appreciation must also go to my golfing colleagues, especially for constantly persuading me to produce my memoirs.

My sincere thanks go to my publishers for agreeing to bring my book to the public, its shortcomings notwithstanding. Their team of dedicated editors and designers went out of their way to ensure this book became available to the public.

Jeremiah Kiereini
March 2014

Abbreviations

ADB	–	African Development Bank
AP	–	Administration Police
ARGA	–	Assistant Regional Government Agent
ASK	–	Agricultural Society of Kenya
BAT	–	British American Tobacco
BBC	–	British Broadcasting Corporation
CDF	–	Constituency Development Fund
CDO	–	Community Development Officer
CEO	–	Chief Executive Officer
CID	–	Criminal Investigation Department
CMA	–	Capital Markets Authority
CMC	–	Cooper Motor Corporation
CMS	–	Church Missionary Society
CPE	–	Certificate of Primary Examination
CSR	–	Corporate Social Responsibility
DA	–	District Assistant
DC	–	District Commissioner
DO	–	District Officer
DRC	–	Democratic Republic of Congo
EABL	–	East African Breweries Limited
EATUC	–	East African Trade Union Congress
EBS	–	Elder of the Order of the Burning Spear
EGH	–	Elder of the Order of the Golden Heart of Kenya
GEMA	–	Gikuyu Embu Meru Association
GMS	–	Gospel Missionary Society
GSU	–	General Service Unit
HQ	–	Headquarters
IBEACo	–	Imperial British East Africa Company

ICDC	–	Industrial and Commercial Development Corporation
ICN	–	International Council of Nurses
KADU	–	Kenya African Democratic Union
KANU	–	Kenya African National Union
KAPE	–	Kenya African Preliminary Examination
KAU	–	Kenya African Union
KBC	–	Kenya Broadcasting Corporation
KBL	–	Kenya Breweries Limited
KCA	–	Kikuyu Central Association
KISA	–	Kikuyu Independent Schools Association
KNTC	–	Kenya National Trading Corporation
KNUT	–	Kenya National Union of Teachers
KPCU	–	Kenya Planters Cooperative Union
KPU	–	Kenya Peoples Party
LegCo	–	Legislative Council
LSE	–	London School of Economics
MND	–	Motor Neurone Disease
MP	–	Member of Parliament
MRA	–	Moral Re-Armament
NEMA	–	National Environmental Management Authority
NFD	–	Northern Frontier District
OAU	–	Organisation of African Unity
ODM	–	Orange Democratic Movement
OHMS	–	On Her Majesty's Service
PC	–	Provincial Commissioner
PCEA	–	Presbyterian Church of East Africa
PNU	–	Party of National Unity
PS	–	Permanent Secretary
PWC	–	PricewaterhouseCoopers
REP	–	Rural Electrification Programme
SABL	–	South African Breweries Limited
UDV	–	United Distiller and Vintners
UK	–	United Kingdom
USA	–	United States of America
VIP	–	Very Important Person
VoK	–	Voice of Kenya

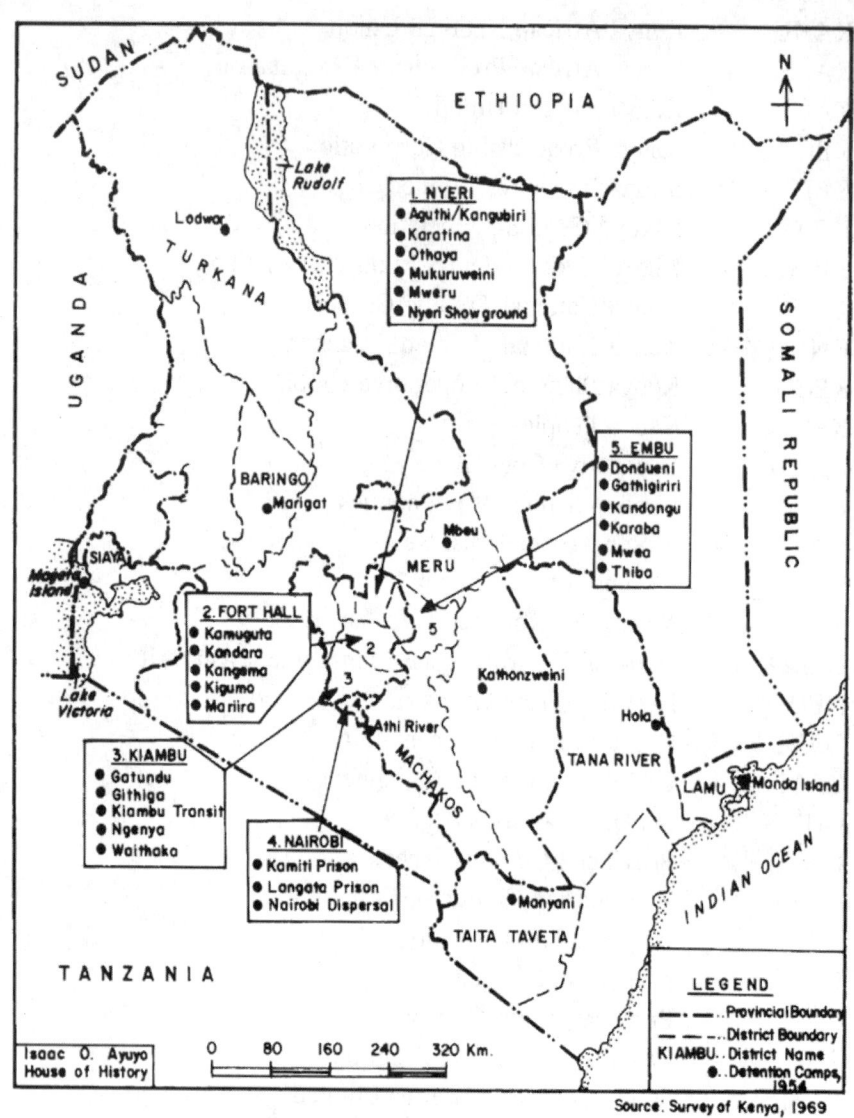

Detention camps in Kenya, 1954.

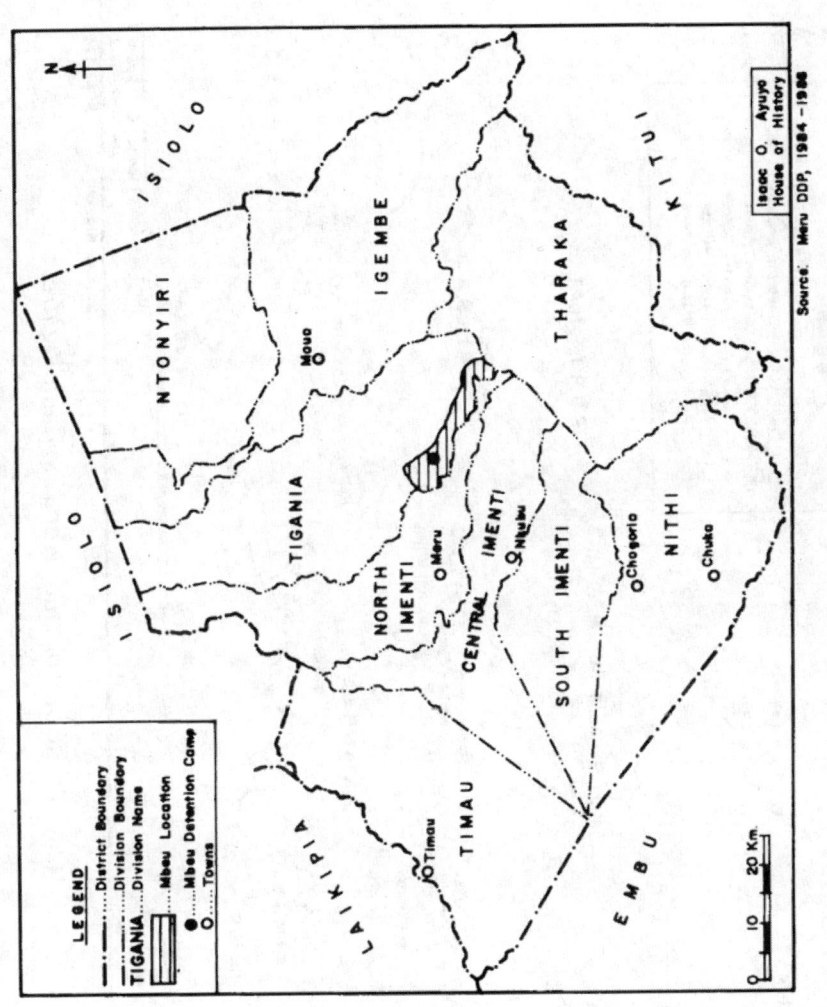

Mbeu detention camp.

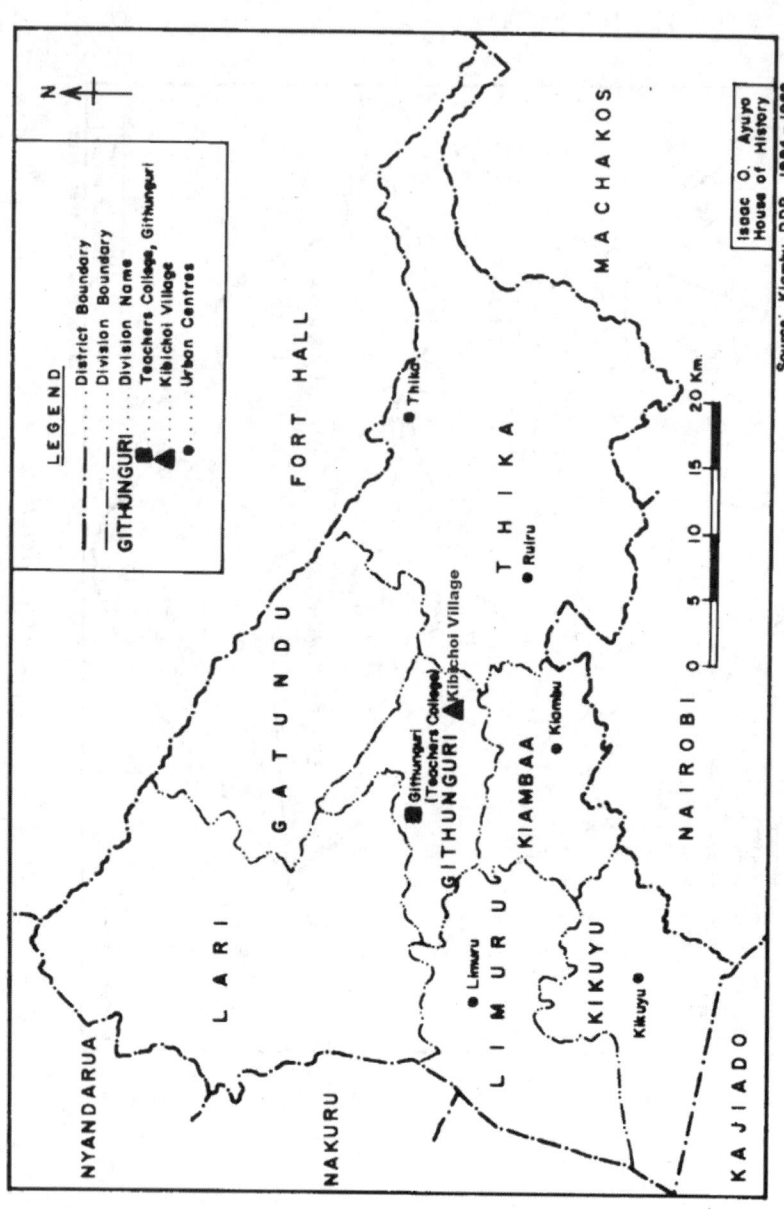

Kibichoi village and surrounding areas.

Prologue

My story does not complete the history of events to which I was witness. There are truths not yet ripe for revelation and I have no desire to attain the short-lived fame that accompanies the loose disclosure of scandal and gossip.

In some cases, I feel the sensitive facts are not mine to tell, as they concern so many family descendants. In others, I was simply not privy to the facts, and the speculation I might occupy myself with serves no purpose. I am still guided by the trust, confidence and loyalty that was once placed in me as a civil servant, and now, as an elder in the community of Kenya.

Discretion, in this case, is strength, while the bald truth is the path to dissention.

There is no doubt in my mind that the details of the few haunting tragedies that Kenya stumbled through in the past and the faltering steps that we still make in the present day will be fully revealed and brought to light. It is inevitable.

But it is not my place to do so.

The reader will find here the story of my struggles, the events I lived through, and the friends and family who accompanied me in my daunting journey through life's challenges. I have done my best to be as accurate as I can, with the facts as I recall them.

Most of all, I wish to give tribute to those who made sacrifices for me, especially early in my life, to those who stepped in with that extra bit of assistance when I needed it, and to those who gave me understanding and trust, in spite of their doubts. My long life has been enriched by the companionship of many individuals and I thank them all.

In a fundamental way, the simplicity of my childhood is in direct contradiction to the course my life has taken over the subsequent years. As a youngster, I had no indication of what type of life I would lead, and this is, I believe, the mystery and adventure of living.

Prologue

It seems natural to contemplate my childhood and my youth, and to appreciate my roots and background. My progression in life to where I am today seems normal and ordinary, one event naturally following another, one stage of life leading to the next, and it all seems logical and systematic. I would like to delude myself that it all came about from my own direction, guided by my own will.

Like any mature experienced man of my age, however, I know well that there were a great many events over which I had no control. These events, and the stream of historical forces that were a background to my life, played a large part in making me what I am, enabling me to transit three distinct government regimes, the colonial experience, Jomo Kenyatta's rule and Moi's administration, not to mention my later life in business and investment.

There were also times when exceptional turns of fate and seemingly extraordinary twists of luck intervened and gave me chances and opportunities that others never had. Perhaps a man is shaped more by chance and opportunity than by any other forces in life.

I am proud of the fact that, although I experienced many problems and difficulties in life, I have survived to see such incredibly vast changes in the world and in my personal circumstances. Today, technical and social developments overwhelm us with such rapid progression that I am virtually certain the younger generation has no idea of the conditions of life in those early days – the painful struggles, the heartbreak and the victories we experienced – as we evolved from a traditional way of life to that of a modern independent Kenyan nation.

In conclusion, I feel the need to add some words of advice for future generations. Yet what can one say that has not been said many times before ... and what can one say that will be taken to heart? These last few years have been characterised by emotional accusations and misinterpretations of my actions in the past, and it troubles me to find myself so misunderstood.

Perhaps that is the fate of all pioneers. Immediate history judges us harshly and emotionally as it awaits the passage of time and gathering objectivity, until the truth and our accomplishments are recognised for what they truly were. I have always tried to do my duty, I have been loyal to my government, and I have cherished my country. I have always acted responsibly, applied myself diligently and exercised all necessary caution and honesty to preserve the dignity and effective service that has given me a fulfilling life.

Above all, I have treasured and valued my family. Without them, everything would have been meaningless.

In moments of contemplation, I sometimes find this transition through life's unpredictable pathways amazing. I believe that fact on its own is a compelling reason to write a memoir. I owe it to my grandchildren and to my countrymen.

Jeremiah Gitau Kiereini (EBS, EGH)
October 2013

Chapter 1

The Early Years

The 'Great Depression' had begun with the Wall Street financial crash in 1929. That year, Vatican City became an independent state and women in Britain were finally declared 'full adults'. The All-India conference in Lahore demanded independence for the sub-continent, and the great American civil rights leader, Martin Luther King, and the future Palestinian leader, Yasser Arafat, were born.

We knew little of what was happening outside the immediate surroundings of Kibichoi village, where I was born on 9 July 1929. My father must have been in his late sixties at the time, whereas my mother must have been in her late thirties or early forties.

Kiereini has not always been our family name. My father was Gakure wa Marai. The 'wa Marai' portion of the name means 'son of Marai', Marai being my paternal grandfather.

As leader of his sub-clan, my father had authority to ensure good parenting practices in the families within the neighbourhood. He had a habit of checking in at various homesteads to verify that the children had been properly fed. If the mothers had millet porridge on hand, he was certain that the children had had something to eat during the day.

Millet was a vital element of the diet of that time. Millet porridge was eaten almost daily, as tea and coffee are taken nowadays. As people did not eat much meat, it was a vital source of protein.

If there was no evidence that porridge had been prepared, my father would suspect that the children had remained without food and would therefore scold the mothers for neglecting their children. He took it as his personal mission to ensure that no child went hungry. He insisted that young mothers be efficient and well-organised, particularly when it concerned nurturing and bringing up children.

Soon, the women started to resent his daily inspections. Moreover, it was not always possible to have millet porridge in the homestead, especially during the dry seasons. If they had no porridge and saw my father approaching, they would hide in their farms or in the nearby

bushes. Eventually they rebelled. They refused to tolerate his surveys and made the remark that he should go live inside clusters of millet grain stalks, *kiere-ini*, so that he could have the ingredients for porridge any time he wanted. Kiereini thus became his nickname.

On occasion, he was also referred to as *Kihumba*, a nickname that means a 'large man', in reference to his stature and size, but perhaps also to his authoritarian character.

My mother, Njuhi, had a severely deprived childhood because she was orphaned when she was just a baby after her parents died of the bubonic plague that swept central Kenya in the late 1800s.

Historically, the eastern coast of Africa is prone to extreme vagaries of the weather, the worst being regular occurrence of long droughts when the two-season monsoon rains fail for a year or more. This impacts heavily on production of food for the human population, and scarcity of water and grass for domestic and wild animals such as happened in 1890s. Unfortunately, at the same time, there also arose major epidemics, such as anthrax and the bubonic plague, which eliminated nearly half of the human and wildlife population, so much so that the low population misled the arriving colonisers to think that much of the fertile Kenyan highlands were not occupied by anyone. This climatic fact combined with the imperial mindset led to land alienation by the Imperial British East Africa Company (IBEACo) and the colonial government that followed.

Njuhi was brought up by a distant relative, Gitau wa Njuguna (who I was named after), but she was pitifully neglected and I have been told that among the other difficulties she encountered as a child, she suffered badly from jiggers.

The jigger is a flea that attacks a person's feet (and sometimes other parts of the body) and prefers boring into toe cuticles but can spread to the whole of the human foot or to other parts of the skin if the infestation is not controlled by good hygiene. The female flea nests under the skin and produces dozens of eggs that fall in the dust to start their life cycle over again.

My mother was much younger than my father, who was more than 25 years her senior.

The manner in which my father came to marry her was unusual. My father's clan and a neighbouring clan fought over issues now long forgotten and an individual in my father's clan was killed. The other clan agreed, as was the custom, to compensate a life for a life. They handed over this young orphan girl, Njuhi, whom they regarded as an unnecessary burden, to replace the individual who had been killed.

My father, as a senior elder, was responsible for placing her with an adoptive family. As deprived as she was, no one seemed to want her, so he assumed her care and eventually, after she reached maturity, took her as his second wife and paid a portion of the dowry to her relatives.

Later in life, my brother, Njoroge, and I 'completed' the outstanding dowry with the payment of a cow. In Kikuyu tradition, dowry could be paid in instalments if the groom did not have enough wealth. Even in cases where he did, the payment of dowry was a lifelong process, which kept both families and clans of the bride and groom together in an everlasting bond. Occasionally, therefore, the man's side had to give tokens to the wife's side to show he was still obligated to them for marrying their daughter.

Polygamy was an accepted customary practice in those days and was regarded as a sign of wealth because only a man who was sufficiently prosperous could afford adequate land and the demands of supporting two or more homesteads. This was how normal society was structured in the past and it was regarded as neither strange nor unusual. To the contrary, divorce, particularly of a wife with children, was unheard of, so much so that we hardly have a word for it in our language. Children grew up accepting such cultural norms and while young, were generally closer to their mothers, while their father adopted a slightly more distant role.

One of the most important qualities demanded by the polygamous family structure was strict fairness and equal treatment of all wives, quite difficult to achieve in practical terms, especially so in modern society.

Therefore, as a comfortably well-to-do man, my father was able to maintain two wives. He had married his first wife, Njanja, long before my mother came into the homestead. He and Njanja had three sons, Marai, Kirika and Jeremiah Mugo, and one daughter, Wambui, who passed away recently.

My father seemed proud of my mother. She was hardworking and an excellent parent who brought up her four children well. In fact, she actually raised us better than many of her contemporaries did their children.

* * *

I had one brother and two sisters. The eldest was my sister Mumbi; second my brother, Zakayo Njoroge. Elizabeth (Beth) Njeri was the third and I was the last.

At that time, men were categorised as members of a particular age group, while women generally adopted the age group of their husbands. My father was of the Mburu age group, circumcised in 1887.

My parents were not Christians. They sincerely did not care for Christians and had no affinity for Christianity. My father saw little difference between the missionaries and the colonialists. He saw both as invaders stealing land and influencing children against their parents. He saw Europeans, in general, as ruthless people without culture, courtesy or tradition. As with many in the Kikuyu community, he honestly tried to maintain his customs and way of life. He sought to protect his family and his community from cultural erosion and from what he saw as the lawless anarchy of the Europeans.

My people came into eastern Africa at the tail end of the gradual Bantu migration of '*andu*' speakers that occurred over a period of 1,500 years. The Kikuyu migrated into the east African region from central Africa together with other Bantu. On arriving in present-day Tanzania, they continued past Kilimanjaro and into Kenya, finally settling around Mount Kenya, along the banks of the river Tana and its tributaries, roughly 500 years ago. While on this slow movement as proto Kikuyu-Kamba-Meru, they were partly cultivators and hunter-gatherers but once they settled, they soon began farming the fertile volcanic soils in the highlands.

My more direct ancestors come from the *Ambui a Mbari ya Mbuu*. The community originally settled in Muruka, in what is now the greater Murang'a district. About a century or so before the first Europeans arrived in the region, my people moved again, when an epidemic hit the community. So many people died that the living just could not bury all the dead.

* * *

It is important to note that the Kikuyu only buried some of their dead – especially the wealthy, clan heads and community leaders (*athamaki*). Ordinary people were left in the wild in the unfortunate event that they died at home. Otherwise, the sick were left in the bush with a little food and water to await their death.

Since they had no awareness of germs or viruses, any illness led them to believe they were bewitched. For them, the only way to escape disease, or witchcraft, as they understood it, was resettlement and this was not too difficult as land was abundant.

There was always one or another natural catastrophe that pushed them onward. Around 1840, guided by Gikera, the clan leader, the people migrated from Muruka village in Metumi (now called Murang'a) and went on to Kigio. Death continued to stalk them, and they moved again. They trekked over the Kiriri river ford *(iriuko)* on the river Chania and then quite a good distance further to a place called Tiiri Mutuune – which literally means 'red soil'. At that time, there was only a sparse population of Dorobo-Gumba laying claim to the area so my ancestors settled and made it their home. They bartered their livestock with the original inhabitants and that way acquired land for the community on which to graze livestock and grow crops.

The population was extremely low by today's standards, and the method of agriculture used ensured that there were plenty of fallow seasons to allow regeneration of farming land. Land did not have ownership as such. Communities used the assets of the environment surrounding them, and acquired a customary right of use in a traditional sense.

As time passed and European colonisers arrived in Kenya, land attained a different status that was alien to the traditional communal African concept. Land was divided, fenced off, and owned. Boundaries were created. By 1900, the boundary separating Trust Land (native reserves for Africans) from Scheduled Areas (land set aside exclusively for Europeans) in central Kenya was demarcated all the way from Kiambu to Murang'a, and from the river Tana towards Nanyuki. The area was alienated by the colonial government to become farming land for settlers, part of the so-called 'White Highlands'.

Unfortunately, the land on which my ancestors settled was where the Europeans set the new boundary. The Europeans moved in and abruptly drove my people away. There was no chance of discussion, argument or retaliation. Family houses were burned down and my people were forced to move to the other side of the boundary into the 'native' reserve. They finally settled in the Kibichoi area in Kiambu District, near Thika. Here they purchased land from a sub-clan called *Mbari ya Kabucho* and made it their community's home.

This foreign and violent interference by the colonial government was incomprehensible to my people. They could not understand how strangers to the area could force the indigenous inhabitants to flee, let alone take over the land on which their homesteads and farms stood.

Gradually there were more and more restrictions imposed by the colonialists. Africans became subject to the Native Registration Amendment Ordinance from 1920 onwards, which made it compulsory for African males above 15 years of age to carry a *kipande*, an identity document with personal details, fingerprints and a history of employment.

This document radically restricted the mobility of Africans and was extremely unpopular.

Furthermore, in order to raise money for the administration of the colony and to force Africans to accept labour under the settlers, the Europeans also introduced various taxes such as the Hut Tax in 1904 and the Poll Tax in 1912. By the early 1920s, women and girls were being conscripted to do work, either clearing roads or working on settler-owned plantations. In later decades, the colonialists even banned Africans from growing lucrative cash crops such as tea, coffee and pyrethrum in order to ensure a steady supply of labour for their own farms.

Once the Europeans took over the land, our people were no longer allowed to set foot anywhere within the scheduled area boundaries unless they were there as hired help.

I have few older surviving relatives who can enlighten me about the particular details of the cultural circumstances that existed in my early childhood, and I cannot recall any folklore about my ancestors. This deficiency could be because my mother had been orphaned so young that she may not have learned many of the traditional stories herself. Nevertheless, my cultural heritage was of course, an essential facet of my personality. I know my ancestors were farmers with the typical traditional background and I too grew up with these beliefs and customs, of which there were quite a number. All the ceremonies I was exposed to were the normal Kikuyu traditions and I grew up as a normal Kikuyu child until I went to school when I was around 10 years old.

Seeing a medicine man (*mundu-mugo*) performing a cleansing ceremony fascinated and terrified me, but there was another incident which I recollect even more clearly. When I was quite young, I had a severe headache and some little cuts were made on my temple. Blood was then drawn from the cuts with a *hihi* (a sucking device made with a small horn and beeswax) in order to 'extract the headache'. There were other rituals I witnessed but none of them made as great an impression on me as this event.

Since modern medicine was virtually out of reach for most Africans, apart from those who went to mission schools or hospitals or who worked for the Europeans, people naturally resorted to traditional healers.

I also recall that when there were circumcision ceremonies, my mother was the 'host mother' to all the circumcised boys and girls at that time. She was responsible for their supervision and health. All the initiates in our area, either groups of boys or groups of girls, would spend about two weeks in one well-to-do homestead to convalesce and receive advice, counselling and instructions on how they were expected to behave, now that they were adults, while their parents would bring food to the chosen home. Most girls were still being circumcised at this time, despite the opposition of the missionaries.

After I went to school, these rituals did not hold the same significance for me and I felt no desire to either observe or participate in them again because they were contrary to my newly adopted Christian beliefs.

Childhood, for most of us, seems to be a time we remember fondly. I recall that when we were quite small, my friends and I used to play with a '*mbiira*', which was a small, round, wooden toy, pointed at the bottom, and shaped like the European toy known as a top. We would hit the *mbiira* along the side with a stick and string to make it spin. It kept us entertained for hours.

When we were a bit older, one of our favourite activities was to make little three-wheeled carts. These were triangular frameworks, all made of wood, with crude steering mechanisms and primitive brakes. The wheels were lubricated with pieces of banana stalk that were fitted onto the axles. We would seat ourselves on these little carts, sometimes alone but more often with a passenger, and roll down hills at tremendous speeds, bounce over rocks and bumps and usually crash to a stop. It was dangerous and fast, but incredible fun.

'*Mbara*' was also a pastime we enjoyed. This was traditionally meant to be practice for when we were to become warriors, but we just saw it as a chance to compete with our friends. We would roll a hoop along the ground and then try to stop it with a sharp well-aimed stick or spear thrown from a distance. Another game we played was similar to 'hopscotch'. We would draw a series of designs on the ground, throw a stone into one of them and then jump through the diagram to the end. It was all delightfully diverting.

My brother, Zakayo Njoroge, did not keep livestock. He was a businessman and a Christian who did not want cow dung or animal waste in the family compound. Christian converts had been taught basic hygiene. Those from 'Christian' homes nearly always had cleaner houses, their yards were nicely fenced with gates, the children wore shirts and shorts and they considered themselves civilised.

My brother's home had proper doors and windows and we considered it a 'modern' house. The first son of my brother, however, felt that he had missed out on an easier life. My nephew, Kiereini wa Njoroge, was not quite as fond of modern ways as his father was. He would watch us enviously as we went out to herd the family goats, wishing he could join in. He was about two years younger than I was and was quite attracted to our carefree attitude. He himself wore a shirt and shorts, so he especially admired the *shukas* (pieces of cloth, draped over the shoulder) we all wore as we went out with the livestock. Adults wore the *shuka* tied at the shoulder to secure it more firmly. It was usually knotted on the shoulder opposite the dominant hand, as this left the stronger arm free to carry weapons or baskets. This boy thought it was novel and distinctive to go out to look after goats and wear a *shuka* without any trousers.

Therefore, my nephew told his father that he wanted to go out with me and the other boys to graze goats. He asked for a *shuka* to wear and, after crying and pleading, he was finally permitted, lent a *shuka*, and we set off to take the animals out to the pastures.

Herding animals takes some skill, but it is not an exceptionally demanding occupation. We would be out the whole day and whenever we felt hungry we would look for something to eat, maybe some sugar cane, or bananas, and occasionally, we might rest, sit in the grass, or even nap.

As we wandered over the meadows, my nephew forgot his *shuka* somewhere. Perhaps he did not know how to wear it properly, but at any rate, he left it behind. He never noticed it was gone. He just walked along with the rest of us, not aware that he was naked, until we arrived back at the homestead late in the afternoon.

Then his father asked, "But where is your *shuka*?"

My nephew looked down at himself and realised that the piece of cloth was gone. He could not even remember where he lost it.

Some of us older boys went out and found the *shuka* that evening. It was not very far out, so it was likely that he had lost it on the way home. I always found it amusing that he was so nonchalant about the matter. For him, the loss was just another one of those strange incidents that inexplicably litter one's childhood.

While we were out with the goats, we would often do a little hunting as well. We hunted rabbits and birds, bringing them down with sticks and stones. Despite the fact that our families had plenty of goats, they were rarely slaughtered for food, and we welcomed any meat we could get in our diets. Game meat was taboo for the adults at home; therefore, instead of taking the meat back to the homestead, we would roast it out in the fields. We would start a fire with a fire stick, twirling it on top of a dry bit of wood. When the tip started to smoulder, we would add dry leaves and tiny sticks, gradually building up a fire. It was a terribly tedious chore, but we had no alternative and the delicious roast meat was a grand compensation.

I was not good at hunting, but I enjoyed it nonetheless.

Chapter 2

Growing up in a Time of Division

Not long before I was born, a split had occurred among those of my people who had converted to Christianity. The missionaries insisted that their converts no longer circumcise girls, and abandon other traditions. Some converts signed on to this condition, or placed a fingerprint on a document as their pledge to abide by it. They were referred to as *Kirore*, (meaning fingerprint). Those who did not agree but continued to accept Christianity and the Bible with reservations, started their own cultural-political Kikuyu Independent Schools Association (KISA). The most radical of this independent schism were the *Karing'a*, cultural purists who strongly opposed the banning of female circumcision.

In fact, the road that passed alongside our homestead became the border separating the *Kirore* from the KISA-*Karing'a* families. Our side of the road was KISA and the other was *Kirore*. KISA and Karing'a formed the third major colonial resistance movement in Kikuyuland after Mwaki wa Icha-Kahanya in Gaaki-Mathira in 1902, and the 1922 protest led by Harry Thuku, angainst the *Kipande,* which was a mandatory identification document. Both of these earlier groups were made up of mainly missionary-converted elders. They were, however, not opposed to the teaching of the Bible or Christianity as such and formed their own churches. The Catholic Church remained more or less neutral during the conflict. I, therefore, grew up keenly aware of the religious schism between us, and gradually came to understand the oppressive colonial systems in Kenya, as well.

All my siblings were already adults when I was born. My sister Elizabeth Njeri, whom I followed in birth order, was 20 years older than I was and already married with a family as I grew up. My mother once told me that after Njeri's birth, she lost five children who died between the ages of three and five years. This explains the huge difference in age between my siblings and I.

Before the Christian converts split into KISA and Kirore factions, my brother had been to Kibichoi mission school, which was just across the road, for about two terms in 1928 when he was already a fully-grown adult. Around this time, few people went to school, and not more than

10 students likely attended school with him. In fact, in order to make up a class, the missionaries enticed pupils to come in to the school by giving them sweets, salt and other treats.

Kibichoi School was run by the old Gospel Missionary Society, an American church that later joined the Church of Scotland Mission in 1946 to form the Presbyterian Church of East Africa. Once the pledge prohibiting female circumcision came into force, many of the converts objected. My brother Njoroge was one of those who rebelled. He and his age mates got together to form their own independent school called Kiamwangi.

Nevertheless, my brother learned to read and write at the mission school and once he had those skills, he did not see the need to continue his education. At any rate, there was no one to encourage him to continue with his studies. Rather than go for further education, he started working.

As a boy, Njoroge had been employed on the coffee farms near our home, guiding the oxen on a string as they pulled a wagonload of harvested coffee for the salary of one rupee (two shillings) every month. Once he had attained basic literacy, he became more ambitious and established a retail shop to support his family.

Quite a few of his contemporaries in the area followed suit. Interestingly enough, nearly all those who started businesses around this time became extremely successful. People had begun to realise the value of education and, as a result, some individuals were employed in clerical and teaching positions.

My brother owned the best retail shop in our village. He was a pioneer businessman who was admired for kilometres around and it was actually he who raised me and influenced me most as I grew up.

Jeremiah Mugo, my stepbrother, also had a bit of schooling at the mission school but did not get as much of an education as Njoroge. After he finished with school, he worked as a houseboy for a settler family. For a short time, he joined my elder brother working in the shop but later went on to work further away from home. By the time I was in high school, he was employed as a driver at the Karen Country Club south of Nairobi.

My childhood was a normal one for the society in which I grew up. My mother, Njuhi, pampered me, since I was the youngest of her children, and the only one still at home. Although the life my family and our neighbours led might be considered as one of extreme poverty by today's standards, it consisted of the typical living conditions for the people of that area and I never considered our circumstances or our hut as inadequate in any way. I had a pleasant and happy childhood and most of my playmates were the sons and daughters of my brother and sisters. All of us, including my stepmother, and half brothers and sister, lived close to each other in one homestead. Although my sisters had married and established homes with their husbands, they were not far away. Beth was just across the river, and Mumbi was only about two kilometres away. We could even see Beth's house from my father's home.

As a little child, my mother looked after me well and there was just the two of us at home. Perhaps, because she had already lost five children, she treated me with great gentleness. I was thoroughly spoiled by her attention, and I am sometimes surprised that I finally grew up to be as independent as I became. I remember I used to cry any time I wanted something and my mother would indulge me. If I became too naughty, however, my mother would lose her patience, get angry and discipline me. However, when I cried, she would be so sympathetic that she would cuddle me on her lap and start crying, too.

My sisters often came home to visit my mother and I remember having a deep relationship with both of them. They pampered me and made a fuss over every little thing, pandering to my wishes even more than my mother did. Now and then, my sister Beth would invite me to stay over at her house, even though her husband did not seem to approve, and I would have a great time playing with her children.

My mother influenced me in many ways, but I mostly recall that she always insisted that I not be idle. She worked hard herself, and disliked seeing me unoccupied. Therefore, as a young child, I performed many chores around the homestead, even some that were traditionally reserved for girls such as fetching firewood and drawing water from the river that was just down the valley. I also remember digging and clearing bush in our farm.

My mother's house was a round hut thatched with dried grass. Instead of the typical mud and wattle structure, it was made of two narrowly concentric circles of interwoven saplings and vines. The slight space between these two circles was then stuffed with dried *mugio* leaves. The leaves were tightly compacted until a solid wall sealed the hut, leaving only an entrance for the door. A barrier, *riigi*, in front of the entrance closed off the interior from the outside world. This *riigi* was a framework of saplings interwoven with other plant fibres, creating a flat surface that looked somewhat like the side of a basket, and allowed the free movement of air in and out of the house.

The hut was insulated and, therefore, warm inside. The main drawback with such a structure was its vulnerability to fire. If the smallest spark touched the wall, there would be no way of saving it.

A further disadvantage was that it was the perfect environment for certain types of insects. For example, during the bubonic plague that returned to afflict us sometime later, the fleas from the rats got into the wall and there was absolutely no way to get rid of them other than burning the hut to the ground.

As was the tradition, earlier in life, my father had lived in his own separate hut, a *thingira*, while each of his wives had their own huts, as well. Normally, as a man grew older, he would move in with his youngest wife, who would be better able to look after his needs. Thus, with increasing age, my father moved in with my mother and me. After all, his older wife, Njanja, was also elderly and would not have been able to do much. As a child, I had the impression that she was somewhat unfriendly and grumpy but when I look back on it, this may merely have been because she was already old, probably in her sixties by the time I formed that notion, and perhaps not in the best of health.

Nevertheless, father shared our little hut. On the left of the entrance, there was an area where the goats would be kept overnight. To the right was the cooking area and hearth. In the back was the sleeping area where we had our beds.

Each bed was a narrow platform of timber off-cuts, supported high above the ground on wooden pegs and crosspieces. Animal skins would be stretched over the platform and that was it. It was reasonably comfortable, and, since it was all we knew, we considered it quite adequate.

My father was an upright and respectable man but somewhat authoritarian and fierce. He was a strict disciplinarian, and his character was perhaps best described by his nickname, 'Kiereini'.

I was born when he was already in his sixties and he did not have the occasion or inclination to spend time with small children. Even my adult brothers and sisters were in awe of him because of his forceful character and no one dared oppose him.

For example, my brother Njoroge had got married in 1927 and he and his wife had their first child before I was even born. According to custom, their first son was named after my father, his paternal grandfather. He was called Kiereini wa Njoroge, but unfortunately, he died within a few months. Later, when the second son was born, the baby should have been named after his maternal grandfather, but my father, being the domineering warrior that he was, intervened.

"He must have my name! No first son will be named after anyone else!" he roared. "Not in my home!"

Therefore, on his insistence, this son was also named Kiereini wa Njoroge.

There was another incident that happened when I was about five or six years old. It impressed me so much that I was always on my best behaviour while I was with my father.

The eldest of my half-brothers, Marai, had two wives. One day he disagreed with one of them and started to beat her. My father heard the screaming and wailing and came out of his house to see what was going on. He became angry.

"What is this noise?" he shouted. "Who dares to upset the peace in my homestead?"

He walked across the compound and found that it was Marai who had caused the uproar. I should explain that Marai was just as hot-blooded as my father was. He became furious, as well.

"What do you mean?" he demanded angrily.

My father scolded him, "How can you beat someone here? This is my home! You should be ashamed of yourself for causing all this disturbance!"

"Is this your wife?" Marai shouted. "This is my wife! What have you got to do with it?"

By this time, my father was absolutely boiling.

"Marai, if you touch that woman again, it will be between you and me!" he bellowed. "Don't you dare!"

Marai seemed not to care. He sneered at my father, went back to his hut and beat his wife again. His temper was out of control.

My father went back to his house and got out his battle sword. This sword was about a metre long, pointed and keenly sharp on both edges. It had a wooden handle that was covered in hide to give it a good grip.

We children who were watching the whole affair filled with apprehension, backed off a little when we saw the weapon. I was not even aware that he had such a sword. We had never before seen such a confrontation and all of us were frightened, wondering what was going to happen next.

When Marai saw my father coming toward him with the weapon in his hand, he ducked back into his house and got out his own sword. He scorned my father.

"Hey, old man! Go back home or you will regret it!"

Marai was, of course, much younger than my father and stronger, too. My father, however, was an excellent and experienced fighter, highly skilled with the blade. Those of his generation and before had used the sword in hand-to-hand combat when in battle. Tribal and clan battles were fought with spears, and bows and arrows. When the combatants were at close range, the sword was used.

They began exchanging blows. We children cringed every time the clash of metal rang out and the women watching gasped and screamed.

Marai was overconfident, certain that he was strong enough to overpower my father, but his confidence made him careless. As soon as my father saw an opening, he hit Marai incredibly hard, high on his right shoulder with the flat of his blade.

Marai fainted and fell like a log onto the ground.

My father looked at him contemptuously. He took his sword and carefully, but with deliberation, cut Marai on the left shoulder. It was just a shallow cut, barely deep enough to break the skin, but blood trickled across Marai's arm. It was a symbolic cut meant to show that my father was the better fighter, that he had won and the battle was over.

It was a great surprise to me when Marai's wife ran into her house to get water to revive her husband. I remember standing there, watching the fight and the aftermath, and wondering to myself, "How can this be? My father is defending her, yet Marai, who beat her, is still most important to her! She should be angry with her husband instead of helping him!"

My father just went back to his hut without a word.

That was the end of the matter, however, things did not return to normal until my brother slaughtered a goat to pacify my father some days later.

*   *   *

I might not have gone to school at all were it not for the insistence of my brother, Njoroge, and I would hate to imagine what would have become of me otherwise. He sent me to school against the wishes of my father.

My father considered education a waste of time and, given his attitude towards Europeans, he both feared and despised anything to do with them. Twice my father beat me, quite severely, for disobeying him and running away to school. He wanted me to work at home and look after the cows and goats. In order to ensure that I was not beaten again, my brother became adamant.

He came to my father's home and told him bluntly, "You will not beat this child again. Next time you want Gitau to herd the goats, I will close my shop and come look after your animals, myself."

The agriculturalist Kikuyu highly valued goats, sheep and cattle. Each family tried to have as large a herd as possible. Most traditional ceremonies involved either the slaughter or exchange of the animals, particularly during marriage. So important was livestock bride price during weddings that the value of marriageable girls was increased because it meant a greater wealth of animals coming to her parents' home. In short, livestock was central to the Kikuyu way of life.

Njoroge insisted, "This boy must go to school! Education has greater value than any herd of goats and he will earn far more money if he becomes a teacher or a clerk."

That ended the beatings from my father.

My father was reasonably well-off and respected, but as he grew older, he became more and more dependent on his children. At the time of the above incident, my brother was supporting my parents, clothing them and giving them provisions and, because of this, they could not actually go against his wishes. Therefore, I started school.

* * *

The road near our home served as a boundary between those who strictly followed the missionaries and those who maintained an independent religious stance. I could not go to Kibichoi Primary School across the road like my elder brother had, because it was a Gospel Missionary Society (GMS), later Presbyterian Church of East Africa (PCEA), missionary school and our family was KISA. As a result, I started attending one of the KISA schools, Kiamwangi, in Kiganjo, towards the end of 1938, before the Second World War. I remember the year clearly because the teacher had written '1938' on the blackboard, and then, not long thereafter, changed it to '1939', before I completely realised what the figures meant.

At any rate, Kiamwangi is about eight kilometres from Kibichoi, and on my way to school, I would cross four streams and valleys – Mugutha, Kibichoi, Kamaratua and Theta. It certainly took me a lot longer to get to Kiamwangi than it would have to get to Kibichoi across the road!

I was in Sub A for a term, then Sub B and then Standard 1. If we learnt quickly, we were advanced to the next class as soon as the teachers felt we were ready. In Sub A and Sub B, we scribbled the alphabet on dusty floors. When we made it to Standard 1 and 2, we were allowed to use slates.

Slate is a fine-grained grey, green or bluish purple metamorphic rock easily split into flat smooth plates. Pieces of such plates were framed in wood and were used for writing on with chalk.

We did not actually have pure chalk to write on these slates, but used a type of soft sandstone that served just as well. Later, we also used pencils and exercise books.

In our first years at school, we sat on the ground and held our slates on our laps, but by Standard 3, three or four students would share a rudimentary bench and table made of wooden planks. Despite these rather simple conditions, I thoroughly enjoyed learning how to read and write and I was quick at my lessons. By the time war was declared in 1939, I was already able to read the newspaper, *Baraza*, which was written in Kiswahili.

My brother's shop was in a market centre called Nembu. People often met and gathered at Nembu to exchange the latest news and gossip and, when the rare newspaper made it to my brother's shop, the villagers, especially the old men, would gather around, and I would read it aloud for them. Most of the news was about the war. Although people had heard about Mussolini, Hitler, Italy and Germany, most of us did not really understand who and where all these people and countries were. We did not understand many of the details, but we did know that some of our young men had joined the British in fighting against Germany, and so we called it the 'German War'.

I was in Standard 3 at the beginning of 1941. After only two terms, the teacher thought I was clever enough to attempt the Common Entrance Examination that year. Because I had not yet acquired sufficient knowledge, I did not pass and had to repeat it the following year when I completed studying the curriculum.

Our syllabus consisted of only four subjects, the three R's (writing, reading, and arithmetic) in addition to vernacular. In the upper classes, if we were proficient, the teacher would occasionally invite one of us to demonstrate our skills on the blackboard in front of everyone. I loved showing off my skills in front of the others.

One of the most pleasant incidents in my early days at Kiamwangi was a consequence of the lack of enough teachers. When I was in Standard 1, I was delighted and proud to be appointed to teach Sub A as a pupil teacher. This procedure was occasionally practiced in those days. Naturally, I took pleasure in teaching because teachers were much respected in our community. I was a *mwalimu*, a teacher, instructing people much older than I was. I felt I was educated and important. Being a teacher was a rewarding experience for me and, although I was not yet circumcised, I felt incredibly advanced. I especially enjoyed teaching numbers and the alphabet.

It might sound amusing, but the first time I got into trouble over girls was while I was teaching in Class 1. I used to take my lunch with the teachers. After all, I was a 'teacher' myself. But soon, a girl student who was fond of me, started to invite me to share the better quality lunch which she often brought from home. Discretely, I stopped eating with the teachers and spent more time with the student.

This girl seemed to fancy me. She would escort me home on occasion and the boys became jealous. According to our culture and their own opinions, older circumcised girls were not supposed to mix with uncircumcised boys such as myself. The older boys complained to the headmaster about my behaviour and I was summoned for a consultation at a teacher's house, together with the girl who was accused alongside me.

As soon as the headmaster asked if we were friends, this girl immediately admitted it. She said, "Yes! What's wrong with that?"

This must have been a bit of a shock to the teachers and as a result, I had no opportunity to tell my side of the story. I was glad when the case was dismissed. After all, we had not got up to anything improper. Nevertheless, the teacher warned me to stop wasting my time mixing with girls, otherwise he would report the matter to my brother. I considered this the worst possible thing that could happen to me and immediately stopped socialising with the older girls. One result of this incident was to lead me to concentrate more on my studies.

My favourite sports activity while at Kiamwangi was 'drill', which was the term we used for a form of quasi-military physical education. Drill consisted of exercises such as jumping jacks, squats, bends, steps, turns and other movements performed in unison by a group of students. I was a squad leader and enjoyed coordinating the group and making sure we all kept time.

Once, we all went up to Matathia to compete with others during an inter-school sports day. I am not sure of the distance, but it was a long way to walk barefoot from Kiamwangi and took us nearly one full day to get there. That night we slept at the venue and then the following day, somehow, we still had enough energy to compete. After that, of course, we had to walk back to Kiamwangi. It was tiring for all of us, but for me it was even more exhausting because once I got back to the school, I still had to cross four river valleys to get home.

At that time, I was the only one from my area who performed well in school. My mother became the envy of the community because her sons had done well. Njoroge owned a prosperous shop and I had gone to school and was moving ahead. It was fortunate that I went to school at my brother's insistence. My brother convinced me that my father was wrong to oppose education and now that I look back on it, I have never regretted siding with this view. Most other people of my age have died and to my knowledge, not one of them did anything out of the ordinary with their lives.

My sister, Elizabeth (Beth) Njeri, also had some ambitions for education and wanted to become a Christian. She was taught knitting and other domestic tasks at the mission, but one day my father walked to the school with his sword out and told the missionaries that his daughter must be released. My father did not want her to have anything to do with the mission because he thought she would never get married, that she would become a nun and that there would be no dowry for him.

He felt his children were losing touch with the culture and traditions that had been our way of life for centuries. We were changing beyond anything he understood. I realise now that when I went to school, my father felt that I was lost to him. It was as though I was abandoning his values and customs, and in a sense, abandoning him. It was regrettable that we no longer saw eye to eye on these issues in the way we had before, but the rapid changes occurring all around forced us to adjust and adopt a completely different lifestyle.

My older sister Mumbi never went near a church until much later in life. Eventually both Mumbi and Elizabeth Njeri were baptised and went on to become members of the PCEA Woman's Guild, the highest organisation for women members of the church.

I selected the name Jeremiah for one particular reason, which now seems rather droll. One of my half-brothers, Jeremiah Mugo, was a houseboy in a European household. Occasionally he would bring us a few slices of bread and jam, a real treat for my nephews and I. We would lick the jam off our fingers as we ate. This brother, Jeremiah, impressed me as such a virtuous and generous man that I selected the name for myself. I was given religious instruction and attended catechism classes at Kiamwangi School and was later baptised in 1941.

The year I was baptised, 1941, was also when I first came to Nairobi. I no longer recall the exact details, but I remember I was ill and, instead of taking me to the small dispensary near home at Kambui, my brother brought me to Nairobi by bicycle, on one of his usual trips to buy provisions for his shop. He took me to Burns Dispensary, which was near the railway headquarters. I believe it was started by the Reverend Burns, who was a missionary. For us, 'Burns' was a particularly difficult word to pronounce and we referred to it as *Kwa-Banji*. I recall there was also a bookshop nearby, in Church House, and it was then the largest building in Nairobi.

An epidemic of bubonic plague broke out in the same year and, unfortunately, my mother caught the disease and died. Bubonic plague is one of the commonest forms of plague in humans, characterised by fever, delirium and the formation of buboes (swollen or inflamed armpit or groin lymph nodes) and transmitted by rat fleas. Various plagues occur from time to time with differing numbers of casualties.

I was very close to my mother and was heartbroken when she passed on. She got sick on a Saturday, and got worse on Sunday. On Monday morning, I went to school as usual and when I came home at the end of the day, she was dead and buried. Her hut had been burned down according to our traditions.

I was terribly affected. I went to lie down on the ground near the ashes of our hut, wondering what was going to happen to me. I did not know where I would go for food, where I would sleep or where I would get the other things my mother normally gave me. I tried to cry but, because I was so traumatised, I was unable to do so. I have never understood why I was unable to express the sad emotions that overwhelmed me.

I found myself motherless at about 12 years of age, with no one to look after me in the special loving way that my mother had. My father loved me, of course, but at that time he was over 70 years old and I regarded him with so much respect and awe that he seemed a distant and almost unapproachable person. It was my brother, Zakayo Njoroge, who became like a father to me.

At this time, my brother spent most of his time at his shop in Nembu market centre. He lived at the back of the shop and I came to live there and assisted him whenever I had time. It was not far from the family homestead, just across the ridge, and I continued to see the rest of the family frequently.

After I adjusted to my new situation, I enjoyed working in my brother's shop and felt important and proud as I waited on customers. Although it was small, the shop was filled with all types of goods piled up to the roof and I would often have to climb up a ladder to reach the stock on the topmost shelves. We sold sugar, salt, tea, pangas, pots and pans, hammers, nails – we had a little of everything. We also sold cloth such as 'mericani', khaki, calico, bafta and sheti, which were mostly cottons and all classed by their various weights and colours. We used a metal yardstick and a tape measure to measure out the length of pieces of cloth, but we also employed a much older measuring standard, the *mkono*, which was the distance from the elbow to the tips of the fingers – in other words, a cubit. When someone came in asking for clothes, I would take his measurements, cut the material with a sharp pair of scissors, and then stitch up the garment while he waited.

There was an old treadle sewing machine in the shop and I became quick and skilled at making clothes. Among other things, I would cut, stitch and hem *shukas* and skirts in advance, which would be hung up as 'ready to wear'. Other than these, we never stocked ready-made clothing nor did we have cast-off European clothes.

It was wonderful to be responsible for running the shop. I was left in charge whenever my brother was away buying supplies from the Indian shops in Nairobi, Ruiru or Kiambu, depending on what sort of items he needed. Mostly, he would travel to Nairobi by bicycle, purchase his requirements and then, coordinating jointly with the other shopkeepers from our area, hire a lorry from a man called Sam, who would transport all the goods back to the countryside. Sam actually had a small local area named after him, called Gwathamu (Sam's place), which was not far from the market centre at Nembu.

Although I had seen Europeans before in the coffee estates, not one of them ever came to my brother's shop. It was meant for African customers. Europeans and Asians would go to buy their supplies from the Asian shops in places like Kiambu and Ruiru.

Around this time, in 1942, my brother Njoroge married his second wife. Since he had not built a house for her, she came to live at the shop. There was not much room for me, so I moved into a small room across the road. Later, after she had her first child, my brother built a house for her in the homestead.

* * *

With regard to my schooling, it is important to bear in mind that during this time, most teachers were neither trained nor well-educated. In general, most had only a small inkling of the concept of what education was meant to be. Just as an example, I had learned English at Kiamwangi, and continued learning the language when I went to Kagumo School, later. Strangely enough, when I came home on school holidays after my first year at Kagumo, even the most proficient English teacher at Kiamwangi was no longer able to understand much of what I was saying when I spoke to him in English.

We were highly conscious of the religious differences between the independent KISA schools on the one hand, and the missionary schools on the other, and the division of people who adhered to either. In fact, KISA adherents were referred to as *Ashenzi* (pagan, or backward) whereas *Kirore* were referred to as *Athomi* (literate or, by implication, modern).

My half-brother, Nahashon Kirika, and families like his, had quite a number of taboos. Kirika was among the original Christian converts in our area. He was *Kirore* and very conservative. Whereas most of us children wandered about fairly freely, Kirika's wife did not even allow her children to visit their grandmother. The reason she made this stricture was that the grandmother might cook some food for the children using fat from an animal slaughtered for a particular traditional ceremony. Alternatively, perhaps the fat would come from an animal that had been killed by strangulation or suffocation. Such things were taboo for these strict Christian families because the early converts had been taught that Christians did not eat meat from an animal that did not have its throat slit.

This and other beliefs had to do with blood. *Kirore* followers would not eat anything with blood, for example, the delicious blood and meat sausage we call *mutura* would never find a place on Kirika's table. *Kirore* families insisted that they believed in Jesus Christ and since he had shed his blood and died for them, it was sufficient.

This split created rifts between families and a breakdown in the links with the culture of the past. Converted families would discuss religion, or read the Bible, rather than tell folk stories or keep up with their culture. They would talk on topics that they considered 'civilised'. Traditional culture was discouraged because it was not in keeping with civilisation. Tradition thus came to be regarded as backward and a regression to native life.

More traditional families, on the other hand, were concerned with their own customs and history and would keep up their cultural practices.

For those of us who were brought up in the 'native' way, our outlook changed completely the moment we went to school and were converted to Christianity. It was new and exciting and we wanted to know as much as we could about everything.

Therefore, I got a hybrid upbringing, somewhere between the traditional culture and the new enlightenment and I feel they both have their own merit. It is something like that saying - taking the best of each culture and discarding what is irrelevant.

As for British schools during the early years of the colony, most Europeans sent their children abroad for their education. Even after they started schools in Kenya, they maintained a purely British curriculum that had nothing to do with the local situation. Parents wanted to ensure that their children had the same background as any child brought up in Great Britain.

Long before I was born, missionaries were the first to take an interest in African education. They wanted to teach Africans about the Bible, and in order to read the Bible, the converts had to be literate. Initially, even missionaries seemed to believe that Africans were not capable of going beyond primary school. It often seemed that the entire inspiration behind education, as envisioned by the British, was to create personnel to cater for Europeans' labour needs in farms, mission centres, business and government. Vernacular was, therefore, treated as the most important subject and the next priorities were reading and writing. That was regarded as sufficient. After all, where would educated Africans go when they finished their education? Their future remained subservient to the Europeans'. The most an African could hope to become was a clerk or a teacher, who would then educate the next generation.

Such basic schools for African children had their own standards and their own philosophy. In 1926, however, educational theories started to change somewhat and children were allowed to go beyond Standard 6 and into secondary school. Nevertheless, up to about 1938 or 1939, students still had to pass an examination in vernacular and for many, it was felt that there was no need to go any further.

Because independent schools were not recognised, we were not permitted to sit our Common Entrance examinations at Kiamwangi. Only missionary schools were authorised to administer the exam and have students admitted to intermediate schools. The Church of Scotland, the Anglican missions and others simply did not permit the registration of independent school students for the examination. Catholics were the only denomination that allowed us to register.

Therefore, I sat for my Common Entrance Examination at the end of 1942 at Lioki Catholic Mission School and I remember I had to walk quite a long distance to get there. The examination was set by the Department of Education in Nairobi, and consisted of a printed form with a copy for each of us. It was in the vernacular and the subjects tested were arithmetic, Kikuyu language, writing and reading. We were not tested in English, Kiswahili, or science subjects. The exams were given in one large classroom and we sat at desks while one teacher supervised and watched as we struggled with the questions.

I found it easy and, because of my previous experiences in teaching others, I was quite confident. There were about four or five of us from Kiamwangi who passed the examination but unfortunately, I do not recall where the others ended up.

Not much later, I was informed that I had passed the 'Common', as it was called, and that I was to report to the intermediate school, Kagumo African Government School, in Nyeri. At the time, this was the only government intermediate school in central Kenya. All the others were mission schools. Kagumo had been established some five kilometres south of Nyeri town on land donated by Chief Wambugu wa Mathangani in 1933.

Before I could join intermediate school, I still had to undergo one traditional rite. Nearly all my friends had already been circumcised and I was desperate not to be left behind when I went to Kagumo. They were now 'men' while I was still a boy.

During those years, most boys were circumcised somewhere between the ages of 16 to 20 and, since I was just 13, my brother, as my guardian, considered me too young to undergo the rite. He was worried that I would neglect my studies and be misled by my fellow initiates. When I begged and cried, my brother finally relented. Shortly before I went to Kagumo, I was circumcised in the usual traditional way after an early morning dip in the numbing, freezing cold, Komothai River. From there we walked to the *iteri*, the site where the ceremony was performed and after the rites were completed, we lived in a *githunu*, a temporary enclosure, for two weeks, until we healed. We received counselling on how to behave, now that we were adults.

My *mutiri* (advisor) was Ngugi wa Mugo, an older cousin. We had little time to interact as I left for school almost immediately. Once I had been to school and got some education, he was no longer able to give me much guidance since I had been exposed to the wider world.

A Daunting Journey

Kagumo School, however, did not open for the new term as scheduled in 1943 because there was a severe drought and there would have been nothing to feed the students. Therefore, sometime later, when it was announced that Kagumo School was to open, many of the students travelled singly to the school as best they could. I received a train ticket from the Kiambu County Council. This would enable me to make my way from Ruiru to Karatina town, which was near Kagumo School.

My brother took me down to Ruiru Railway Station on his bicycle, and then put me on the 'mixed train'.

A 'mixed' train was one that carried both cargo and passengers. The Kikuyu could not pronounce 'mixed train' and so shortened it to *mugithi*. The popular evangelical song, *Mugithi,* borrows its name from this title. The dance normally performed with this song, had people holding each other in a chain, like the coaches of a train, and symbolised that they were in the train headed for heaven.

I clearly remember it was 10 January 1943 because one of my brother's daughters was born on that date. I had never even seen a train before and perhaps I should have been frightened, but my brother seemed to know what to do and the other people in the vicinity were behaving normally. I was not scared at all and just embraced each new experience as it came.

I entered one of the coaches and sat on a hard wooden bench, watching everything and everyone with great curiosity. Once the train started heading down the track, I had the strange feeling that the buildings, trees and landscape were moving backwards. It was a trick of perception, of course, the same feeling one gets in a moving car, when two other cars overtake on either side. I enjoyed the journey immensely.

My brother had never been to Karatina or Nyeri, so the only advice he had given me was to get off the train at Karatina, ask for directions to Kagumo School, and walk until I got there. Neither he nor I realised it was quite a distance, nearly 25 kilometres.

Therefore, when I got off the train at Karatina, I assumed the school would be somewhere close, along the track towards Kiganjo. I followed the railway line from the station, searching for the school, but the farther I went, the more deserted it became, so I returned to the station.

Since I had been told I would be given a uniform and all my necessities once I arrived at the school, I had carried absolutely nothing with me, neither money, nor extra clothing. It was getting cold, the sun was starting to set, and I was shivering and desperate. I knew I would have to ask for directions, something I had been avoiding until then, and luckily, I found someone to assist me near the station platform.

After greeting him, I stated my problem.

"I'm a student," I told him. "I'm supposed to go to Kagumo, but I don't know where it is."

"Eh! Kagumo is not near here," he replied. "It's quite a bit further on."

He looked at me and I suppose he felt sympathetic. "You come with me," he said, "let's see if we can get you settled for the night and you can leave for Kagumo tomorrow."

He took me to the Karatina shops and led me to a small restaurant, a traditional type of rest house, *mukawa*, which unfortunately no longer exists. In such an establishment, a stranger would always be well received, even if he had no money.

I was ravenous. Luckily, the people I met at the restaurant were generous and I was given some food and tea. Later, after the place closed for the night and all the customers were gone, the landlord told me I could sleep on a table. I ended up napping fitfully on top of a table, sticky with spilled sugar, shivering from the cold because I had no blanket. I did not actually get much sleep of course, but near morning, I fell into a doze and was finally awoken by customers coming in for their morning tea.

I was disoriented, exhausted, and therefore extremely thankful to the landlord, who gave me a mug of hot, sweet, milky tea for my breakfast. After I finished, he took me outside and showed me a trail.

"If you follow this path and go right across the valley, you'll get to those shops in the distance there. Just ask those people around the shops and they will tell you the way to get to Kagumo. Just keep on asking as you go."

With that bit of advice, I set off toward the shops, got my directions and started onward to school.

As I was walking along, I encountered a number of women coming toward me, carrying bags packed with cabbages and baskets of foodstuff heading for the market in Karatina. Once again, I asked and they said I was going in the right direction. Every person I met declared I should keep going.

"Follow this road until you reach Wariruta, then ask for directions to Kirurumo Falls, and keep on walking. You can't go wrong."

That 25-kilometre walk was the longest journey I had ever undertaken on my own. I was about 13 at the time and I felt dreadfully alone.

Finally, I arrived at Kagumo in the mid-afternoon and showed my admission letter to the headmaster. He immediately admitted me, but instead of granting me an opportunity to have a rest or eat a meal, he instructed his clerk to take me directly to Class 4B.

The clerk led me down the corridor, opened a classroom door, and said to the teacher inside, "Aloys, here's your student."

I remember his words very well, but I did not have any clue what was to follow.

Class 4B was taught by the haughtiest teacher I have ever met. Aloys Mwande was a teacher from Mang'u. He proved to be a brute and was exceedingly severe with all of us students.

Here I was, starving, exhausted after my long trek, not having slept at all well the night before, and he didn't even notice my condition.

He glowered at me critically and said, in Kikuyu, *"Riu nakio giiki kihii kioima na ku kina maitho matune ta ma mburi?"* That is to say, "Where has this uncircumcised thug with red eyes like a goat come from?"

After that humiliating introduction, I hardly knew where I was and wondered if I had made a mistake to come.

I sat down and noticed that the students were learning a subject I had never studied or even heard of, called geometry. The other students had been instructed and directed but, given that I had never learned geometry before, I was lost. The teacher gave me a book, a piece of paper and pencil and I studied the blackboard to see if there was anything I could discover from the diagram that had been drawn there. All I could see were two lines, one thick and one thin, about a foot apart. I saw the other students drawing and then taking their papers up to the teacher for marking at the front table, but no one told me what to do, and I did not have the slightest idea. I thought the thick line looked a bit more promising, so I drew a nice thick line on my sheet with the help of a ruler and took my paper up to the teacher.

Aloys looked at what I had drawn and then he glared at me. I started shaking like a leaf. He wrenched me up by my hair, and said in Kikuyu, *"Uyu ni nyukwa wachora?"* meaning, "Is this your mother you have drawn?"

I decided that, if this was the type of education provided at Kagumo, I wanted nothing more than to go straight home. But after I calmed down, I reconsidered. I knew that if I were to go home, my brother would never be able to understand it and I would receive a severe beating. I stayed on despite my misgivings.

It was truly a baptism of fire and I became especially wary of Aloys. I was determined to get out of his class, so I studied as hard as I could, concentrating on getting enough knowledge to move on and within a term, I graduated to the next class, which was 4A. I have to say that Aloys was the most unpleasant teacher I ever studied under in my life. I understand he later went to teach at Kilimambogo Teachers' Training College.

Of my other teachers at Kagumo, only one is still alive today and that is Peter Muhoho. His daughter comes to one of the clubs I frequent. I also recollect James Mbotela, who taught English and Maths. He was upright and dedicated and I learned a great deal from him. He taught with zeal and commitment.

The headteacher was A. F. Bull, who was an ex-British Army officer. He had no deputy and was the only European in the school. V. A. Ottaway, who later became the Director of Education of the colony, had been his predecessor.

In general, we fared reasonably well in the school. In the classrooms, we had proper individual desks with lids, so we could keep our papers safely inside. The food was more or less up to the standard that was conventional in African schools those days. We ate in one large hall and the menu was usually *ugali* (maize meal) with vegetables, or *githeri* (a mix of maize and beans). We had a few pieces of meat twice weekly.

The chief annoyance I recall were the beds in the dormitories that both physically and mentally left an impression on me and on other students. We slept on planks without mattresses. All we had were two blankets, which we folded in such a way that they were both under and over us, but the boards were so appallingly hard that by the time we left school, we had virtually permanent bruises on our sides. We even had to use our clothes as pillows. Three years of that was harsh!

Then, in the mornings, we had to fold the blankets and have everything neat, ready for inspection. This inspection was sometimes embarrassing to the younger boys who had not outgrown the habit of bed-wetting. They were the objects of merciless teasing by the older bullies.

Although it would have easily been feasible, we were never permitted to make our own mattresses, a procedure that was commonplace in later years. One could sew together a few gunny bags, stuff them with grass, sew up the opening and there would be a perfectly comfortable mattress to sleep on. I presume that by denying us permission to stitch together our own mattresses, the Kagumo administration was attempting to 'harden' us to become men.

The institution was established about 10 years before I arrived, and all the teachers were male. There was no religious instruction at Kagumo, so there were neither church services nor prayer sessions. Occasionally, there would be a visiting priest or pastor who would preach to us, but there was no interaction with missionary schools.

The school had nine dormitories, each identified by number. There was a large hall in the middle of the school complex and the rest of the buildings were classrooms. The fees were 45 shillings a year, which we considered rather high.

We did not socialise much with the local people; we hardly had anything to do with them. We tried to organise secret dances a few times, behind Dormitory 8, and invited several girls and some local youngsters to join us, but the occasions were never successful. One way or another, the teachers always found out that something was afoot. Luckily, we never got into trouble because there was no fence round the school and as soon as we saw an adult coming, we would all scatter and disappear. I have no idea how the girls made it home but none of us was ever discovered. Naturally, this sort of thing was against school discipline and I think there was some petty theft that occurred as well, which made the school even stricter about such matters.

Just to clarify the situation, when my generation talks of having been in Kagumo, many people think of it as being in Kiganjo, near the Kiganjo Police College, where it is located today. At the time I was a student, however, Kagumo Primary School and Kagumo High School were located at Gatitu along the Karatina-Nyeri road, which was locally known as Kiambuiri, and there was nothing but bush in Kiganjo. Later the school moved and the older site at Gatitu was then turned into Kagumo Teachers' College.

There was no library at the school while I was a student there, and we had hardly any textbooks. The few that existed were mostly for maths and languages. We had to rely on the notes we took as the teachers dictated them. I do remember reading several books in Kikuyu while at Kagumo, although I can no longer remember how I got them. Among the earliest Kikuyu books I read was *Gitune,* by Rev. Barlow. Later I read *Mwendwo ni Iri na Iriri,* written by Justin Itotia wa Kimacia in 1929, and *Miikarire ya Agikuyu,* by Stanley Gathigira Kiama written in 1933. I read others written in Kiswahili, most notably *Hekaya za Abunwasi,* and *Alfu Lela Ulela,* a translation of *Tales of Arabian Nights.*

There was insignificant activity at the school apart from lessons. We had some extracurricular sports such as 'drill', which I enjoyed, and football, but there were no inter-school competitions. We simply competed between dormitories.

At the conclusion of every term, we trooped out of the school in a group. We had to walk up and down hills and valleys, all the way to Karatina and take the train from there, since there were no buses. There were no commercial buildings at Gatitu market, either. It was just a rough dirt road. If we wanted to buy anything, we had to walk to Nyeri, which was about eight kilometres away, but we walked without complainting.

In 1944, a teacher training college opened at Kagumo, with the Reverend Richard Arthur Lockhart as the principal. Lockhart was an Irish missionary who worked exceptionally hard. His wife *'King'oo'* (a nickname alluding to the nasal quality of her speech) was like a mother to the boys in the school, but we could hardly understand what she was saying because of her strong Irish accent.

Our class was the first to experience changes coming from the expansion of Kagumo to a teacher training school. The adults who were studying to become teachers would come over to our side of the school and practise teaching on us. Sometimes we felt like we were part of an experiment, like guinea pigs in a new environment. It was often fun to be taught by these trainee teachers because they were much more sympathetic to our difficulties and were not that strict about following the syllabus. Since they had not yet qualified, they were ready to tackle any subject without boundaries and we learned fascinating extraneous information from them. I recall that Joe Koinange, who later became Dean of Students at the University of Nairobi, was one of the trainees during our time.

We benefited in other ways as well. One of the advantages of having the teacher training school on the same compound was to observe the example of people who had a superior education. Not many students ever thought about higher learning because we could have got jobs straight out of Kagumo. The presence of the student teachers, therefore, led us to reflect more seriously on our future and gave us an even greater motivation to succeed.

At Kagumo, there were four of us from the Kiereini family. There was my cousin David Mugo Marai, my nephew Steven Kiereini, another nephew, John Kirika Kiereini, and I. At the time, and many years thereafter, I used the name Gitau to avoid confusion. Other people I recall who went to Kagumo while I was there were Duncan Ndegwa, who was two years ahead of me, and Geoffrey Kariithi, who was a year ahead. There were also a few students from outside Nyeri such as Maina Wanjigi from Murang'a and Godfrey Mviti from Embu. Others were Mwangi Ayubu, Eliud Gikaru, and Josephat Karanja. A number of these later held prominent positions in the Kenya government.

Kiswahili was the medium of instruction for all subjects except maths and English. Even our primary examination papers were in Kiswahili and I am proud of my proficiency in the language to this day.

We never worried much about taking the examinations. We were daring and perhaps one of the reasons for our attitude was that this was during the Second World War. We students called ourselves *Majemedari,* meaning 'generals'. We pretended to give ourselves high military ranks since we considered ourselves leaders, among the first in our generation to acquire higher primary education, and we were exceedingly proud of it.

I was at Kagumo Primary School for three years, for Standards 4, 5 and 6. Subsequently, I sat the Kenya Primary Examination (KPE) at the end of 1945, under classroom conditions similar to the circumstances under which I had sat the Common Entrance Examination, and passed.

The Kenya Primary Examination became the Kenya African Preliminary Examination (KAPE), and later Certificate of Primary Examination (CPE).

Although I learnt a great deal at Kagumo, I was more impressed with Kiamwangi and the concept of independent schools. The whole idea of education that suited the world of the Africans was more exciting and inspiring to me than a syllabus that was basically Eurocentric.

After Kagumo, I did not have a notion of where to go next. I considered investigating the possibilities of finding a job in Nairobi but the Second World War had just ended and the job market was flooded with thousands of young ex-soldiers looking for employment. The African soldiers who had returned from serving the Crown were a dejected lot. They thought they would be rewarded by the government but there was nothing forthcoming. Whereas British soldiers received cash grants to buy farms or invest, the Africans were given overcoats and told to go back to the village. These angry young people were among the ones who crystallised the Mau Mau movement a few years later.

In any case, there were not many jobs available. The few opportunities open to educated Africans were for clerical work or teaching.

Returning to school for further education had never been on my mind and besides, secondary school places were extremely limited. The few upper schools open to Africans at the time were Shimo La Tewa at the coast, Maseno in what was then Kavirondo (today's Nyanza), and

Mathari in Nyeri, none of which had classes beyond Form 2. Alliance and Mang'u were the only ones with classes up to Form 4, and with facilities for students to sit the Cambridge Ordinary Level examinations, but at the time, I was unaware of their existence.

* * *

While at Kagumo, my father died of food poisoning.

The men of the community arranged a particular type of feasting, called *'kiruugu'* or *'kimandi'*, every now and again. Old men would each contribute a goat and all of them would go away from home, down into one of the river valleys. They would be gone for a month and do nothing but gorge themselves on the goats, one by one, eating meat and soup and growing fat. This did not have any spiritual significance. It was just an elitist male get-together to socialise. Although no women were allowed to go down into the valley, they would leave other types of food, such as vegetables, up on the ridges and young boys would bring them down to the men to eat.

My father and my brother, Zakayo Njoroge, attended such an occasion in 1944 and, although the river was nearby as a convenient site for washing up, hygiene was never observed at these feasts. My father was infected and became very ill. I remember that my brother and I carried him up the hill and then wheeled him on a bicycle up to my brother's shop where we put him on one of the beds to rest. I had to return to Kagumo that day, so I left soon afterwards. Regrettably, my father died the same day.

My brother wrote to me at Kagumo, to tell me about his death, but when I received the letter, I did not return home for the funeral. As was the custom, my father had already been buried on the same day he died, so it would have been meaningless to make the trip back.

Today, the unmarked graves of both my parents lie at Kibichoi. Perhaps I inherited a certain amount of an authoritarian outlook from my father and I doubt it is such a bad thing. My father probably influenced me in my determination to accomplish my goals but as I grew older, it was my brother, Zakayo Njoroge, who raised me with the same care and attention he gave to his own children, guiding me through life. My work ethic is definitely from my brother. He became my mentor and my role model throughout his life.

Chapter 3

School in a Season of War

While I was occupied with school, the world around me was changing. The Second World War started in 1939 and Kenyan soldiers served abroad. The Kings African Rifles, a multi-battalion British colonial regiment, which had served in First World War, had, by 1940, a strength of over 800 officers, over 1,300 non-commissioned officers and more than 20,000 Africans in other ranks, mostly Kenyan but also including Ghanaian, Nigerian and South African troops. They fought against the Italians in Italian East Africa, against the Vichy French in Madagascar and against the Japanese in Burma.

Earlier, Kenyan soldiers who had served in the First World War had been exposed and influenced by what they saw of the outside world. This exposure had played a part in the first agitation against the British, especially against the *kipande* (an identity document by which the colonial administration controlled the movement of Africans), against the hut tax and against land alienation. After the First World War, the additional contact with other countries brought about an increased awareness of people and nations free of colonial control.

During these early years of my life, the colonial presence completely changed the situation in Kenya. Although the European community was predominantly upper middle-class and upper-class British, in Kenya they were divided into two groups, the settlers on the one hand, and the colonial officials and tradesmen on the other. The officials belittled the settlers and regarded them with a certain amount of disdain. They disagreed with them on a number of issues, mainly land allocation. During the 1920s up to the 1940s, socially elite settlers were renowned as the 'Happy Valley' group and became notorious for their decadent lifestyle. Their treatment of 'natives' did nothing to endear them to Africans. On the other hand, their counterparts, that is government officials and missionaries, considered the settlers overbearing and uncultured.

In the 'White Highlands', Europeans now 'permitted' Africans to cultivate small parcels of land as tenant farmers, or squatters, on the farms that the Kikuyu community had previously called their own, in exchange for a certain number of days of labour. While I was happily at school, Europeans demanded more and more toil from their tenants and attempted to reduce them to mere agricultural labourers in addition to increasing restrictions on Africans' access to land. According to some studies, this led to a drop in the income of Kikuyu squatters by 30 to 40 per cent. By the end of the 1940s, their income had fallen even further.

The fact that European settlers could occupy African land with impunity became a fundamental point of conflict. Resentment and hostility that had resulted in agitation from the 1920s onward now grew more vociferous as more limitations were placed on Africans. By 1948, in central Kenya, just under a million Kikuyu were limited to the occupation of 5,200 square kilometres. On the other hand, about 30,000 settlers were given prime agricultural land of about 31,000 square kilometres.[1] About five years later, nearly half of the Kikuyu had nowhere to cultivate their crops or graze their livestock. Interestingly, the few Kikuyu who were more firmly established on the land began to build powerful ties within the colonial structures. In addition to the initial split between *Kirore* and KISA, this loyalty to the colonials led to a further split into the factions that later divided the Kikuyu down the middle.

Consequently, thousands of Kikuyu drifted into Nairobi and other towns looking for employment. In the period between 1938 and 1952, such migrations nearly doubled Nairobi's population, which gave rise to the trade union movement that started to form in the 1940s. Trade unions became active, not only in agitating for the welfare of the workers, but also heightened the political agitation.

The country was in a state of flux. At the end of the Second World War, demobilised African soldiers came back with strong feelings of nationalism and, for the most part, these returning soldiers led and inspired the Kenyan nationalist movement. Like the soldiers in the First World War, they too had seen that Europeans were ordinary human beings. Furthermore, they had witnessed the spirit of nationalism that welded countries into cohesive societies. They had become aware that other countries such as India were fighting for their independence. Organisations such as the 'Forty Group' was formed. The 'Forty Group' was composed mostly of African ex-servicemen who had been recruited into the military in 1940. The name is a translation of *Anake a Fote,* meaning 'The Young Men of Forty', and they were also known as *Kiama Kia Fote*, that is 'The Party of Forty'. The Forty Group later became a powerful section of the Kikuyu Central Association (KCA).

1 "The History of Kenya Agriculture" by L. Winston Cone, Ph.D. and J. F. Lipscomb O.B.E.

The Kikuyu Central Association had been started much earlier in 1924 by James Beauttah and Joseph Kang'ethe to act on behalf of the community in making representations to the British Government, especially in regard to land issues. In turn, its predecessor had been the Young Kikuyu Association founded by Harry Thuku, which was banned by the colonial government, and in 1940, the Kikuyu Central Association was banned as well when East Africa became involved in the Second World War, and survived only clandestinely.

As youngsters, we were conscious of these groups and admired their nationalistic spirit.

Society became increasingly divided and there was growing suspicion between Africans and Europeans. Surreptitious mutterings about rebellion, liberation, agitation and protest continued to build up.

For many of the older generation of Africans, life under colonial rule had dimmed their vision of the prospect of new or revolutionary circumstances. On the other hand, countless young people were well aware that the country was inching gradually forward into some variety of a transition and they sought to be part of it. They believed that the *status quo* in Kenya had to inevitably undergo modification.

These changes were occurring with great speed. Everywhere, Africans were critical of the humiliating colour bar and racial discrimination. More and more people became disinclined to be passive, obedient and submissive.

Even in our insulated situation at school, students were well aware of the political situation in Kenya. We students were from diverse places and our principle sentiment was that we were fortunate to be there in school. After all, there were multitudes that were unable to acquire an education.

Although we did not discuss politics at Kagumo, it was a constant dynamic in the background. Students puzzled over the manner in which Europeans obtained such power and influence, and we could not grasp the rationale behind the status of races and categories of discrimination among the Europeans, Indians, Arabs, Somalis and ourselves.

Why had we been relegated to the bottom of this list? Other races had much easier restrictions and circumstances, yet, before the Europeans arrived, the country had belonged to us. It seemed unfathomable and unacceptable.

Simply put, we did not comprehend the Europeans or their actions. We speculated about the factors that made them so dissimilar and distinct, why they were arrogant without any sense of justice and why they felt they were superior to all others. We hypothesised on the methods they used to acquire so much land and influence. Personally, I was puzzled over how the British could have callously taken our community's land and cold-bloodedly burned down my family's houses while my people watched in dismay, yet the same people preached Christian love and compassion.

That story – the one about how our houses were burnt down – was one that gave me a lingering sense of outrage. As a boy, I often went to pick coffee in that European estate to earn some money, but I could not enter or leave the farm without express permission by the supervisors. As an adult, and much later in life, I deliberately went back and bought some of that land. Although I had to buy the land that had once belonged to my community, it nevertheless gave me great pleasure that the first piece of land I ever purchased was part of the coffee farm on which I used to work. I felt that justice had at last been done for me, my father and our people.

* * *

After completing my education at Kagumo, I thought I would most likely become a clerk. I built a hut on my father's land and I had a girlfriend I wanted to marry.

One day, after I had put up some finishing touches to my new house, I was resting in the hut, dreaming vaguely of the future, when my brother Njoroge burst in. He had gone to the post office at Ruiru and found a letter for me. A letter, in those days, was an unusual occurrence and he waited impatiently for me to open it.

I no longer remember what I expected, but I never thought that all my plans and future would be transformed forever by the paper I found in that envelope.

It was from Alliance High School, and stated something like, "You have been accepted at Alliance High School and are expected to report on such and such day, between these hours, for enrolment."

The letter was late. The date I had to report was the very day that I received the letter and I had to report by 4 or 5 o'clock!

I was bewildered, my clothes were dirty and I needed to bathe, but my brother immediately got me on the bus to Kikuyu, which was about 96 kilometres away. When I arrived, I enrolled that afternoon, just as I was. I had no decent clothes or other necessities suitable for a boarding school. Not even a bag or box.

Nevertheless, my brother did not want me to miss this opportunity. He was an exceptionally steadfast and loyal man with a firm belief in the advantages of education. Some days later, he brought me my luggage.

However, at the back of my mind was regret that I had not even informed my brother about my girlfriend. I was sorry that I did not even find an occasion to say goodbye to that girl. My outlook absolutely switched over as the opportunity to attend Alliance arose. My thoughts changed from marriage and employment to going back to school.

Naturally, when I had the opportunity to meet my girlfriend sometime later, she forgave me for my abrupt departure. It was a shock to discover that, by that time, she had already married someone else. Just imagine, I could have married at the age of 16 and my life would be thoroughly different today. I would probably have become a school teacher and remained so for the rest of my working life.

At the beginning of 1946, I settled in at Alliance. This was an incredible opportunity for me. Only a small number of people were fortunate enough to attend secondary school and I certainly felt justified in being proud of myself.

There were several students from Kagumo who went to Alliance along with me, and we were all well received. Josephat Karanja, Mugo Marai and Gitau wa Kimuri joined me at Alliance, but they were unhappy with the strict discipline. Once they had taken the Junior Secondary Examination at the end of Form 2, they went back to Kagumo for their third and fourth years of high school.

Alliance received the best students from all over Kenya. Once students arrived in Alliance, there were no longer any ethnic divisions. Tribal differentiation was not encouraged at Alliance. The spirit was a Kenyan one and it was a wonderful little community. The students were extremely close and lived admirably together. I had a chance to meet people from all over the country.

At Alliance, all classes were conducted in English but those of us from Kagumo had been taught in Swahili. Although we had been taught to write excellent English at Kagumo, we had never actually conversed in the language, so the first two terms at Alliance were difficult. It was a challenge just to comprehend what the European teachers were saying.

The first year was spent in learning topics both academic and social. Because of our diverse backgrounds, some boys were more enlightened than others, but within the first year, we all came to be of a similar level and were all expected to have the same principles and values as Alliance boys.

Inequality at Alliance was highly discouraged by the Principal, Carey Francis. The transformation to a common status was extraordinarily quick because we were together all the time. As an example, not everyone could afford a pair of shoes. I was one of them. Due to this diversity in our backgrounds, it was a rule that we were not permitted to wear shoes except on Sundays. Carey Francis wanted us to concentrate on education and discouraged any other talk or distraction.

There were a good number of students from Kikuyuland in Alliance. I consider this disparity more a consequence of various circumstances rather than any tribal factors. For example, the Kikuyu were closer to the metropolitan area of Nairobi and as such, had greater awareness of the benefits of education. The construction of the Kenya-Uganda Railway and the location of Nairobi as the capital of Kenya, in addition to the focus of the missionary thrust, also brought the agriculturalist Kikuyu into immediate and deep interaction with Europeans and Asians. Therefore, this interplay of societies, traditions and customs resulted in quick assimilation of western ways for the neighbouring cultures like the Kikuyu.

The feeling of tribalism or ethnicity, during those days at Alliance, and even later at Makerere University College, did not really exist. We were one community of our own, that is 'Africans', and we saw ourselves consigned to the lowest level of society, treated differently, unfairly and without justice. As such, we had a common purpose and a common enemy and this enhanced our sense of mutual commitment.

There were a few other dissimilarities in the environment at Alliance to which those of us from Kagumo had to adjust. For instance, at Kagumo, the school was established by the government but Alliance was set up by missionaries. While the teaching at Kagumo aimed purely at enabling pupils to pass examinations with no attempt made to shape personalities, at Alliance the education was spiritually inclined and concentrated on character and community building. There was a serious religious disposition.

I should also mention that, at this point, almost halfway into the twentieth century, the colonial government had started actively promoting higher education for Africans. Although the missionaries had founded their schools around the beginning of the century with the intention of educating future teachers and priests, there were no government secondary schools until about 1933, after the Phelps Stokes Commission.

The first Phelps Stokes Education Commission was established in 1922, while the second was set up in 1925 and was chaired by Prof. Thomas Jesse Jones, with Dr Arthur Kwei Aggrey as the sole African member. Thereafter, it published a Colonial Office White Paper, *Education Policy in British Tropical Africa* (1925).

The commissions were privately financed and were inspired by the missionaries. The report called for partnership between missions and government, not separate development, and this policy was set forth in a subsequent Colonial Office Memorandum of 1925 entitled, "Education Policy in British Tropical Africa". There was also a significant "Protestant Lobby" at Westminster, which supported the partnership concept. The report also emphasised the need for agricultural and vocational education in Africa, criticising the then African educational system "as too literary and impractical for the realities of peasant-based African societies".

Martin Carnoy and Donald Schilling have argued that the education system supposedly adapted to meet local colonial conditions was, in fact, a means of social control intended to inculcate Africans with a sense of inferiority and keep them permanently in a secondary position. Africans received "industrial" training that included village-based agriculture, hygiene, and some reading and writing. The underlying premise was that the Kikuyu would remain in agriculture and work either on a large European settler farm or on his own plot indefinitely. There was no university preparatory secondary school in British Africa; according to S. J. Ball, secondary education for Africans was associated by the colonial administration with political activism and, therefore, condemned.

Then, later realising the need to provide educated labour to meet the needs of the European population, the government created high schools in each region of the country and established educational programmes. Alliance itself had been started about nine years earlier, in March 1926, by the Alliance of Protestant Churches – including the Church of Scotland (later known as the Presbyterian Church of East Africa), the Anglican Church of the Province of Kenya, and the Methodist Church. It was the first school in Kenya to offer secondary education to Africans.

Alliance had students from all denominations but Mang'u High School, our main rival in academics and sports, was mainly for Catholics. I am pleased and proud to have attended Alliance. It was a wonderful school which to this day continues to enjoy a reputation of high quality education and academic excellence. It has a long history of producing leaders both at national and international levels.

Our teachers were committed and skilled and did not need to intimidate or bully students. Carey Francis himself taught maths and English, and James Stevens Smith was his deputy.

Francis had the nickname *Kihiuria,* which means swinging or swaying. Whichever student got the bright idea of giving him that nickname was inspired by Carey Francis's odd habit of lurching forward in a rocking motion, with his finger rubbing across his upper lip, a characteristic and quaint movement he adopted, especially when agitated or annoyed.

Smith also had a nickname and the students referred to him as *Muturi,* which was natural enough, seeing that the word means a smith, or blacksmith, in the Kikuyu language. He was Scottish, a dedicated and thorough teacher, but not as much of an intellectual as Carey Francis. There were only one or two African teachers, one of whom was J. M. Ojal, who taught history. I believe he was a graduate of Alliance himself, and he later became a Permanent Secretary in 1963 when Kenya became independent. Earlier on, Eliud Mathu and James Gichuru, who both became prominent politicians in the run-up to and after independence, had also spent some time teaching at the school.

The few African teachers at Alliance had studied at Makerere and received a diploma in education, while the rest of the teachers were Europeans. I would say that all the teachers were enthusiastic about educating their students.

Alliance had a number of streams and we were approximately 200 students altogether. The courses were English, maths, literature, Kiswahili, history, geography, and general science, which included biology, chemistry and physics.

The curriculum was demanding and arduous. In addition to other topics, we were taught the history of the British Empire, about India and about the USA. There were no books at all about Kenya. In fact, the only subject in which Kenya actually featured was concerning the geological formation of the Rift Valley.

We also had religious studies at Alliance and my spiritual growth progressed as well. As I mentioned, religion was one of the subjects we had studied at Kiamwangi and I had already been baptised in 1941 when I was about 12 years old. I was committed to my faith and while at Alliance, I attended an Anglican confirmation class and was subsequently given a letter to take to the independent KISA Bishop, Harrison Gachukia, and was thereafter confirmed back home at Kiamwangi. As a result, I considered myself a full member of the church.

As far as our studies were concerned, there were no locally produced setbooks, and if our education seemed rather foreign, we nevertheless had no choice in the matter. It was the only education available to us. The main rationale for not teaching about Kenya was simply because there was no written material available. It is true that some Kikuyu books had been published. Tumutumu Church Missionary Society at Tumutumu had produced a number of vernacular books at this time, but no teachers used them because they had to follow the standard syllabus from Nairobi.

There was one small book, *Safari kutoka Mombasa,* which gave details of geographical sights along the railway line. There was, as I mentioned, *Hekaya za Abunwasi* and *Alfu Lela Ulela.* There were not many others written in Kiswahili, but I recall a very funny book written in Kikuyu called *Kaguraru na Waithera,* about a character who was so ugly that he just could not attract girls. We laughed our heads off when we read it. It was wonderful to be exposed to these books and the many others we found at school, but I have been unable to trace the authors. This was the first time I came across that famous character, Biggles!

Carey Francis also wrote books later. I remember *Highway Mathematics,* a series that later became the main mathematics textbook for schools.

Some people might wonder if the use of British books was an attempt to brainwash us, and I would not rule that out altogether, but personally, I doubt the philosophy was that deep. Most likely, the Europeans intended to pass along their own beliefs and, they possibly sought to convince us that everything should be done in the European 'civilised' manner.

While I was in school, I never really thought about who had written these books and never aspired to write because most of us were satisfied to read what was available. There was a West African, Dr Arthur Kwei Aggrey, who made a great contribution to education in the Gold Coast, today's Ghana. There was one other person, Henry Kiama Gathigira, who started writing and was a writer by nature. He became an editor for the *East African Standard*, and later one of his sons did the same. As time passed, of course, many other writers pioneered books for schools that had more Kenyan content.

I felt I was growing and learning. My concepts of the world I lived in naturally became more mature and gradually universal, yet my basic perceptions never really changed. It is important to remember that we would return to our homes at the end of every term and revisit the same people and same situations we grew up with. Our early influences remained within us. Merely learning how to read, learning how to speak English, acquiring facts or becoming Christians did not alienate us from our origins. Perhaps the most significant inspiration was the impact made by the constant repetition of the phrase, 'You are the leaders of the future', which we frequently heard from our elders. These words gave us motivation, encouragement, pride and a great sense of responsibility.

Throughout these years, it was government policy to divide and segregate the races at work, in social life and in education, and this was enforced by law. It was just not possible for a European or an Asian to study at Alliance High School just as no African could attend the Prince of Wales (now Nairobi School) or Duke of York High Schools. In towns, there were separate residential areas and even public toilets were distinct. No European at that time would have let it cross his mind to send his child to the same school with Africans. Alliance students like James Nesbit, Bill Martin and John Keen, who were of mixed race, were unsure of where to fit in.

One of the most pleasant and interesting diversions we undertook while at Alliance was a school trip to Mount Longonot. This was one of the annual educational tours that the school organised and any number of us who wished to go was able to travel there. The school authorities hired a number of train coaches and during our visit, the coaches were parked along a siding at Longonot station. We cooked and ate outside, but at night, we slept in the coaches.

Mount Longonot was, and still is, an impressive sight. It was the first example I ever saw of the volcanic craters we learned about in our geography classes. We hiked right up to the top and walked all around the crater rim. Dolimore, who taught science at Alliance was our guide. He took us round and explained everything.

We were enormously proud to be at Alliance and ecstatic at the chance to prove ourselves. We held triangular sports meetings with Prince of Wales and Duke of Gloucester (now Jamhuri High School).

I took a great deal of pleasure in sporting activities while at Alliance. My field was athletics, especially sprints. My favourite speciality was the 100 yard and 220 yard sprints. However, when I attempted the 880 yards a few times, I found it too demanding. Although I never won any trophies, I could say that I just barely missed winning prizes.

At that time, trophies and certificates were rare. I cannot recall anything other than a teacher patting me on the shoulder and giving me a resounding, "Well done!" At any rate, I would represent the school and represent my boarding house in athletics events, and it was great fun.

In addition, I did extremely well in hockey as goalkeeper and I recall that one of my teammates, both at Alliance and later at Makerere, was Samuel Onyango Ayodo, who later became a Government minister. We played a lot of football in the school, as well.

We excelled in everything but were especially excited at trouncing the European schools in sports. We defeated the Prince of Wales in football all the time, and it must have been a shock when we thrashed them in the English language exams, as well. We students were supremely pleased and I remember Carey Francis was extraordinarily proud of us.

We constantly sought to prove that we were not at the bottom. Due to the racial discrimination we experienced, we had a chip on our shoulders and at Alliance, we had the opportunity to demonstrate that we were educated and that we were as knowledgeable as the European students were.

We also competed against Mang'u High School. Mang'u was an African school comparable to Alliance and I recollect we consistently beat Mang'u in sports over a few years when we were on a long winning streak. Our relations with Mang'u were more congenial than with European schools. Our motives in dealing with European schools and fellow African students were poles apart. We understood that we students from Alliance and Mang'u were going to leave school concurrently and we would confront and tackle the same situations after graduation. We would be undergoing the same difficulties together, yet the Europeans would be our supervisors, taking charge over us.

Alliance Girls started around 1948, but even before that time, we already had four girls studying with us at Alliance. They had no dorms but resided in a teacher's house. They were Joan Gitau, later Joan Waithaka, who became Headmistress of Alliance Girls, Margaret Kenyatta, Isabella Muthoni and a Meru girl called Mukwa-Mugo. Joan was one year ahead of me, Isabella in my year and Margaret and Mukwa-Mugo a year behind me. The four girls at Alliance attended the same classes with the boys but their presence was never disruptive. They were clever girls but opportunities to talk to them personally were rare and no boy would dare disturb them for fear that he might be expelled.

There were other junior girls' schools in existence, such as at Thogoto, but in general, after the girls sat the primary examination, their parents were not willing to encourage them to prolong their education.

Parents felt the girls had reached the stage to get married. In addition, in the context of those days, not every parent valued girls' education. It was only as they became more enlightened that girls' education received the necessary attention it deserved.

For the European community, this educational disparity for girls was not so noticeable. There was Kenya High, Limuru Girls, and other schools, but no African girls went to these institutions during those early years.

There were plenty of activities at Alliance, and we were incredibly busy. On occasion, as young men, we naturally were interested in the company of girls but there were no opportunities to meet them. Dances or mixed social events were never held at the school and if Carey Francis ever caught us talking to girls, we were punished.

I remember there was a girls' school just across the valley. One day a friend, Mugo Waiyaki, and I met two girls on the lower slopes and started up a conversation. We were just beginning to get acquainted when Carey Francis spotted us as he drove his pickup to school.

"Boys, get in the car!" he ordered us.

We climbed up in the back. We were quite nervous and scared, and a thousand thoughts must have rushed through my mind at the time, but the memory that first strikes me is that Carey Francis's dog Mickey was there in the back of the pickup with us.

When we arrived at the school, we were each taken to our separate dorms.

"Sleep! And don't leave this bed until I give you permission!" Carey Francis commanded me, and I assume he told Mugo the same. This was a little strange, but I suppose it gave Carey Francis some time to consider our punishment in a calm and equitable way. The following day, he ordered us to cut the grass and do a few other chores, the usual penalties that were current in schools at the time.

To get back to my education, all the schools – Alliance, Mang'u and the European schools – sat the Cambridge School Certificate, which was set, naturally, in Cambridge, England. We took the examinations seriously because we were competing with European schools on an equal footing.

Just as it is today, the classroom and all the desks were cleaned and inspected and no piece of paper was permitted to remain during the test. We entered the examination room with our mathematical sets and pencils only, and our invigilators were teachers from other schools.

History, geography, and English were my favourite subjects and I did well in them. I sat for the Cambridge 'Ordinary' level examination in 1949 and achieved a Second Division. Division 1 was the top grade and Division 4 the lowest.

The exam was not as gruelling as I had feared although I never contemplated failure. I would have liked to pass at the highest level; nevertheless, I had distinctions in English and geography and in Kiswahili.

What let me down was literature. I was taught by James Stevens Smith, the deputy head, who seemed to detest me for reasons I have never understood and consequently I did not do as well as I had in my other subjects.

While still at Alliance, I did the Makerere Entrance Examination and received an A in literature. My passes were so high that I was vindicated. I would like to point out that some people passing in First Division in the School Certificate could still fail the Makerere Entrance Examination, as the criteria were not the same.

I also recollect another teacher at Alliance called Fred Welch. One evening I forgot to send in my prep book to him for marking and, although it was purely an oversight, he never forgave me. He believed that I withheld it deliberately and from then onward, no matter what I did, he never gave me a good mark.

Welch was also the school bursar, so at the end of my final year, I had to approach him in order to receive a refund of my caution money. When Welch handed me my leaving certificate and the balance of my money, he glowered off to the side without meeting my eyes and said, "Jeremiah, these Makerere teachers must have been asleep when marking your English paper."

I waited until I had received my money and had the certificate in my hand and then told him, "Thank you, sir, but if Makerere teachers think my English is satisfactory, I'm not bothered by the opinion of a mere school teacher." I was angered by his rudeness and never sought to see him again. That is how I left Alliance at the end of 1949.

* * *

Looking back at my school days, I believe Alliance had a wonderful influence on me. It enabled me, as well as others, to gain sufficient knowledge to reason, analyse events and formulate decisions about the future. By the time we returned to the village, we were aware that we were going to be among the select few. We were regarded as role models and, as I mentioned earlier, the old men frequently told us that we were the leaders of the future. We were held up as examples. How could we help but feel that we had great responsibilities ahead of us?

The Alliance motto, 'Strong to Serve', can be interpreted in a number of ways, but I believe it referred to the fact that, if one belonged to the school, one was obliged to be at the service of the school. Just as strongly, the words of the motto incorporated the sense of serving the country. I feel that this was not in a political sense and I do not believe it was intended to make us subservient. On the contrary, it made us deliberate on how we could best use our skills in serving the people and as schoolboys, it seemed a spiritually rewarding thing to do.

Leadership and leadership qualities were respected at Alliance. For example, all prefects at Alliance were carefully selected and their attributes were well recognised. Later in life, those who had been acknowledged to have these characteristics actually did become leaders, or prominent persons in their fields.

There were never sufficient places for everyone who wanted to go to school, so there was a great wastage of talent in this respect, merely because government revenue was not adequate to ensure an acceptable number of schools for Africans. Alliance, as a government-sponsored school, received a grant from the government and later there were other government-assisted high schools established in each region, in an attempt to educate a few from every area of the country. In addition, there were also government-funded primary schools. Kagumo African Government School, which I had attended before joining Alliance, was one of these.

The type of education we were getting did not exceedingly bother us, provided we acquired knowledge. Nevertheless, it was disturbing to realise that educating one European child cost as much as educating 20 African students. If we compared the diet of the European schools with that of the African ones, for example, there was a huge disparity between them. We could see this disparity, even as school boys.

One of the explanations for Alliance's success was the distinguished and impressive leadership of Carey Francis. He was an excellent educator although I believe he originally came to Kenya as a missionary. He was a staunch Anglican and believed, quite compellingly, in the goals he was undertaking to achieve. He came to Alliance in 1941, administered the institution as his own, and treated the students like his children.

Carey Francis had his individual idiosyncrasies and occasionally clashed with other Europeans. He was solely engaged in education, teaching, and service to the country and discouraged politics deliberately. He was highly respected, even in the Ministry of Education.

At that time, I assume he reflected only vaguely on independence. I doubt he ever saw this country as self-governing. Carey Francis believed that he was part of the process of civilising and educating Africans, and probably never considered that this education could lead to African rule. In that respect, he may have been as short-sighted as many other Europeans. He did not see that independence was imminent and he believed, like the settlers, that the Europeans were in Kenya to stay, that this was a 'White man's country'.

In addition to his dislike for politics, Carey Francis also despised and detested women. I remember there was one woman stationed in the Ministry of Education as a physical education supervisor. Whenever she arrived to check on the Physical Education (PE) programme at Alliance, Carey Francis would get physically sick.

Carey Francis would occasionally invite selected boys for dinner and I know there are people who question the motives of certain of these European teachers who remained bachelors for life. In hindsight, I do not believe Carey Francis ever had a hidden agenda. He gave the impression that he was wholeheartedly dedicated to facilitating our development into idealistic young men. Furthermore, many years later, after his retirement, when he was at Pumwani School in Nairobi, he assisted children who were orphaned by the Mau Mau war, and his exertions on their behalf led to notable accomplishments. He simply delighted in giving service to young people, just like Geoffrey Griffin who founded the academically excellent Starehe Boys' Centre for destitute boys.

Carey Francis was an extraordinary individual and as far as I know, other schools did not have an equivalent. Father McGill, who was the headmaster at Mang'u, never had the force of character that Carey Francis had. Lockhart from Kagumo and Carey Francis never got on well and were constantly critical of each other. They were in direct competition, both in recruiting the best students, and in achieving the highest results in their schools.

* * *

While I was at Alliance, and shortly after my graduation, events in Kenya and in the world were rapidly changing. As I mentioned earlier, soldiers returned from the Second World War and the sentiment among Africans who had served in the armed forces grew more and more nationalistic. Furthermore, India had gained Independence in 1947, creating immense anticipation and encouragement for those Africans who were agitating to remove the settlers and colonial officials from their positions of privilege.

Although the Kikuyu Central Association had been banned, it went underground in the late 1940s. The General Council of the association started calling for civil disobedience to bring colonial attention to the problems of landlessness and over-crowding as well as to force reform in that sector. The preparations for the campaign were initiated by certain leaders of the KCA through traditional secret oaths. The KCA formed clandestine teams throughout central Kenya and the oaths, which initially required acts of civil disobedience, transformed to become more radical.

In addition, by 1949, the fledgling trade unions also took up the challenge. On 1 May 1949, the East African Trade Union Congress (EATUC) was formed by a coalition of six trade unions. One of the first campaigns EATUC undertook in 1950, and which proved incredibly awkward for the colonial government, was to boycott the festivities surrounding the granting of a Royal Charter to the city of Nairobi. The Duke and Duchess of Gloucester had flown in from London for the ceremony, in order to hand over Letters of Patent to the Mayor, Alderman Woodley, on 30 March.² At that time, the Governor was Philip Mitchell.

The general rumour among Africans was that the Royal Charter would put the city of Nairobi under direct control of the King and that he intended to annex all the land therein and the 16 kilometres surrounding it. This naturally caused extreme concern and bitterness.

The nationalists justified the boycott with the claim that Nairobi Municipal Council was undemocratic and was under the control of Europeans who were the minority in the country. This precipitated furious conflict between African militant activists and those Africans loyal to the colonial administration. For example, political activist, Fred Kubai, and two others were arrested for allegedly attempting to murder a councillor, Muchohi Gikonyo. The councillor was shot at while he was in Eastlands. Although Gikonyo was not hit, Kubai was arrested for this, though he was later set free for lack of evidence.

Later the same year, EATUC put forth an ultimatum pressing for Kenya's independence. This led to the arrest of the executive members of EATUC and later, on 16 May 1950, the few officials who had eluded the police called for a general strike. This strike paralysed Nairobi for nine days and ended only after 300 workers had been jailed. Other towns took up the demonstrations and some sources say that up to 100,000 workers were involved altogether. For two days, all activities in the port city of Mombasa were at a standstill, as well. The colonial forces eventually arrested all the EATUC officials and the strike collapsed.

---

2   "History of Kenya's Trade Union Movement to 1952", Makhan Singh, East African Publishing House, 1969.

The trade union activists then began to concentrate on KCA oath-taking activities, and used the organisation as a foundation for further achievements in the conflict. In order to strengthen their impact, they joined the Forty Group, founded by Mwangi Macharia, among others. The oaths administered by the Forty Group were still more radical and differed significantly from the ones adopted in the so-called 'White Highlands' because they were dedicated to the violent overthrow of colonial rule.

I was studying at Makerere while most of this was going on, and we Kenya students were electrified by the happenings back home.

Chapter 4

Makerere and After

Even before I received my results for the Cambridge School Certificate, I had decided on going into teaching. The teaching profession appealed to me greatly. It remained my intense ambition. In any case, what alternatives were available? There were scarcely any opportunities other than teaching and we could only aspire to what was possible. I could have become a clerk but the majority of such positions were held by Goans and other Asians. Furthermore, if I were to be employed in a clerical post I would be on the same level and job group as someone with only primary school education.

I often thought about my old school at Kiamwangi and the education I obtained there. The teachers did not actually understand much about the theory and purpose of education and I was convinced that it was essential to uplift the quality of the education such schools provided. I saw discrepancies and incongruity because, for example, in cookery classes, the girls were instructed in baking bread and cakes and yet they did not even have ovens at home. Naturally, they had the opportunity to learn how to prepare African dishes from their mothers, but in school, they were taught material that was mainly foreign to our ways of life.

I felt there was a need to re-examine the curriculum and evaluate it afresh. As it were, the more we were educated, the more alienated and 'foreign' we became. The exams I took while I was at Alliance High School were related to the British Empire, the USA, European and Asian history, for example the life of Genghis Khan, and there was nothing about Kenya. I realised that I knew exceedingly little about my own country and I disliked the irrelevant and unfamiliar view of reality presented to the students. I felt I could make the greatest contribution to my community by introducing significant and pertinent teaching and this ambition became a driving force in my life.

My focus changed when I received my results of the Makerere entrance exam. Although the results of the School Certificate were to be announced later, the results of the Makerere entrance exam were declared while we were still at Alliance High School.

The names of all those who had passed were posted on the notice board and you can just imagine the shouts of joy and the noisy excited laughter that erupted when we spotted our names on the list. We were thrilled and delighted and I was absolutely jubilant. It was one of the most exhilarating experiences I ever had at Alliance.

For me the joy was a little delayed. Joan Gitau and I shared the same initials, as I was going by Jeremiah Gitau at the time. Initially, there was a bit of confusion as to which of us had passed, but when Welch, the bursar, checked the list, it was found that both of us had been successful.

The Makerere entrance exam was unique and had little relevance to the curriculum we studied for the Cambridge School Certificate. For example, Joan Gitau and Joseph Kariuki, who were one year ahead of me at Alliance and who both received a First Division in the Cambridge School Certificate, did not pass the Makerere entrance exam on their first attempt. They sat for the exam again in the same year in which I did the test for the first time and since we all passed, we began at Makerere together.

Those of us bound for Makerere boarded the train at 10 am in Nairobi, one day, and arrived in Kampala the following day at 4 pm. Although I had seen the Rift Valley when I climbed Mt. Longonot on a school field trip, it was quite a different experience travelling by train and seeing the vistas passing by in one long panoramic series of spectacular landscapes.

On arrival in Uganda, we were met at the station by the college bus. We did not have a formal orientation, but some of the other students were kind enough to show us around the college, which is located on one of the small hills that dot Kampala.

In those days, it was impossible to select one's own courses at Makerere. The field of study was determined by the results obtained in the entrance exam. In this respect, I had never seen myself as a scientist and had a strong preference for arts subjects. My school certificates show that I excelled in them, For example, at Alliance my best subjects were English, history and geography. At heart, I knew I was an arts student. Nevertheless, through some quirk of fate, when we wrote the Makerere entrance examination, although I did well in English, I got my best results in science subjects.

Therefore, since I had passed so well in the sciences, Professor Beadle, who was the head of the Science Department, informed me that I would have to study full science, that is, physics, chemistry and biology, in order to become a doctor. I was traumatised! I pleaded to be allowed to change my subjects but Professor Beadle turned down my appeal, and for two years I struggled with sciences and considered it a punishment.

I just could not tolerate biology. The immediate basis for my revulsion was that we were sometimes expected to study in the morgue, where they cut up human cadavers. My only thoughts were that I just could not accomplish anything in this field of study and that I would be obliged to go home.

Luckily, I ended up studying physics, chemistry and geography, and managed to discontinue biology. I was upset that I was unable to study history, a subject that fascinated me. Eventually, I had to accept the reality of studying sciences. In spite of the fact that I was studying subjects for which I had little affinity, I would never have dared turn down the chance to study at Makerere. I would have looked foolish.

I would like to give a little background on this illustrious school. Makerere began as a technical and post-secondary school in 1922 and was the first institution of higher learning in eastern Africa. It accepted students from the whole region and central Africa as well.

In 1949, it became a university linked to the University of London for purposes of offering degree courses. In 1950, there were 90 students from Kenya in Makerere and in 1953, it produced its first-degree graduates. The Royal Technical College was opened in Kenya in 1954. In 1961, it started offering degree courses and was renamed 'Royal College'. It became a university college in 1963 and was later renamed the University of Nairobi.

Makerere was considered to have similar standards to those of the same-level schools abroad. The first two years of study were spent on Foundation Courses, and after that, one could proceed onward to one of the four professional fields of study offered. These were education, medicine (which was a seven-year course), veterinary science and agricultural science. Makerere did not award degrees at the time but conferred a lower qualification referred to as 'Licentiate' – an attestation of a student's competence. I recall, for example, that later, after Makerere was sanctioned to do so, Mwai Kibaki was among the first students awarded degrees under the auspices of the University of London.

About 16 students from Alliance went to Makerere with me, which was the largest group yet. Students came from all over eastern Africa and the majority came from Kenya, Uganda, Tanganyika and Zanzibar, but the proportions varied from year to year.

Makerere and the situation in Uganda were a revelation to me. First, one of the major differences we found in Uganda was the freedom to come and go as we pleased, in contrast to the strict control we had experienced in boarding school.

Secondly, Uganda was extraordinarily unlike Kenya and had a distinct form of colonialism, which was entirely dissimilar to what I had experienced at home. There were few Europeans and their influence in the country was limited. Ugandans enjoyed basic freedoms of movement, of expression, of politics, of society and so on. We found delight in the freedom to travel anywhere we wished without restriction and to see well-to-do Ugandans mingling without restraint with their European superiors at entertainment spots and restaurants. As students, we did not have much money to engage in these pastimes ourselves. It was surprising to see that, although non-Africans were treated with a certain degree of deference, discrimination based on race was insignificant.

In great contrast to Kenya, there was no talk of rebellion or of oaths by Africans in Uganda. Although both Kenya and Uganda were under British rule, the Ugandans retained their kings and their social associations, resulting in a significant measure of independence, and there was diluted enforcement of the colour bar in evidence. The traditional kings were semi-autonomous and largely cooperated with the colonial administrators in the process of governing the country. For example, the ruler of the Buganda Kingdom, the Kabaka, reigned over a substantial portion of Uganda and thus was among one of the most powerful rulers. The traditional rulers in Uganda were respected by their subjects. Therefore, the British were able to rule through them (indirect rule). The situation in Kenya was different as the ordinary man had little regard for the sub-chiefs and chiefs appointed by the colonial authorities.

The new liberty and lack of restrictions that we Kenyans enjoyed at Makerere was intoxicating. A small number of students plunged into a happy-go-lucky lifestyle and unfortunately acquired the inclination for overindulgence in alcohol and thus did not complete their college courses. The majority of us, however, undertook our education absolutely seriously and after completing two years of study, we successfully passed our exams and were awarded our certificates.

I never happened to get into trouble. I was, in general, well-behaved and concentrated on my studies. Just after I left, Josephat Karanja, Omolo Okero, John Malechela and Hamduni were expelled from Makerere during what was called the 'Mammoth Strike' when the students protested over the quality of food. Luckily enough, they all ended up in good schools later and did well.

We did not have much money, and, since the college did not close down and continued to provide food for us even while on term breaks, we saved money by staying at school. I used to go home just once a year, from December to March, for vacation and during that time, I would return to Kiamwangi as a temporary teacher.

During my time at Makerere, Prof. Elizabeth Hoyt was one of my lecturers. She was an elderly woman, intense and dedicated to her work, and was a professor on an exchange programme from Iowa State College in the United States of America. Although I cannot recall what prompted me into my original discussions with her, I remember that I discussed my feeling of personal commitment in improving the curriculum for African students at KISA schools, particularly for girls. I told her about my dissatisfaction with the subjects which appeared to have little or no relevance to the everyday life of the pupils. I recollect that I used the same example (quoted earlier), that is, the irrelevance of learning to bake cakes and exotic European dishes, yet students had no ovens in their homes. She was something of an intellectual mentor to me. She was quite interested in the independent schools and I recall that I prepared a few background papers for her on the subject.

We became friends and Prof. Hoyt assured me that she would assist me to obtain a scholarship, so that I could study for a degree in Iowa. I filled out the application forms and received my letter of admission. When Prof. Hoyt returned to the USA, she wrote to say she would expect me in the fall. I have to confess that at the time, I had no idea which months fell within that season. She also sent me books and even a warm winter coat to enable me to prepare for university.

Once I left Makerere, therefore, I merely had to acquire a passport and be on my way to the USA. I found this prospect enormously exciting because, not only would I be flying for the first time, but I would also experience the Western world personally and would be returning to Kenya with a degree in education.

I could have continued with my studies at Makerere in order to obtain a teacher's diploma but since Prof. Hoyt had assured me that I would get a scholarship, I felt it wiser to leave after my foundation courses and make it my priority to obtain a degree and specialised qualifications elsewhere. A degree would enable me to teach education professionally and, more importantly, to develop a system of education incorporating a curriculum more appropriate to the students. I felt I would be able to garner respect for such a new system by proving its relevance and importance to Kenyan students.

Therefore, I left Makerere at the end of 1951 and went home for what I was convinced would be a temporary stay until I got my travelling documents and funds organised.

By the time I started teaching at Kiamwangi in early 1952, it had become a secondary school under Headmaster Stephen Kioni. He was an incredibly committed educationalist who had trained at Makerere and later became head of the Kenya National Union of Teachers (KNUT). Because many of the teachers at Kiamwangi were untrained, he actually took the time to train the staff in the various skills they needed as teachers, during lunch time and during break. By this time, Kiamwangi had become a prominent educational institution which attracted students from all over Kenya, even as far afield as Nyanza and Coast provinces.

One of the main reasons independent schools were so successful was that they had a more national outlook, unlike village schools that admitted people from the surrounding areas. Kiamwangi even had international students, such as those from Uganda, and at one stage, it had students from most of the major tribes in Kenya. Just before the Declaration of the State of Emergency in October 1952, when the school closed down, we had students from Ukambani, from the Coast, from the Rift Valley, Western Province ... everywhere in Kenya. Kiamwangi, Gikumbo and Githunguri were considered prominent schools within the family of independent schools.

I enjoyed being a teacher at the school and concentrated on teaching geography and English. The special class we taught in order to prepare our pupils for the national exams consisted of about 20 to 25 students.

As is natural, some of my students did well in life, but others did not. G. G. Kariuki ended up as a Member of Parliament and a minister under the Moi administration and Joe Mugambi became a wealthy businessman. I did not meet G.G. often, but I met Mugambi many times. He always referred to me as *Mwalimu* (Teacher). G.G., on the other hand, did not quite recognise me as his *Mwalimu*, perhaps because he became a senior politician and I was a senior civil servant. It seems that politicians always think they are more important than civil servants. Nevertheless, at one time we served together well. He was a Minister of State and I was the Head of the Civil Service and Secretary to the Cabinet at that time.

There were about four or five other students of mine who were later employed in the oil industry. I clearly remember their faces, but I cannot recall their names. Once they were employed, I used to meet them in Nairobi. They had all done extremely well in their careers. I was always happy to see them.

I was proud of my students and pleased with all those who went to school and survived. Life was difficult for them and they were in a particular category of their own. Just the fact that they went to independent schools would be a stigma when they went to look for jobs. It is important to remember that grades, marks or certificates from independent schools were not officially approved or accepted by anyone. As a result, they did not have a recognised document which they could show and which would be respected. Therefore, for these people, success came purely through their own efforts.

Furthermore, despite the political agitation that was going on and the feelings of oppression and isolation, the students were well-behaved, well-disciplined, showed respect for teachers and had a desire for education. Education was seen as the key to progress and success.

Although there were girls in the primary sections, as far as I can recall, there were no girls at the secondary school level at that time. Most parents felt it was a waste and that their daughters would be better off married.

While teaching at Kiamwangi Primary and Secondary schools, I had two intentions in mind. Firstly, I would be facilitating the students in their scholarly pursuits, a task I felt drawn to, and secondly, I would be earning money for my airfare and expenses when I went to the USA. In addition to the funds I saved myself, a number of the elders and friends of my brother's made contributions to assist me.

When the schools closed for holiday in early 1952, I travelled to Nairobi to get clearance documents, which would enable me to get a passport. I went to see the officer in charge of higher education, Arnold Curtis, an impressively tall man who was responsible for giving recommendations in such matters.

Curtis refused to recommend me.

"You young people! You are too ambitious! Even if it means going back next year, you must return to Makerere," he told me, "and get a teacher's diploma!"

He stated that as long as he was in charge of Higher Education, he would never allow me to obtain a passport.

Later I understood that he was confronted with a shortage of teachers in Kenya, and he did not want to lose me, but at the time, I was extremely disturbed and disappointed, even angry. The stubbornness of one individual blocked the ambitions I had been envisioning for my future, my education and travel abroad. Finding myself at this dead end, I had to force myself to re-evaluate the opportunities that were still available around me. For a protracted length of time, I continued hoping to study abroad, yet eventually, other things intervened. I returned to Kiamwangi, thwarted and downhearted, but there was little I could do about realising my personal dream at that difficult juncture in the history of the country.

* * *

The decade after the Second World War turned out to be tumultuous throughout the country and quite unsettling for me, irrespective of my success and matriculation from Makerere. Political dynamics were now an inferno and the return of the nationalist Jomo Kenyatta from the UK on 14 August 1947, fanned the flames even higher. Civil disobedience, which was supposed to commit people to a cause, started in earnest.

From December 1944 to 1952, the Governor in Kenya was Sir Philip Mitchell and from December 1952 to 1959, the Governor was Sir Evelyn Baring. During this period, the political situation in Kenya became extremely difficult because the amplification of the struggle for rights and liberties merely resulted in greater repression of Africans and there was a great deal of upheaval, particularly in the few years between 1951 and 1953.

Although African opposition to colonialism and agitation for independence was widespread throughout the country, the oath was, for the most part, a phenomenon peculiar to central Kenya. The oath-taking culture had taken root while I was away in Uganda, mounting by the day and was administered to many men and women throughout Kikuyuland. The oath was meant to bind and unite all members of the Kikuyu tribe in their struggle for independence from British colonialists. Young adults of my age and above were expected to undergo the oath and contribute to the hostilities against the British. The oath was intended to inspire terror and to guarantee faithful allegiance to the movement's principles of self-determination, independence and the restoration of our land.

As a result, across central Kenya, thousands of men and women were taken into custody and incarcerated in detention camps without trial. Those suspected of subscribing to the oath and supporting the Mau Mau were dragged off to these detention camps. This crackdown added fervour to the oath-taking as additional supporters enlisted in the struggle.

The immediate events that led up to the declaration of a State of Emergency in Kenya reveal that the increasing agitation for African rights was met with stern oppression and force rather than cooperation and compromise which, had they been adopted as policies of administration, may have made the Kenyan path to independence less traumatic.

In May 1951, the Kenya African Union (KAU) presented the visiting British Colonial Secretary, James Griffiths, with a list of African demands including the removal of discriminatory legislation and the appointment of at least 12 elected African representatives to the Kenya Legislative Council (LegCo). KAU was a political organisation formed in 1944 to articulate African grievances against the British colonial administration and was led by Jomo Kenyatta from 1947 onwards.

Jomo had been sent to London in 1929 by the Kikuyu Central Association, of which he was secretary, to agitate for Kikuyu rights and freedom before the Secretary for Colonies. He returned to Kenya in 1930 and left again for England in 1931. He stayed there until 1946 when he came back and took over the chairmanship of KAU, which was the biggest political party then. KAU was banned by the government in 1953.

KAU had attempted to be more inclusive than its predecessor, the Kikuyu Central Association, by espousing a national outlook. When he came back from Britain in 1947, Kenyatta took over the helm of KAU leadership from James Gichuru, who was its chairman. Gichuru was an educated political activist and he was very articulate about the rights of Africans.

Instead of giving in to KAU demands, Griffiths introduced a system in which 14 delegates were elected to represent 30,000 settlers; another 100,000 Asians elected six representatives, and Arabs elected one representative. However, over 5 million Africans had only five representatives – and these were nominated by the government, rather than elected by the people.

By June 1951, radical trade union members forced their way into the formerly moderate KAU and gained control of the Nairobi branch. By this time, Tom Mboya had already started his political career after he was employed by the Nairobi City Council in 1950. A year after joining the African Staff Association, he was elected its president and immediately embarked on moulding the association into a trade union named the Kenya Local Government Workers Union.

As it happened, the militants in KAU created a secret Central Committee to organise an oath-administration campaign throughout Nairobi and formed armed squads to enforce its policies, protect members from the police and eliminate informers and those who sympathised with the

British. Radicals also attempted to take control of KAU at a countrywide conference convened in November 1951 but were outmanoeuvred by the moderate Jomo Kenyatta (who preferred the constitutional approach rather than violence) and he again secured election for himself. Nevertheless, pressure from the radicals forced KAU to adopt a pro-independence position for the first time.

The Central Committee also began to extend its oath administration campaign outside Nairobi. Their resistance won them many adherents in committees throughout the 'White Highlands' and the Kikuyu reserves. Central Committee activists grew bolder, often killing opponents in broad daylight. A few European farmhouses were set on fire and their livestock hamstrung. The Governor, Sir Philip Mitchell, who was only months away from retirement, ignored these warning signs. Therefore, Mau Mau activities remained unchecked.

Since 1950, the Mau Mau oath had been administered secretly but extensively throughout Kikuyuland but colonial intelligence services did not seem to grasp the facts or the intensity surrounding the movement. Even before the Mau Mau war flared up in 1952, incidents such as the murders of loyalists were occurring, but the authorities did not seem to link them with the rebellion.

By June 1952, Henry Potter briefly replaced Mitchell, who had gone on sick leave, as acting Governor. One month later, he was informed by the colonial police intelligence that a Mau Mau plan for rebellion was in the works. Collective fines were levied and punishment enforced on particularly unstable areas, oath administrators were arrested and Kikuyu loyal to the government were encouraged to denounce the resistance.

Several times in mid-1952, Jomo Kenyatta gave in to colonial pressure and agreed to give speeches purportedly critical of the Mau Mau, yet he never once openly criticised the Mau Mau. He spoke in such circuitous and ambiguous proverbs that even the Kikuyu themselves could not decipher the true meaning of his words. One phrase I recall was his advice to the Mau Mau to "disappear". The way in which he said it could be interpreted in two ways, that is, "no longer exist" or "go underground". There is no evidence that Kenyatta ever took the oath himself.

In terms of law, no one knew what 'Mau Mau' was as an entity. I believe Kenyatta was being subtle and discerningly precise when he denied knowledge of it. He was doing so, 'tongue in cheek', and if such a problem had ever come to me, I might have done the same. Nevertheless, this prompted the creation of at least two plots within the Nairobi Central Committee militants to assassinate Kenyatta.

It was around this time, October 1952, that Ambrose Ofafa and Walter Mbotela, both moderate councillors, were killed. Walter Mbotela was a member of the Nairobi African District Council and was killed by the Mau Mau at night while on his way home. In addition to being the Councillor for Nairobi's Eastlands, Mbotela, by the way, had been working as a freelance translator at the Indian High Commission, where I was later employed.

I first heard about the Mau Mau around 1950 while at Makerere. We heard reports about some trouble in Naivasha. I believe there had been some incidents such as breaking into a police post. I read a report in the newspapers about that event and about some people taking oaths and I recall that Fred Kubai was mentioned. The colonial government was just starting to take a serious look at what those fighting for freedom were doing, their intentions and the implications for security.

It may be of interest to note that the name Mau Mau may not have been coined by members of the movement itself. There are many unverified versions on the origin of the word.

The organisers intended the movement to be widespread and the oath served to bind them together. The Mau Mau movement was led by the elders who made the decisions while the youth were the foot soldiers, the infantry. A great many other supporters delivered supplies, sent messages, hid Mau Mau agents and, in general, gave them financial and logistical help.

The District Commissioners (DCs) in the affected areas were well aware of what was going on and viewed the Mau Mau as a political movement whose aim was to force Europeans out of the country. Reporters who were writing stories about KAU and dealing with the local politicians were also well aware it was a political movement yet this perception was deliberately obscured by the colonial propagandists in order to discredit the movement. It was, therefore, presented as a primitive and bloodthirsty movement, a civil war with murder and atrocities as the main focus.

* * *

Around March or April 1952, while I was teaching at Kiamwangi, Waira Kamau, a fiery nationalist who led the Mau Mau movement in the Githunguri area approached me on the issue of taking the Mau Mau oath. Most people of my age had pledged the oath and it was inevitable that I would be coerced to follow suit. Waira, who was at the time, the

Secretary to the *Mariika* (age-groups) Association, began to increasingly gain political influence when he and other like-minded nationalists from the area started collecting funds for the Kenya Teachers' College at Githunguri, which was spearheaded by Mbiyu Koinange. Africans felt they were being denied access to higher education because training for them was severely limited.

Funds for education mostly went to the European schools. Nationalists like Mbiyu Koinange then felt that the easiest way to overcome this disparity was to produce well-trained teachers for the independent schools. In 1929, they demanded an end to the monopoly on education held by missions, asking the colonial government either to establish more government schools or to authorise Kikuyu parents to start their own independent institutions. The Kikuyu were also prompted by a desire to preserve as many of their traditions as possible in the face of colonialism. They hoped to provide greater educational opportunities, free of government or mission control, and at the same time avoid the corrosive influence of adopting colonial education policy. Koinange eventually helped launch the first independent teacher training institution – the Kenya Teachers' College at Githunguri, which trained teachers for East and Central Africa in 1938. It found a home in Githunguri as the area was the stormy centre of pre-independence nationalist activities.

Mbiyu Koinange was Jomo Kenyatta's best friend and was among the most educated Africans at the time. He was a moderate, who emphasised the need for Africans to get education in order to come up to the level of the Europeans. His father, Senior Chief Koinange, had been a supporter of the colonialists but altered his view after it dawned on him that the British had never intended to treat Africans as equals. It is said that the so-called Kiambaa parliament met in his house. It was also rumoured that the arms that were gathered in Nairobi immediately before the declaration of the State of Emergency were stored in an armoury in his house. He rebelled against the colonialists, was sacked and then ultimately, imprisoned.

Waira was quite cautious because he was aware that he was being followed by informers and carried out most of his activities at night.

He and his brother, Babu, were my friends and would call on me at home every now and then. Due to my level of education, I was well known and Waira requested that I accompany him during visits to meet foreign dignitaries, British politicians and other prominent individuals who occasionally toured the countryside in order to evaluate the volatile state of affairs in Kenya. Waira often invited me to become part of the escort because he believed that I spoke better English and would effectively communicate with such international visitors about African concerns and grievances.

Waira also informed me that I could be of invaluable service to the country. He declared that an educated person like me could influence others more than he (Waira) could. He frequently called on me, continually attempting to convince me that I could perform far more vital work for the country if I took the oath.

"You have to be with the people. It does not matter how well-educated you are. Unless you get the confidence of the people, you will get nowhere. You have to be in a position where people trust you. You have to be one of them."

He felt that until I took the oath, people would never have trust in me. *"Mundu ni andu na andu nio indo,"* he said, persuading me with a proverb stating, "One is nothing without others because wealth is rooted in people" or "No man is an island."

Finally, after some time had passed, Waira again asked me why I had not taken the oath.

"You know, Waira, I'm a Christian and I've also had an education. There is no way anyone is going to intimidate me by saying I will die if I go against the oath. It won't bind me in any way."

"But people will not trust you!" he exclaimed.

I tried to explain my view more clearly. "I'm not one of those people who are going to be afraid of spirits or whatever. I just do not believe in them. Whether I take it or not is irrelevant."

Waira insisted, "But unless you do this, you can never be among the people. Look, I cannot do anything about the fact that you do not feel bound by the oath, but no one will trust you until you have taken it. It is the only way you will be able to communicate with other like-minded nationalists. You better take it, whether you believe in it or not."

It was a difficult decision for me. The oath was irrelevant, but for the ordinary man, it was everything. I finally agreed.

After all, I definitely believed in the principles behind the movement, and I sincerely wanted the colonialists out of our country. I was strongly convinced that it was the moment for Africans to seize control of their affairs. Education and nearly all other aspects of life were dictated by colonial whims. Waira merely stressed a point that was already a conviction in my own mind.

Under the cover of darkness, Waira escorted me to an out-of-the-way little hut in the neighbourhood. There were three people inside and everything was arranged to horrify the superstitious mind. I was quite disgusted with the concoction we were forced to swallow!

I went through the motions, took the oath and from then onward, I was regarded as a dependable comrade who was faithful to the cause and trusted with the secrets of the freedom movement. By taking the oath, I had demonstrated my determination and commitment to fight the Europeans. I promised that if called upon, I would obey my orders and never disclose the oath or anything to do with the movement.

Oaths were given at various levels of seriousness and commitment. I took the initiation oath to show commitment, but none of the higher oaths. I do not believe I would have ever been called upon to kill anyone, but nothing was excluded. As I said, once one was given an order, one was obliged to obey it, no matter what it was. I am afraid that if I had been told to kill someone, I would have been unable to do so. I would never be able to kill. This was just not in my nature and I have never been a physically violent person.

* * *

In the greater Kiambu District, some men opted to take up arms and go to the bush to wage guerrilla warfare against the British and the loyalist Home Guard. The Kikuyu Home Guard forces were informally established around 1952, in response to attacks by the Mau Mau. It was a collection of several hundred Tribal Police and private armies established by loyalist leaders in the wake of Mau Mau attacks. Officially sanctioned by the colonial government, at its peak, in 1954, the Home Guard numbered more than 25,000 men – more than the number of Mau Mau fighters in the reserves.

It is said that, unlike many other Kikuyu, Embu and Meru warriors who went to fight and hide in the Aberdares and Mount Kenya forests, most people in Kiambu stayed behind and waged the war from their homes. I cannot sufficiently explain or account for this difference; however, one factor was simply due to the geographical detail that few forests existed in the area. Another factor might be that they concentrated their efforts on the resistance taking place in Nairobi, which was not far away. There was essentially an enormous quantity of activity taking place in Kiambu and people raised considerable amounts of money and other resources for the cause. The funds and supplies were dispatched to the Mau Mau leadership in Nairobi to buy arms and supplies for the forces in the city and in the forests.

We had heard that Bildad Kaggia and Fred Kubai headed the Mau Mau Central Committee (or Mau Mau War Council, as it was sometimes called) but information was so limited and confidential that we were never sure.

In Kibichoi, we established our own secret cell of the Mau Mau. One day, Waira Kamau informed me of the need to create a façade in order to disguise the regular secret night meetings of our men. These meetings were risky and hazardous as the colonial authorities or the home guards would unquestionably arrest us and drag us off to detention camps if they discovered the nature of our stealthy gatherings. Therefore, in April 1952, Waira and I initiated plans to rent a building and created phoney business premises with a sign, "Mariigi Bakery".

Once this 'Bakery' cooperative was set up, the Mau Mau leaders in the area would convene in various places, collecting members' dues, discussing how they should raise funds for the business and recruiting more members from villages. Oaths were then administered on the sidelines. Waira selected me to be the secretary since I was the most literate in the group and I would write the 'minutes' of the meetings every time we met. Should the authorities burst into the meetings, the minutes would act as backup evidence that we were not Mau Mau, but just a group of enterprising investors. The ruse worked very well for us for a while.

One night, a British District Officer (DO) accompanied by a number of African home guards stormed into our meeting on suspicion that we were planning Mau Mau activities. Obviously, he had received intelligence from an informer, perhaps one of our 10 regular core members, or one of those in our network or someone who had taken the oath at one of our meetings.

"What's going on here?" the DO demanded.

I knew precisely why he had come in and that he must have been tipped off. I therefore adopted a confident attitude and informed him, "We are planning to start a bakery. We want this to be a bakery of the people, a cooperative, and we are raising funds."

I showed him the minutes of the previous meetings, all written in perfect English, in a clear hand, which were nevertheless purely fake, just to cover up the oath-taking and other activities in the place.

One way or another, he was partially convinced. He took a copy of the minutes, but I could see that he was nonetheless still doubtful and suspicious. I considered the fact that I might be arrested, even though we had taken the precaution of operating under the guise of a bakery. If that front failed, it would have meant detention for us all. Therefore, as soon as the DO left, we immediately stopped and postponed our activities until the next meeting. We realised that a traitor must have infiltrated us.

A short time later, due to this uncertainty and knowing that we were being watched, we let it be known that we were bringing our efforts to establish a bakery to a close. We put out the excuse that people were not willing to contribute, and therefore we had to discontinue the effort.

Things were getting incredibly hotter for the Mau Mau due to intensified surveillance by government agents. The first European to be killed by the Mau Mau was Steven Emhurst in his Naivasha farm and by August 1952, the colonial office in London received its first indication of the seriousness of the rebellion in a report from acting Governor Potter.

On 6 October of the same year, Sir Evelyn Baring arrived in Kenya to assume the post of Governor. Three days later, on 9 October 1952, Senior Chief Waruhiu wa Kung'u was shot and killed by Mau Mau gunmen at Gachie, a few kilometres north of Nairobi.

Chief Waruhiu was returning from a *baraza* (public meeting) in Gachie, part of his location, when a car drove up in front of him and blocked the road, forcing his driver to stop. A man emerged from the other vehicle, came up to Waruhiu's car and shot him dead, leaving his driver and another passenger unharmed.

Quickly realising that he had a serious problem on his hands, Baring asked for permission to declare a State of Emergency in the colony. On 20 October 1952, he declared the State of Emergency, which took effect on 21 October. Baring also signed the arrest warrants for the 120 people who were thought to be Mau Mau leaders, among them the so-called Kapenguria Six, that is, Jomo Kenyatta, Bildad Kaggia, Kung'u Karumba, Fred Kubai, Paul Ngei and Achieng' Oneko.

As soon as the Emergency was declared, troops from the Lancashire Fusiliers were flown in and later that day, they were patrolling the African areas of the segregated Nairobi. During the first 25 days of this operation, dubbed 'Jock Scott', up to 8,000 people, mostly Kikuyu, were arrested.

It was thought that Operation Jock Scott would decapitate the rebel leadership and that the Emergency would be lifted in several weeks' time. On the contrary, the violence intensified as did the secret oath administration. The Emergency would not be lifted until 1961.

While much of the senior political leadership of the Nairobi Central Committee was arrested, several of its military leaders went underground and took refuge in the forests and reserves. The freedom fighters were already too well-entrenched to be uprooted by mass arrests. With the encouragement from the leadership of the military wing, the local rebel committees took the decision to strike back over the next few weeks. There was an abrupt rise in the destruction of European property and attacks on Africans who were perceived to support the colonialists. In Nyeri, Chief Nderi was set upon by a mob and brutally murdered in broad daylight.

A section of settlers treated the declaration of the State of Emergency as a licence to perpetrate excesses against suspected Mau Mau, further exacerbating hostilities. It reached a stage where the governor had to warn the settlers against taking the law into their hands. At one time, hundreds of settlers from the 'White Highlands' camped outside Government House demanding to be granted power to shoot and kill Mau Mau suspects on sight.

As for the Kapenguria Six, they were brought to trial in Kapenguria, a fairly remote town near the western borders of Kenya. Anthony Somerhough was the prosecutor and the defence was represented by Denis Pritt, QC, together with H. O. Davies (a Nigerian), Chaman Lall (an Indian) and three Kenya resident lawyers, Fitz De Souza, Achroo Kapila and Jaswant Singh. This defence team was selected mainly by political leaders interested in the case and, as it became an international affair, additional advice was offered by prominent individuals such as Thurgood Marshall, an American lawyer. At this time, there were no Kenyan African lawyers of sufficient stature practising in the country, a situation that continued until the University of Dar es Salaam opened a School of Law in 1965.

The prosecution covertly bribed and rewarded the witnesses for the Crown. The key witness for the prosecution was Rawson Macharia, and although he was later convicted of perjury, all six defendants were convicted and jailed for seven years in Kapenguria. When the others were released in 1960, Kenyatta continued being held in Lokitaung. He was eventually released in 1961 after virtual house arrest in Maralal for close to three months.

* * *

As for my association with the Mau Mau, I no longer had much to do with oath-taking after our 'bakery' closed down. I had assisted Waira for an exceedingly short time and my role was limited to giving support. I was never an insider, in the real sense, and therefore had nothing to do with the intricacies of administering oaths, and had merely acted as a diversion.

Shortly thereafter, Waira Kamau and other Mau Mau leaders were arrested and detained for many years. Other than the fact that I was not an insider, I do not know how I escaped, but I am convinced that my life could have easily taken a turn for the worse.

Such was the situation at the time. A Kikuyu man had little chance of avoiding detention. Hundreds of thousands of Kikuyu men were detained with or without evidence of their involvement in the freedom struggle. I was fortunate. With the exception of a short time during Operation Anvil, I was never imprisoned, perhaps because I was not a radical and I kept my involvement with the Mau Mau secret.

* * *

The Declaration of the State of Emergency on 20 October affected everyone, including our school at Kiamwangi. That day, around 4 o'clock, while holding the final parade at Kiamwangi, we heard the announcement of the Declaration on the school radio. We all went home quickly, uncertain of how this would affect the school and then, the following day, the radio broadcast stated that all Independent schools were closed. A little later, the elders finalised the closure more formally by paying the teachers their final monthly salaries and that was the end of it. There were no more classes and no one ever went near Kiamwangi again. It ceased to be a school and much later became the site of a Catholic Church.

As for the Kenya Teachers' College at Githunguri, it was razed down during the Emergency. The government knew it was a centre of political agitation and rebellion against the British. In fact, the elders who oversaw the institution were the intellectual leadership of the independence movement. There is a church there now and a District Officer's office.

The closing of all Independent schools effectively meant the end of the KISA movement. As a network spreading out from Githunguri, KISA schools and churches were recognised as effective centres of oath administration and it was assumed that students who underwent training there came out indoctrinated with an anti-government mentality. Government troops just walked in and declared these schools and churches closed. Although the land on which these churches stood had belonged to the community, there were no title deeds and after the churches were proscribed, the land reverted to the government.

Later, the government allowed churches of different denominations, such as the Anglicans, Catholics and others to parcel out the church and school land among themselves. For all practical purposes, these churches were under the influence of European and American missionaries who did nothing to save the predecessor churches set up under the KISA movement.

Once Kiamwangi closed, I was jobless and began looking for work. It was fortunate that I was not yet married at the time, because I would have been devastated by family responsibilities.

In November of 1952, I went to Nairobi to look for employment. Initially I approached the Railways, but was offered a mere 120 shillings a month. I felt quite sorry for myself at this point. I tried other places but found it difficult to get an offer. I needed a job and I needed to earn money to support myself, yet throughout this period, my main motivation and ambition was still focused on getting an opportunity to go to the USA for a degree in education.

As I mentioned earlier, before the Declaration of Emergency, I had also been involved in escorting visiting dignitaries on tours around Gatundu. While on one of these tours, I met the High Commissioner and the First Secretary at the Indian High Commission and some other officials. We discussed various matters and I informed them of my complete inner conviction about independence.

Therefore, as I went about searching for employment, I decided to give the Indian High Commission a try. Luckily, I was immediately offered a position in their news office, at a salary of 500 rupees a month, which was about 750 shillings a month, a considerable amount at that time.

The Indian High Commissioner at the time was Apa Pant, who was the author of *A Moment in Time* and *Undiplomatic Services*, books on his experiences in the diplomatic corps. He was expelled from Kenya by the British authorities in 1956 on claims that he was aiding the rebellious independence movement.

It was at the Indian High Commission that I met Dr Njuguna Gakuo who had previously studied in India. He was also working at the Commission but he left fairly quickly. There were rumours alleging that he was to be detained and he therefore felt unsafe. With assistance from the Commission, he travelled secretly back to India by ship. While there, he was employed by All India Radio and broadcast from Delhi in Kiswahili.

A little later, the Indian High Commission got into difficulties because of its association with nationalists and, therefore, the colonial government treated it as suspect. Shortly thereafter, Apa Pant, the High Commissioner, was quietly asked to leave.

India had been a British colony, and had acquired its independence several years back in 1947. As such, the Indian government understood the colonial experience we were going through and sympathised with us. The Commission staff were very understanding of the plight of Kenyans and assisted wherever they could, albeit covertly. In my opinion, I thought that in taking up the job, I would be working with people who were friendly to our liberation cause. I also assumed that the High Commissioner might possibly help me to get a passport, but that proved unfeasible.

Others who were working there at that time were John Kamba, a Ugandan, John Kamau Cauri and Douglas Njiiri Karago.

The High Commission employed me to compile a newsletter called *News of India*, which I did until June 1955. In addition, I translated the newsletter into a Kiswahili edition, which was called *Sauti ya India*. The newsletter was meant for the Indians living in Kenya and the diaspora, and for any persons interested in Indian affairs. Since this job only occupied me for a short period every month, I was also recruited by the *Colonial Times*, which was a local Indian newspaper, as editor of *Jicho*, its Kiswahili version. This gave me an additional 200 rupees a month. The exchange rate at that time was one rupee to one and a half shillings and it was an excellent salary during that day and age.

I was interviewed for the job by the Press Attaché, Panjabi, but I have to admit that I was not totally honest in answering all the questions he put to me. I was asked if I knew how to type. Although I said yes, it was a complete fabrication. The reason I lied about my typing skills was because I found out that I would not be working on the premises. I would just be given the papers and then be responsible for preparing the article for printing. Since I would be working elsewhere, no one would discover that I could not type.

It was a bit of a tricky situation but I had a good friend, David Nyahe, who was employed by D. L. Patel Press, one of the largest printing presses in Nairobi at the time. He was a fine typist and I would take the work home, translate the material into Kiswahili in longhand and then pass it along to Nyahe to type up and cut stencils. He was of great assistance to me.

Gradually, I tried to take over the work but I found typing and especially cutting stencils difficult. Finally, I asked Nyahe to recommend a typing school and he took me to Premier College. For a whole week, I did nothing but learn to type. After those five days, I had learned how to type and cut a stencil. A little later, by the time I was given an office at the High Commission, I was able to do all my own work without help.

Since that time, I have always been grateful to Nyahe because of his support and encouragement at a time when I needed it most. Nyahe, by the way, is still alive and well, living at home. He worked most of his life as a clerk and typist, and at one time, he even worked for the Thika County Council.

In my position as editor of *Jicho*, I was an accredited pressman and as such, I had the opportunity to attend the Denis Pritt trial.

Denis Pritt was one of the lawyers who represented Kenyatta and his group (the Kapenguria Six) and he was charged with contempt of court for something he said during the trial. While the case in Kapenguria was still going on, he was tried in Nairobi at the High Court, Court Number 1. The courtroom was extremely crowded because we Africans were incredibly proud of him, but we were orderly and quiet. Pritt's case did not take long because he was excellently defended by the rest of the defence team and the charge was speedily dismissed.

At the beginning of my stay in Nairobi, I lived in Kaloleni with a friend called Kuria Mungai wa Thangwa, who was from my home area. He offered me refuge when I had nowhere else to go. He had a nice house and I stayed there for approximately one year. He was a house servant for a European family and his employer rented the house for him. This practice was common at the time. European families would live in the upmarket estates, and rent quarters for their African domestic help in estates like Kaloleni and Makongeni.

While at the High Commission, I did my utmost to support the liberation movement in the position I occupied. My own contribution was intellectual rather than physical or financial. I assisted with the surreptitious preparation and transmission of secret documents that we knew we could not send through normal mail. At that time, letters and circulars going through the regular post were checked, censored and followed up by colonial security.

The confidential documents we sent out were from the Mau Mau and were mostly intended for high-level individuals supporting the liberation struggle, such as British Members of Parliament. Such top-secret documents contained details of torture, massacres, detention practices, and outrageous incidents, which revealed the dishonourable and disgraceful acts of the colonial government. I was very proud to be part of this effort in the liberation struggle.

My colleague, Njiiri Karago, also an excellent typist, would spend many hours at night typing these documents. Once they were typed, the rest of us would assist in proofreading and checking their accuracy and from there, the papers would be transmitted, usually through the diplomatic bag, to New Delhi and onward to London. In many cases, the reception of such documents in England would create a furore in the British Parliament and press.

In addition to such clandestine work, we often furtively hosted British delegations who were visiting Kenya with the intention of examining the excesses of the colonial government for themselves.

* * *

In 1952 and 1953 many Kikuyu adults in and around Nairobi were swept into detention camps and a great deal of brutality accompanied the arrests.

I had gone home to Komothai for the weekend when news reached the authorities that the family of a suspected loyalist called Ndegwa, who lived just across the river from us, had been slaughtered in the night, most probably by Mau Mau fighters. A contingent of about five British officers and local loyalists then descended on the area on Sunday morning and started rounding people up, particularly those suspected of being Mau Mau adherents and supporters. About 10 prominent people from the area were arrested, taken round the village in the back of an open pickup truck and driven into the nearby forest.

We all assumed they were going to be interrogated, but when they were brought back to the shopping centre at Kibichoi, they were all dead. They had been shot in the forest and their corpses were dropped by the side of the road in the shopping centre and left there for a number of hours.

It was quite a dreadful and macabre exhibition. The colonial authorities resorted to this horrible method of displaying dead bodies to warn the people of what would befall them if they joined the Mau Mau. My friends and I as well as the rest of the crowd at the shopping centre, numbering roughly 100 people, were naturally shocked and deeply saddened, most particularly because the whole series of events seemed to be without cause.

The Ndegwa family had never been extremists and people wondered why they had been murdered. Those who had been shot by the British officers were well-known, important people and it was not at all likely that they had been involved in the Ndegwa murders, either. We all wondered if these actions would be repeated again and again. I was astonished and angry.

My family was, in general, apolitical, but my brother, Jeremiah Mugo, was swept up in one of the screening operations and was detained in Manyani and other places. Luckily, he became sick with a skin infection and was released fairly soon. He later recovered from his sickness and never showed any ill effects throughout his life until he passed away in 1993.

As the Mau Mau heightened their activities, the atmosphere in Nairobi and in Kenya became more turbulent. Many people started coming under suspicion as Mau Mau supporters, and I was one of them. Several times, after coming home from work in the evenings, my neighbours would inform me that some European Special Branch officers had been to the house during the day, looking for me. My neighbours would stare at me as they told me about the visits and I could see the questions in their eyes, wondering just what I had done to deserve such personal attention from the police.

Since I was getting increasingly concerned about these visits, I decided to go and see the District Commissioner about the matter and went to his office in Pumwani.

Once I managed to get in to see him, I explained the purpose of my visit.

"I've been told that the Special Branch have been coming to my house while I'm away at work. Apparently, they are looking for me, but I do not know what they want. I don't know what they are looking for and I don't want them to think I'm hiding, so I've come to see what it is all about."

"I see," the District Commissioner said. "And what is your name?"

After I told him my name, he asked me to wait and when he came back, he was accompanied by two Europeans with guns.

The two Special Branch officers put me between them and escorted me to a saloon car. They put me in the back seat and then they got into the front and drove me to an area beyond Eastleigh Airstrip, out in the middle of nowhere.

I was worried because the area was so remote. If anything happened to me, it was likely that no one would ever know.

Then they started asking questions, trying to get information from me.

One of them accused me of being involved in the Mau Mau. He said that the Indian High Commission was providing facilities for the Kikuyu to take the oath. He produced photographs of me and several other people at a function at Highridge where the Commission staff was staying, and asked me to identify the people in the picture.

The pictures the intelligence officer showed me were taken at a High Commission party to celebrate India's Independence Day, so I recognised the people immediately. A few of us were entertaining the guests by performing *muthuo*, a Kikuyu boys' dance, in some improvised costumes and I was leading.

As I looked at the photos, I pointed out the others and myself and explained that it was a party.

"But what were you doing?" the officer demanded.

"We were just entertaining the guests," I said.

"Who were the guests?"

I explained that the guests had been invited by the staff of the High Commission. "This was a party to celebrate India's Independence Day."

Then they asked me if I had taken the oath and I said I had not. After all, it was no business of theirs. They asked me quite a lot of routine questions but I was stunned when they showed me a photograph of myself in costume and, written on the bottom of the picture were the words, "Oath Administrator".

"Me?" I exclaimed in outrage. "Gentlemen," I said to the two young British officers, "it appears that you have an agenda and it appears that you have been told quite a lot about me. Why don't you just ask me about myself before you start writing such things? You really ought to know who and what type of a person I am."

The two officers just looked at me so I continued to explain. "You need to know how to spot the typical behaviour of an oath administrator. You should be aware of the type of circumstances and conditions he would likely have in his past."

I told them about my educational background and about the fact that I was a Christian.

"I am just not the type to administer a Mau Mau oath. My Christian background and my education – and, by the way, not many Kenyans have an education like mine – make it impossible for me to take up such a role. In fact, if you ever come across an oath administrator with a background like mine, then come for me, arrest me and I will go with you freely. It is futile to look for oath administrators among people with my background!"

I have to admit I was quite furious by then and I knew who had put me in this fix. One of the office messengers must have seen the chance to use these innocuous and innocent photos, which had been taken by the official photographer attached to the Indian High Commission, as a chance to make some money on the side by pretending to pass information to the colonial Special Branch.

The Indian High Commission was constantly under surveillance at this time, under suspicion that they were helping the forces behind

Kenya's independence struggle, as indeed they were, but I was not going to admit that I was part of it.

"So in that case, will you help us?" the officers asked.

"In which way?"

One of them said, "You know this country is in trouble and we need people with understanding to help stop this nonsense."

I am sure they thought that if they could recruit me, I would be a prime source of intelligence for them.

I shook my head. "Look, I will not help you to oppress or suppress my people. If you are telling me to try to convince my people not to demand equal rights, not to demand education, or not to demand the right to govern themselves, I'm sorry, I cannot do so." I thought for a moment and decided to add to that statement. "Even though I am not engaged in these activities myself, there are people who are fully convinced that what they are doing is right and I will not be recruited to spy or inform on them."

"Would you be prepared to work with us in any other capacity?"

"Yes," I said casually and sarcastically, "any time. And now that you know where I live and where I work, if you want me to help you, now that we understand each other, just let me know."

Well, they took me back to the office of the District Commissioner and I was thankful that they never approached me again. They obviously wanted me to be an informer but I think I had given them a clear picture of my integrity and my loyalty to the cause of freedom. They also understood that there were certain things I just would not do.

The whole episode left me enraged.

I took a taxi back to the High Commission and went in to talk to the High Commissioner, Krishna Menon, who had replaced Apa Pant. I bluntly informed him that I wanted to resign.

"I don't want to go round in fear of my life, under suspicion that I am a subversive, just because I work here," I explained. "I'm very upset that people should be coming to my house to interfere with my peace. And I took myself to the DC to find out what they wanted and now ... now ... I want to resign."

The High Commissioner said, "No, no. Don't worry! We will deal with this."

He actually took it up with State House and went to see the Governor over the matter.

No one ever bothered me again on this matter and I felt free to resume my assistance with the preparation of secret documents headed for sympathetic Members of Parliament in the UK.

* * *

In 1953, while I was at the Indian High Commission, the Nairobi Central Committee had reconstituted its senior ranks and renamed itself the War Council. In contrast to other liberation movements of the time, the Kenyan urban revolt had no socialist inclination.

The declaration of a war of liberation may be seen as a strategic mistake that the War Council was pushed into by its more aggressive members. The resistance did not have a national strategy for victory, had no cadres trained in guerrilla warfare, had few modern weapons and no arrangements to get more, and had not spread beyond the communities of the central highlands. Nevertheless, the initial lack of large numbers of British troops, a high degree of popular support and the low quality of colonial intelligence gave the Land and Freedom Army the upper hand for the first half of 1953.

Large bands of Mau Mau were able to move around their bases in the highland forests of the Aberdares mountain range and Mount Kenya, killing Africans loyal to the government and attacking isolated police and Home Guard posts, generally spreading terror. Three of the dominant Active Wing leaders were Stanley Mathenge, Waruhiu Itote (aka General China) who was leader of the Mount Kenya Mau Mau and Dedan Kimathi Waciuri, the leader of the Mau Mau in Aberdares Forest.

One of the well-known events at this time was the Lari Massacre. What is little known, however, is that the Lari Massacre had its origins in the early 1900s, when the members of ten *mbari (*sub-clan) families and their tenants were evicted from their land in Tigoni to make way for White settlers. The most prominent of the senior elders fighting against the relocation to Lari during the long years of struggle to keep the land in Tigoni in the 1920s and 1930s was Luka wa Kahangara. By 1927, Luka, realising that the colonial forces would acquire Tigoni land, no matter what they did, indicated that the elders had agreed to consider an exchange of land, provided that the new lands were equal in every respect, acreage, fertility and most especially water supply as Tigoni.

Luka appeared to cooperate with the colonial authorities and settlers. Despite the fact that the land at Lari was inferior, Luka accepted the exchange, and the Tigoni people became bitterly divided, especially since, in settling at Lari, Luka and his relatives had taken the best land and benefitted most. Thus, they became an obvious focus for Mau Mau fighters.

On the evening of 26 March 1953, hundreds of Mau Mau fighters attacked the homesteads at Lari. They particularly targeted the homes of retired Chief Luka wa Kahangara, his relatives and friends. The fighters set the houses on fire, killing everyone who tried to escape.

In the counteroffensive by security forces, scores of suspected Mau Mau and members of their families were killed. More than 2,000 men and some women were rounded up in the area around Githunguri.

One could thus say that there were actually two massacres that took place. First, the Mau Mau attack and second, the brutal retaliation by the authorities and their collaborators. The Press gave considerable distortion to the events during the Lari Massacre, in order to slant the occurrence in line with British propaganda.

In my opinion, the Lari Massacre was an extremely unfortunate event, which occurred, at its deepest level, primarily over land issues. One must understand that the local people were put at tremendous harm and disadvantage by actions of the loyalist chiefs, and as such, the Mau Mau felt they had justifiable motives. It was a shameful and terrible thing to see innocent people killed. These contradictions happened repeatedly in the liberation struggle.

We see it again later, when land was distributed. The leaders grabbed land for themselves and their families, forgetting the original purpose of the struggle, while the landless remained without recourse.

By May 1953, the Kikuyu Home Guards had officially joined the security forces and become a significant part of the anti-Mau Mau effort.

In June 1953, General Sir George Erskine arrived from London and took up the post of Director of Operations, and revitalised the British effort in Kenya. A military draft brought in 20,000 troops who were used aggressively. The Kikuyu reserves were designated 'Special Areas' where anyone failing to halt when challenged could be shot. This was often used as an excuse for shooting suspects, so this provision was subsequently abandoned. The Aberdares Range and Mount Kenya were declared 'prohibited areas' within which no person could enter without government clearance. Those found within the area could be shot on sight.

In late 1953, security forces swept the Aberdares Forest in 'Operation Blitz', captured and killed 125 freedom fighters. Despite such large-scale offensive operations, the British found themselves unable to stem the tide of insurgency because, at the time, there were approximately 15,000 Mau Mau insurgents in the forests.

By January 1954, the King's African Rifles had begun 'Operation Hammer' in the forests of Mount Kenya and the Aberdares.

Then, on 24 April 1954, after weeks of planning, the colonial army, launched 'Operation Anvil' in Nairobi and the city was put under military control.

The Commander of the British military forces, General Sir George Erskine, planned and implemented Operation Anvil intended to rid Nairobi and other areas of all Mau Mau elements. To assist in the operation, a battalion, the Lancashire Fusiliers, was flown in from Egypt in what was then the longest airlift in British military history. Assisted chiefly by loyalist African home guards and British troops, more than 24,000 people, most of them Kikuyu, were arrested in Nairobi over a period of one month and sent to detention camps for either allegedly taking the Mau Mau oath or being Mau Mau supporters or sympathisers.

In the first few days of the operation, security forces screened 30,000 Africans and arrested 17,000 on suspicion of complicity in Mau Mau activities. They were then moved to detention camps, including many people who were later found to be innocent. The so-called screening managed to convict over 10,000 Mau Mau within two months. By the end of the exercise, possibly 150,000 alleged Mau Mau adherents were in detention camps.

The city remained under military control for the rest of the year. Many thousands of Kikuyu were interned and thousands more were deported to the Kikuyu reserves in the highlands west of Mount Kenya. The sheer numbers were overwhelming and the conditions in the camps were grim, all in violation of the United Nations Universal Declaration of Human Rights. Entire rebel passive wing leadership structures, including the War Council, were swept away to detention camps and the most important source of supplies and recruits for the resistance evaporated. Just as an example of the attitude of the British forces, one sergeant major decided he could "shoot anyone he liked as long as they were Black".

* * *

On the day 'Operation Anvil' was launched, the sweep occurred in the neighbourhoods around us. While we were at work, we locked ourselves in the Indian High Commission offices, because we were well-aware that we had extra diplomatic protection while on its grounds. Despite this immunity, quite suddenly, a large group of young British soldiers burst in and began ransacking the offices. They broke into filing cabinets and cupboards and threw papers everywhere.

It was a frightening situation, but these things were happening so often, and to so many people, that we actually anticipated it. We never knew what could happen on any given day and were no longer capable of being terrified by the threat of arrest or detention. The soldiers ignored the Asians and the junior office staff and arrested the senior African personnel – John Kamba, Douglas Njiiri Karago, John Kamau Cauri and I. Although the High Commissioner protested and spoke on our behalf, we were bunched together like a herd of goats, roughly packed into a crowded lorry and taken directly from the office of the Indian High Commission located on Duke Street (now Ronald Ngala) to Lang'ata Screening Camp, where a cemetery is now located. About 80,000 people were held in this small area but there were so many coming and going that there may have been many more who passed through.

It was a brutal experience. At Lang'ata, we were beaten as though it was a crime to be working for the Indian High Commission. John Kamba was quickly released when the authorities realised he was a Ugandan.

The rest of us were put in custody with everyone else who had been arrested. As we arrived, we were put in a small tent. There were quite a lot of these tents, all placed within barbed wire enclosures, and there were about 30 enclosures in total, each identified by a number. Although we were in suits when we were arrested, our clothes were splashed with paint of various colours, either to identify us, or perhaps to humiliate us.

Every morning and evening, we would be paraded before hooded informers – called *tukunia*, in reference to the gunny sacks that covered them to hide their identities – as they pointed out members of the Mau Mau. There was no real interrogation. We would be paraded in front of them and beaten with sticks on our heads for no reason at all.

Although the Mau Mau hierarchy within the camps ensured that inmates maintained discipline, conditions were terrible and inhuman. For example, the food we were given was placed outside the gate of the enclosure and we had to cook it ourselves. We threw it into large pots and had to struggle to prepare it – you can imagine trying to stir a huge pot of ugali over firewood – so it often ended up not properly cooked, despite the fact that we always selected a strong person just for that purpose. In addition, we had no blankets and had to pull our jackets up over our heads, just to try to keep warm while we slept on the ground.

Later on, we learned that the British officers in charge of this camp at Lang'ata and other camps, lied to the outside world about the terrible conditions, and that official medical reports detailing shortcomings were ignored.

Our arrest developed into a serious case and caused a diplomatic row that ended up in the British Parliament because the colonial administration had breached diplomatic convention. The High Commissioner complained to Delhi and from there the Indian government complained to London. Finally, after one week in detention, orders came to release us and instructions were given from London that the people from the Indian High Commission, were to be given priority in screening. Since the anonymous informers pointed none of us out, we were released.

From there, we were escorted out of Lang'ata. The officer in charge was told to deliver us to the High Commissioner's house on Limuru Road and get a receipt. The receipt was to acknowledge that we had been delivered safely. If we were to disappear, or be killed, the British government would be held responsible. We were full of relief at being released and joked with the officer and when he dropped us off, he thanked us for giving him an opportunity to have a day off.

The colonial administration decided that all Kikuyu workers in Nairobi would be required to live in Bahati, an estate that was still under construction. This meant that we were no longer able to return to our previous places of residence. So Douglas Njiiri Karago, John Kamau Cauri and I were briefly given living quarters in one of the High Commission's large staff houses on 2nd Avenue Parklands before we moved on to Bahati Estate, which was under curfew from seven in the evening until six in the morning. The Luo, on the other hand, were free to live anywhere in Nairobi. Most of them lived in Makongeni and in Kaloleni. Makongeni was mainly railway quarters but Kaloleni was a City Council estate where most of the senior Africans lived. Majengo and Pumwani estates were much older. Later Makadara estate was constructed.

At any rate, shortly after the terrible experience we had had in Lang'ata, Kamau Cauri, Douglas Njiiri Karago, Wanjama, who was Peter Gachathi's brother, and I, moved into prototype 'model' houses in Bahati. We were the first people to move into the estate. The houses were a little more expensive to rent than other places but they were fairly nice bungalows with two bedrooms and a lounge. We considered it 'high class' because most other Africans were living in single rooms. Njiiri and I lived in one house, Kamau Cauri in another and Wanjama, who was married, lived in one with his family.

There was no running water in the house, only a communal tap outside where we could fetch water, and there were bucket latrines outside as well. There was no power, so we did our cooking on a *jiko* (small charcoal stove).

We could not afford luxuries like hiring someone to do our laundry. Instead, Njiiri, Kamau and I had an arrangement and more or less divided the household chores into three. These were shopping and cooking, washing laundry, and ironing. We took these duties in turn and would change round our duties every week. If one of us was the cook for the week, he would shop for food from the money that we pooled, then cook and wash the utensils. As for the laundry, I remember we always were properly dressed when we went to work, and wore ties but I really cannot remember how often we changed our clothes or washed them. Yet that was how we survived our bachelor experience.

The only person who did not much like the arrangement was Kamau Cauri. He would have preferred to do everything by himself and persisted in doing his own laundry, but he joined us in the rest of the duties.

Back in the village, of course, none of us would have agreed to cook. That was considered a woman's job!

* * *

Since I had a regular, well-paying job, the time came that I wished to marry and the girl I intended to marry, Esther Njeri, was a Presbyterian. She insisted on a wedding in the Presbyterian Church at Kambui.

We went to the minister at Kambui Mission, who enquired if I was baptised. When I told him my background, he disclosed that Presbyterians did not recognise baptism by independent churches and, therefore, he declined to perform the ceremony.

"As far as I'm concerned," he said, "you are a pagan and you cannot marry in any Presbyterian church."

I tried to explain that I had been baptised and even confirmed, but he would not listen.

"So what will I have to do?" I asked.

"As a first step, you will have to come to my church and start catechism classes."

This came as a considerable shock to me, but there was nothing I could accomplish by arguing. He complicated the matter and gave several more conditions. He was adamant and became hostile when I protested.

I was despondent and depressed about the circumstances and attempted to discover means by which I could shorten the waiting period to my wedding. Finally, my future father-in-law advised me to take a small quantity of sugar (an expensive commodity for most Africans) to the minister, lend him a hand and be as cooperative as possible.

Thereafter, on those occasions when the minister and I were headed to the church, the minister would get off his bicycle when we got to a hill and I would push it for him. It was extremely awkward because I was not only pushing his bicycle, but my own, too. I must have presented an amusing spectacle.

I managed to get through the course of catechism studies and when I had completed the first stage, I was permitted to marry Esther Njeri from Kibichoi. We were married on 4 December 1954.

While I was working at the High Commission, I travelled by bicycle to see my new wife, and later our children, at home in the countryside on the weekends. I was reasonably happy to travel like this. Naturally, I saw people driving cars, although there were extremely few Africans with cars in those days. Having a bicycle was considered a great step forward in terms of status.

By the way, I had initially learned to ride a bicycle during the time I was helping my brother in his shop. Whenever he was away, I would borrow his bicycle and, since I was still too short at the time to reach the pedals if I sat on the seat, I would put my leg through the frame, under the crossbar, and ride in that somewhat lopsided position. I bought my first bicycle, a Raleigh, in 1954. Later I bought a Raja, and then a Hercules.

In reflecting on my youth, while I was in school I had a number of friends, but we were all young and it seemed most of these friendships did not outlast our youth. However, Douglas Njiiri Karago and John Kamau Cauri were among the close friends I met at the Indian High Commission.

Karago later became my closest friend. In fact, in 1954, when I decided to marry, he was my best man. In him, I saw an honest man, a Christian and a mentor. Although he did not go far in education, he progressed faster than any of us.

While we were working at the Indian High Commission, his feet were already firmly planted on the ground of reality. For example, he never touched alcohol and the little money he earned was invested in a small yet profitable enterprise. We were surprised by what he managed to accomplish. Little by little, he became independent and ended up with a happy family life.

As we became closer, I got to know about his investments. He was actually among the initial few who kept poultry for commercial purposes.

He was among the first few Africans to import a hundred day-old chicks in the early 1950s. He imported them, 100 at a time, from Britain and went to the airport to collect them on arrival.

The first time he did so, he borrowed 500 shillings from me because he could not raise enough from his own resources to pay for the chicks. I was paid back many times over, in faithfulness and in friendship.

We called him the 'Bishop' because, among us, he was the best Christian, and if there was ever any need for prayers, we turned to him. As I will relate later, he was the man who bought a loan application form for me for one shilling. I do not think I have ever had a friend like him, and I do not expect to ever find someone like him again. No one else was ever as close.

Yet he was also very humorous. I remember at my sixtieth birthday party in 1989, he was the main speaker. In reference to me, he said something like, "One thing about this man ... I found him when he was *mshenzi* (pagan) and there is nothing I have not done to turn him into a civilised Christian, but I have failed."

He also said I was "incorrigible". He was joking of course, but in terms of his way of life, he was much more earnest and committed than I could ever be. Although he was a short man, he had a large, warm and wonderful wit. He passed away around 1991 and I miss his presence in my life.

There is a photo I had, of the two of us together before my wedding in 1954. We were both wearing suits, and were on the way to the church. We were still young and when I looked at the picture, I felt we both looked like little boys, very slender, and straight. As I said, he was my best friend but these days, as I get older, I try to regard everyone as a friend.

* * *

There were many changes going on in Kenya and the situation in Nairobi and elsewhere was quite volatile. We never knew what to expect from day to day. A unique passbook, for the Kikuyu only, was introduced. Every Kikuyu adult had to carry the book at all times and administration officials would track his or her movements with annotations.

One of the most annoying colonial rules that came up during the 1950s while I was working at the High Commission was the requirement that everyone with a bicycle must write his or her name on the crosspiece of the frame. This was because the administration had realised that the

Mau Mau were using bicycles to ferry supplies and travel when gathering to attack a certain place. With their names on the frame, it was easy to single out the Kikuyu and stop them for searches. They were constantly harassed and it came to a point that they could no longer use their bicycles at all.

Subsequently, the only means of transport became the segregated Nairobi City Council buses. There was first class for Europeans, with nicely padded seats, second class for Asians, and third class for Africans with wooden seats. There were even three doors on each bus, labelled with the class, to ensure one did not blunder and enter into the wrong class. If an African entered the second-class section by mistake, people would stare and redirect him, and he would most likely be forgiven. If an African entered the first class compartment, it was considered a serious crime and he would probably be arrested by the police. Such buses would go up to Dagoretti Corner, but would not travel outside the city. There simply were no long distance buses and the only other means of travel was by train, which was segregated, as well.

I often travelled in the buses since they were the only means of transport in the city. The fares at that time were very little although I cannot now remember the exact amount. What I do remember is that the most common denominations in use at the time were the one-cent coin *(kahera),* the five-cent coin *(ndururu)* and the ten-cent coin *(king'otore).* There was no twenty-cent coin. In fact, a fifty-cent coin was already considered a substantial amount of money.

When the Mau Mau realised that their movement by bicycle was being restricted, they retaliated and called for a boycott of the buses. A few people who tried to board the buses were shot.

Those of us in town then had to walk long distances to work and eventually the buses stopped running altogether. I remember walking all the way back and forth from Duke Street (now Ronald Ngala) down to Bahati. We did not complain because we were fully in support of such actions.

Incidentally, the roads in Nairobi were all tarmac up to Muthurwa. Beyond that point, it was murram, but there was no such thing as sidewalks. Since there were few cars on the road at this time, it was not difficult to walk along the street.

* * *

I continued working at the Indian High Commission and, due to its strong support for Kenya's struggle for independence, we Africans working on the premises became acquainted with Tom Mboya and Pio Gama Pinto, and even became good friends. The two of them were young, educated trade unionists and were among the most powerful agitators against colonial rule. They would invite us to their conferences and clandestine meetings in Nairobi, where they would deliberate on strategies to fight the colonialists. I felt privileged to get to know them and participate in the struggle for independence.

Due to the large number of complaints against discrimination, Britain would occasionally send parliamentary committees to Kenya on fact-finding missions. Personalities like Mboya and Pinto would present their grievances and they would always be accompanied by delegations of supporters. In some instances, such meetings were secret, and I recall that I attended a number of them in J. M. Desai's house on 2nd Parklands Avenue. Through this sort of anti-government activity, I came to meet British MPs such as Arthur Bottomley, Fenner Brockway and Richard Maudling, when we offered our views. The Kenya Government stand throughout this period was that the Mau Mau was not an anti-government movement but a civil war army among the Africans. On the other hand, our stand was that there was no civil war, but civil strife to claim freedom.

Despite the good salary and the easy working conditions at the Commission, I felt unhappy with my position and the limited contribution I was able to make to the freedom struggle. I had seen terrible things occurring in the screening camp at Lang'ata and felt frustrated. I had not gone through all my education just to engage in a simple career where the biggest challenges were to type and translate documents. I felt stifled and aggravated, as if I had reached a dead end, while all around me terrible forces were destroying my country.

At this stage in my life, I would remember the guidance I received at Alliance. Carey Francis had taught us to try our best in whatever circumstances we found ourselves. I felt it would be silly to indulge in self-pity but I started questioning myself about my future.

John Kamba was a steno typist and he was earning a higher salary than I, despite the fact that he had lower educational qualifications. I contemplated becoming a steno typist as well. I bought the Pittman's Shorthand textbook and started teaching myself shorthand in the house during my free time. It was not complicated, and before long, I had progressed up to Exercise Number 43, and was able to read and transcribe.

The thought of doing something more meaningful, something more spiritually significant was still in me and I finally was convinced I should search for alternatives. One evening while studying in our house in Bahati, I had an epiphany, a sudden breakthrough and my concentration on the lessons snapped. I asked myself, "Why am I doing this? With all my education? To sit on the other side of the desk and let someone tell me what to write and never be able to think for myself?"

It was one of those instances when one sees life with crystal clarity and evaluates all aspects of one's existence without mercy. Here I was, Jeremiah Gitau Kiereini, one of the few Makerere graduates in the country, studying shorthand. Was I only capable of taking down what was dictated to me? I felt I was not born for such limited horizons and, on impulse, I seized the shorthand book and all my notes and hurled them through the window out into the street. I determined that I would never study shorthand again. From that time onward, I persisted in my job at the Commission, but with a great deal less enthusiasm and conviction.

Chapter 5

Working on the 'Pipeline'

My dissatisfaction at the Indian High Commission led to the circumstances that eventually changed my destiny and by June 1955, I had entered the employ of the government. This fateful intervention created the beginning of a long and unbroken career in the civil service that would last 30 years.

In this case, providence came in the form of one of my friends, Wilson Gitangu Kibathi, who would occasionally come to see me at the High Commission. He would come with a friend of his, Isaiah Mwai Mathenge. Both were trainees at Jeanes School.

Jeanes School was started in 1925 after the recommendations of the Phelp Stokes Commission, which sat in Kenya in 1923, to give Africans basic training for lower cadre government jobs, such as teaching and accounting. The students were adults who had received elementary education and were trying to improve or specialise their skills in various fields. Technical courses such as masonry and carpentry were taught at the Native Industrial Training Depot in the neighbouring school. The institution later became the Kenya Institute of Administration and is now part of the University of Nairobi.

Kibathi was a former schoolmate in Kagumo and, as we came from the same area, we had a common background. In fact, we became still more closely related when I married Esther Njeri, and he married her sister.

Mathenge and Kibathi informed me that the country would always require persons such as me in one job or another. They mentioned that there were good jobs available in government service so I decided to consider it.

I was actually emotional about it. I saw myself at the High Commission with no future, serving a foreign country and believed that I would be better off serving my country instead. I had seen the terrible conditions in the detention camps during the short while I was in Lang'ata, and felt driven to do something about it.

As a result, I applied for a job in community development in the Kenya Government and, in order to take up the job, I had to be trained at Jeans School for three months. I was informed that I would be required to produce a letter of recommendation from a government officer in order to be accepted and, therefore, I approached my former teacher, Wanyutu Waweru, who was a brother to Chief Magugu Waweru of Komothai, where I had come from.

Both the chief and his brother, the teacher, were proud of me because I was one of the educated people in Komothai location. In the past, the chief had always insisted on seeing my school reports at the end of every term and he had been consistently delighted with my results.

I paid a visit to Wanyutu Waweru – a former senior education officer in the Ministry of Education before he was nominated to the Kenya Legislative Council (LegCo) and appointed an Assistant Minister for Education – to ask him for a recommendation. He had been nominated as one of the first Africans to sit in Parliament in 1952, with others like B. A. Ohanga and later Musa Amalemba.

He said, "Why don't you go and draft the required letter and bring it to me?"

After that, I prepared a draft for Wanyutu Waweru. I no longer remember the exact wording but it was something like, "I know this man. He's a good loyal man," and other flattering things. I typed it nicely, but I also put in a lie. I stated that I had never taken the Mau Mau oath. When I finished, I took the letter to him and he signed it. However, since I was concealing the truth, I felt guilty because he had been so kind to me. My conscience continued to bother me, and finally, some two years later, I went to him and apologised.

"I'm very sorry that I told a lie," I explained. "But I needed the job. And you know I could never be a Mau Mau terrorist. There just didn't seem to be any other way of getting the position."

He was obviously not happy about it, caught as he was in a position he could not change, but he advised me not to worry about it and I felt relieved and my conscience was then clear. I think I was forgiven. Waira Kamau and some other colleagues in detention and in my home area, on the other hand, considered me a traitor for accepting employment with the administration that had arrested my colleagues. Waira became bitter about my taking up the position and I have reason to believe that he never forgave me until his death.

When I started in Jeanes School on 1 June 1955, I found a class of about 20 people. We lived in the hostels there, and took a three-month course in Community Development, which entailed sociology, civics and basic human psychology. The policy from the top was that the colonial government had done nothing wrong in handling the Mau Mau and it was up to us supposedly to convince the detainees of the same.

It was an impossible task. The detainees had been treated atrociously and there was no way anyone would convince them otherwise. In addition, three months were not adequate to prepare us. We were expected to have sufficient psychological knowledge to carry out our task but the course was too brief to make an impact on us, or to enable us to have any impact on the psychology of the detainees.

Actually rehabilitating the detainees would have required professionals who had done extensive studies on the subject, but they were simply not there. We were chosen because we were among the few educated Africans, and for the fact that we were Kikuyu, as were the majority of detainees with whom we would interact.

We were expected to divert and transform the detainees' minds from anger and the feeling of oppression and subjugation. We were to convince them to turn to positive thinking and supposedly remove the Mau Mau attitude and viewpoint. We were taught that we should hold discussions with the detainees on topics such as the reason for their internment in the camps. We were instructed in various methods of engaging the detainees' attention and occupying them with diverse activities. We had classes in sports and social subjects. We were also expected to teach the detainees how to read and write in order to show them that they could lead normal lives after renouncing the Mau Mau movement.

Furthermore, our task entailed making them realise that they were not, after all, unscrupulous people and they could return to society and interact with others in a natural and ordinary manner. Detention had been traumatising for them, and we were required to offer some sort of therapy.

My position was not an easy one. Because I had taken the oath, yet was working with the colonial government, I was treated with suspicion by both the Mau Mau and the authorities. My sincere motive, to alleviate the suffering of detainees, was disregarded.

It was unfortunate that many of my former friends and colleagues who had taken the Mau Mau oath now considered me a traitor in view of the fact that I was employed by the government. I felt extremely troubled by this attitude, because I never considered myself a collaborator. It was hard to deal with because I believed I was an honest Kenyan citizen, and under no circumstances did I abandon my political leanings. Oath or no oath, I was a supporter of the cause of freedom with all my heart. As an educated Christian, the oath held no power over me. For me, it was better to champion a revolution with one's full heart and mind, rather than be coerced into the position by superstition.

I was aware that independence was fast approaching and I felt there was dire need to pull the detainees out of the camps as quickly as possible and re-integrate them back into society. I was convinced that my task was indispensable and crucial and that it was for the benefit of the community.

My earnings were considerably lower than my remuneration in the Indian High Commission and therefore it could not possibly be construed that I had joined the government with greed as my motive. Many of my friends could not understand why I would take up employment with lower financial returns.

My explanation was straightforward. I was making a sacrifice to serve my country by attempting to hasten the progress of re-absorbing the suffering detainees into the community.

I was also considering my future career. Whereas the probability of promotion and professional growth in the Indian High Commission was minimal, the likelihood of further career development in the government, once Independence was achieved, was infinite. I was especially unambiguous on this and very focused.

Upon completion of the course at Jeanes School, I was posted to Thiba Detention Camp in Embu in September 1955 as a Community Development Assistant or, to put it simply, a rehabilitation assistant in a detention camp. Thiba was one of the Mwea camps. The others were Mwea, Tebere, Gathigiriri, Kandongu, Karaba and Wamumu, the last being mainly for juveniles. There were also many other detention camps scattered throughout Kenya. At that time, John Cowan was the Commissioner of Prisons and he was thus in charge of all detention camps, in addition to the normal prisons.

Major J. B. W. Breckenridge[1] was the officer in charge of rehabilitation in all the Mwea camps and he was based in Thiba. Despite some differences in outlook, he and I managed to develop a good working relationship. The Mwea camps were at the end of the pipeline and there were no hardcore detainees in these camps.

---

1   Breckenridge later wrote "Up the Pipeline" about his experiences in rehabilitation.

In order to fully understand the structure of the detention camps, it is necessary to explain the arrangement that was set up to deal with the Mau Mau. There was a routine in place right from the beginning of the detention process, but in the original concept, there was officially never any violence towards the detainees. This system was later formalised as the 'Pipeline' and I believe this version was created by Terence Gavaghan who came to Mwea from the Provincial Administration and was made a Special District Officer in charge of rehabilitation, although he had no experience in that field.

He had his own ideas of how to deal with the detainees and discussed his theories with John Cowan, who was in charge of Prisons. Because Kenyan colonial authorities were under so much pressure to release most of the detainees, I assume he convinced the authorities in Nairobi to adopt his plan, mainly the official and systematised use of brutal force, which he felt would expedite the process. Sadly, I believe that someone somewhere must have decided that the end justified the means.

As a result, prison warders used severe methods to 'break' the spirit of the prisoners while they were in Manyani and other hardship camps, or even on the train as they were being transported from one camp to another. Throughout the journey from Manyani to Sagana, they were brutally handled and intimidated. When they came to Sagana, before the detainees were moved on to the camps, the prisons warders roughed them up. From there, they were generally sent to Kandongu. Within a day or two, the authorities would decide if the detainees were fit for Mwea and able to stay with the others already there. When some did not quite fit in, they were sent away to Hola as so-called "exiles".

All this was handled by prisons and, I must reiterate, at no point were rehabilitation staff ever involved. Only prison warders handled detainees. It was the prison authorities, headed by the Commissioner of Prisons, who handled the detainees. They were responsible for making the detainees work during the mornings and instilling discipline, and they looked after camp security issues.

Those of us involved in rehabilitation would talk to the detainees later in the day when they were released to us after they had finished their work. We were supposed to counsel them, take down their statements and, where necessary, recommend their release. This arrangement meant that those who were prepared to 'confess' would not go out to work that day. They would remain with the clerks who would prepare their statements. It was never within our mandate to punish detainees in any way.

When suspects were swept out of Nairobi and elsewhere, they all went to screening camps (like Lang'ata, where I had been held) where they were interrogated. According to the attitude they maintained during the screening, and the intelligence that had been received on their activities, they were sorted out into three categories, Black, Grey and White.

The hardcore or so-called 'Black' detainees were those who were accused of serious crimes. They would be sent to high security camps where living conditions were unequivocally disheartening and demoralising. Such facilities included desolate places like Manyani, Hola, McKinnon Road, Manda Island and Mageta Island. In these detention camps, the detainees undertook forced labour, although so-called 'incorrigible' and committed Mau Mau adherents would refuse to work and repeatedly go on strike. A number of the hardcore detainees held such stalwart and resilient loyalty to the Mau Mau cause that they absolutely rejected commands, at times refusing to work and going on hunger strikes. Despite continued existence in the hardship detention camps, some individuals like Josiah Mwangi Kariuki adamantly refused to cooperate and survived in the camps until 1960 when the detention programme was finally abandoned. In early 1975, JM Kariuki was murdered under mysterious circumstances. 'JM', as he was known, was the Member of Parliament for Nyandarua North constituency. He was critical of the founding President Jomo Kenyatta and the government in many respects. He was especially known for condemning the growing gap between the rich and the poor.

Numerous detainees died in these camps since the prison warders and their British supervisors were exceedingly violent and totally without compassion. The basis for this vicious conduct was the presumption that the Mau Mau attitude and spirit had to be crushed, and individual officers employed diverse tactics to achieve this goal.

The camps were terribly congested and the environment grim and unhygienic. Consequently, there were frequent outbreaks of diseases such as cholera, dysentery and skin infections.

The second category of detainees was the 'Grey'. They were either 'Blacks' who had changed their attitude and complied with the orders they were given, or they were detainees who had never been extreme enough to be classified as 'Black'. The theory was that when the detainees changed their behaviour, either through torture or through their own conviction, and admitted to taking the oath, they would be 'down-graded' to a lower category and would eventually be released. 'Greys', therefore, were individuals who were gradually on their way out.

The final category of detainees were the 'White', who were either 'Greys' who had willingly complied with orders, admitted to taking the oath and confessed, or those who had proved cooperative and confessed right at the beginning of the screening process. These were released at the earliest opportunity.

Thus the process of moving from 'Black' through 'Grey' to 'White' was considered a 'pipeline', that is, a progression of 'mental adjustment', which was supposed to bring them all back to normal life.

Both 'Grey' and 'White' were taken to places like Mwea, Kangema, Kirigiti and Kangubiri. At Thiba, where I was first stationed, detainees had left behind the arduous conditions in hardcore camps. They had supposedly changed their attitudes and were on the verge of returning to normal life.

* * *

The philosophy (if it can be called that) behind the incarceration of Mau Mau detainees was based on ideas developed by various individuals. The colonial authorities particularly believed in the theory, developed by Thomas Askwith, that if an individual admitted to having taken the oath and mentioned collaborators, the oath he or she had taken was no longer binding.

Askwith had arrived in Kenya in 1938 and in 1945, he became the Municipal African Affairs Officer in Nairobi. Four years later he was appointed Commissioner of the Community Development Department. He was also the principal of Jeanes School, where he promoted his concepts of African Betterment and Social Change. In 1946, he formed the United Kenya Club for all races to intermingle.

When the Mau Mau crisis arose, Askwith was handpicked by Governor Baring to go to Malaya colony and train in rehabilitation. Malaya had been under a State of Emergency since 1948 and the Governor, Sir Gerald Templer, had already provided Baring with a blueprint of Emergency Regulations. Rehabilitation was meant to be a way of luring the Kikuyu away from "Mau Mau savagery" and towards the enlightenment of Western civilisation, to make them 'vomit' the poison of the Mau Mau and integrate.

Askwith came up with a rehabilitation plan that advocated a humane approach to making the detainees confess before being integrated back to society. However, the rehabilitation he envisaged was turned into an operation of terror through the mistaken beliefs of Baring, Lyttleton, Gavaghan and other officials and settlers who did not understand the nature and essence of the Kikuyu and the Mau Mau war.

Askwith was later relieved of his duties when he suggested that the Kenyan government should rely less on force and harsh conditions to impose order in the camps. A number of other Europeans were also involved in formulating the rehabilitation theory. One was Dr J. C. Carothers, who was in charge of Mathare Mental Hospital in Nairobi. Dr Carothers was a psychiatrist whose analysis of the Kikuyu was twisted and perverse. He disparaged the Kikuyu and compared the oath to those taken by witches in the European middle ages. Governor Baring and many of his officials believed his theories and set upon the detainees as though they were inhuman beasts. As a point of interest, Carothers also claimed that Kikuyu were a non-musical community, which was simply not true.

He held that Kikuyu possessed a 'forest psychology', which compelled them to be warlike, and unless that mentality was eradicated, they would persist in combat. He did not comprehend the significance of the Kikuyu or Mau Mau oaths, believing that they were evidence and proof of primitivity and savagery. Neither did he grasp that the central issues of the Mau Mau struggle were land and freedom.

Since the colonial authorities considered L. S. B. Leakey to be one of the individuals who was acquainted with Africans, specifically the Kikuyu, he was no doubt also consulted. He was an archaeologist who was highly conversant with the Kikuyu language. The world famous archeologist was the son of Canon Leakey of Kabete. He grew up among the Kikuyu while living with Senior Chief Koinange, and he was very fluent in Kikuyu. He underwent the circumcision rite of passage according to the community's traditions. In addition, he wrote a comprehensive treatise, "The History of the Southern Kikuyu before 1903", and Europeans considered him to be the leading (White) authority on the Kikuyu. He also acted as the translator during Kenyatta's Kapenguria trial. He suggested that the power of the oath could be removed if the taker confessed and that a traditional cleansing ceremony was then needed to rid his mind and body of the oath's polluting vestiges.

He began to occupy a position somewhat like Kenya's Rasputin, and greatly influenced Governor Evelyn Baring on the procedures he adopted in dealing with the Kikuyu. He even wrote a book about the Mau Mau, *Defeating the Mau Mau*, in which he expounded on the nature of the Kikuyu oath as he understood it. It was said that it was his idea to create closed villages for the Kikuyu to stem their support for the Mau Mau. The creation of these villages brought social upheaval, mental and material hardship, malnutrition, famine and victimisation. Without the permission of the Kikuyu guards who oversaw the villages, no one could leave. This dealt a killer blow to the Mau Mau, whose source of supplies was effectively closed.

At any rate, despite being on familiar terms with the Kikuyu, Leakey did not trust them as was evident when he acted as a translator for the prosecution in the infamous Kapenguria trial of Jomo Kenyatta in 1953.

The Moral Rearmament was a religious group that was given the mandate by the government to convert prisoners. Their Christian beliefs were controversial, the movement was not successful and their role was discontinued in 1956 by Thomas G. Askwith after they took prostitutes to Athi River detainees' camp in a bid to make the prisoners lust for flesh and confess. Needless to say, the prisoners did not confess.

The Moral Rearmament people, the churches and similar associations gave some advice but other than the ill-defined scheme of the 'pipeline', the government had no blueprint on the psychological methods of rehabilitation, yet the process was executed all the same. There was actually no effective forum for consultations on the various theories of handling detainees. This may perhaps be yet another reason that unconventional methods were used by individual British rehabilitation officers.

* * *

Breckenridge was a humane fellow who did not believe in mistreating detainees through torture and other violent means. He tried to treat the detainees as decently as possible. His wife, Caroline, voluntarily helped staff and detainees in the camp, as well.

During the day, the detainees were managed by prison authorities to work on various projects under the supervision of the warders. Unfortunately, we had no control over what happened at that time.

In the afternoons, the detainees were handed over to the rehabilitation staff. My responsibility in Thiba was to instruct the detainees in civics and social education. I supervised and ensured there were sufficient social welfare activities for all the prisoners. These included games such as football, volleyball, draughts and dance sessions. The objective of these recreational pastimes was to establish a sense of bonding separate from the prison atmosphere. The entire rationale behind rehabilitation was to prepare the detainees for integration into society once again.

With this purpose in mind, we frequently brought in their families to visit them. There were also church elders who were concerned with their spiritual welfare, and they preached and attempted to convert the prisoners to Christianity. The entire notion of having non-prison staff, such as ourselves, available was to persuade, influence and win over the prisoners to the belief that there was no benefit to be gained by continuing hostilities towards the government. It should be noted that not all Mau Mau suspects were in these detention camps. There were thousands of Mau Mau adherents who had been tried in courts of law and committed to serve sentences in ordinary prisons. This occurred shortly before the declaration of the State of Emergency in 1952 when the detention system started. Those who were charged in court or were in prison did not pass through the pipeline system.

According to what we had been taught at Jeanes School, we were to assist the detainees to resume their previous normal way of life. When we actually undertook the assignment, however, we managed the task in a fashion somewhat contradictory to the directives of our British superiors. As African rehabilitation staff, we more clearly understood and sympathised with the objectives of the Mau Mau, unlike most of the European administrators. Therefore, when we operated in camps such as Thiba, we made it a point to discuss matters compassionately and with tolerance and understanding.

It should be kept in mind that there was no single African rehabilitation officer at this time; we were merely considered 'staff'. It was the British officers who drew up our programme and all of them condemned the Mau Mau entirely.

I would say that, given the colonial circumstances and compared with other detention camps, conditions at Thiba were reasonably civilised. Every detainee worked but no one was ever forced through any inhumane punishment. In fact, all the earthworks that one now sees in the Mwea rice schemes were done by hand, by these detainees who were paid a tiny allowance for their labour. The colonial authorities believed that, by agreeing to work, a detainee was considered ready to be reintegrated.

About a year later, the Ministry of Home Affairs set up a team of 10 African rehabilitation staff from Mwea to go to Manyani and I became part of this unit. At this time, there were about 80,000 detainees in Manyani. It was terribly overcrowded and it became increasingly necessary to move the detainees back into the world. Our team was assigned the task of holding discussions with the detainees in Manyani in order to convince them that there was no need for them to continue their supposedly aggressive and hostile stance. In fact, we knew that many of the detainees held in this camp were actually quite innocent and there was absolutely no reason to continue holding them in such harsh conditions.

I often felt that the terribly poor conditions in these hardcore camps were unnecessarily severe. They were not right for any human being. Our assignment was, therefore, to encourage and persuade the detainees to open up and talk to us. We made sure that those who showed the smallest sign of cooperation were swiftly moved to more humane camps like the Mwea, or camps nearer their home areas. Such camps were generally the last site of detention before detainees went home.

I was in Manyani for a very short time with this team and returned to Mwea by early 1957. Breckenridge was releasing a good number of detainees quite rapidly, with my full cooperation, and someone in authority must have become aware of the high numbers and concluded that Breckenridge was being too soft on the prisoners.

Therefore, Breckenridge was transferred to Athi River, a high security camp, where senior Mau Mau detainees were held. When his orders came through, he requested that I be transferred along with him, and McGuiness then took over in Mwea.

I had no difficulty over the transfer since I agreed with the methods Breckenridge used to handle this unfortunate situation.

On arrival at the detention camp, I discovered I knew a number of the detainees from back home in Kiambu. Some of them were well-aware that I had taken the Mau Mau oath and I made the decision to admit the fact to Breckenridge before he found out from the prisoners. I made the admission to Breckenridge and the Special Branch officer in charge of the department at Athi River. I was ready to face the consequences, even if it meant I was to be dismissed. I also informed them about my view of the oath and gave my assurance that it would in no way affect my efficiency.

This was noted in the records and no action was ever taken against me, although I failed to obtain a Loyalty Certificate in order to vote in the countrywide elections for the Legislative Council that occurred during the year.

Breckenridge, as I said, was a humane person and did not condone the mistreatment of prisoners. He found conditions in Athi River harsh and depressing. This camp was meant for the defiant hardcore Mau Mau leaders, while the environment in Mwea had been for those considered pacified and ready to go home. Breckenridge made his discontent known to the authorities but he was reprimanded and reminded that detention camps were not luxury hotels for the relaxation and indulgence of the detainees.

Breckenridge then resigned from government service in protest and I believe he subsequently left the country. The authorities at Athi River Detention Camp knew that I shared his point of view over the treatment of prisoners. They felt that I was his protégé, and soon after Breckenridge left, I was transferred back to Mwea, this time to Kandongu. I actually served for less than three months in Athi River and was glad to get back to my old station. Like Breckenridge, I did not agree with the tight and disheartening security and conditions in that camp.

I always held the opinion that brutality was not the way to change the thinking of the Mau Mau detainees. After all, they were seeking justice. In such a case, it was not possible to change people's minds. How could there be change? People still wanted their land. They still wanted freedom and education. In respect to changing people's outlook and their political beliefs, rehabilitation failed miserably. People do not easily change their minds on their fundamental beliefs. They were totally convinced of the justice and truth of their cause. One cannot cure a disease without addressing the root causes and symptoms, yet this was what the colonial government was trying to do. It stubbornly failed to realise that all the Africans wanted was liberty and justice.

As far as the colonial government was concerned, the focus of the detention camps was to get detainees to admit they had taken the oath. To get round having to acknowledge oath-taking, detainees invented a system among themselves. Detainees called it *Muma wa ndaka* – or 'oath of mud' which was a symbolic manner of saying that it was a false confession. The reference to mud was to indicate the insubstantial or malleable pretence of their declaration of guilt.

In order not to implicate a living person, they would thereby purport to make a clean breast of it by making up a fictitious person, identifying the oath administrator as someone who had died in the village, or otherwise specify someone who was already in detention or in jail and had already been named by several others. All the detainees would designate the same person as the oath administrator and be cleared.

Although we in the rehabilitation system knew the confessions were not genuine, I did nothing to discourage the system and colluded with the scheme. I would have done nearly anything to enable the detainees be released. There were substantial numbers of detainees released in this manner. On occasion, there were such large crowds that some of those who were ready to confess had to remain behind and wait for clerks to record their specifics. I ignored this deceit because I understood the underlying issues and deeply empathised. I knew that most detainees were not murderers, and the majority of them were well aware that they would not die if they confessed the oath. They merely did not want to capitulate to the colonial authorities.

While I was at Kandongu in Mwea, David Base was my immediate superior and McGuiness took over from Breckenridge as the officer in charge of all the Mwea camps. McGuiness and I established a friendship, although it took time for him to accept me.

A short time later, McGuiness left and Terence Gavaghan, the Special District Officer in charge of Rehabilitation, took over the position in charge of all the Mwea camps. Gavaghan, unfortunately, was an arrogant and unfriendly man who believed in humiliating the detainees. When interviewed in a BBC programme, *White Terror* (aired in 2006), he said, "I have no regrets," when asked about the atrocities committed by the British against the Mau Mau. He also vehemently denied Caroline Elkins allegations in her book, *The British Gulag*, on the same subject, in which he is mentioned negatively along with various others.

At that time, the performance of staff was judged by how many detainees went home after the so-called rehabilitation. When we, the African staff, talked to the detainees, convinced them it was time to go home and brought about their release, David Base, who knew neither Kiswahili nor Kikuyu, would take all the credit despite the fact that he could not even communicate with the detainees directly.

Gavaghan would write letters congratulating Base for a job well done, even though the rehabilitation staff was actually doing the task. I was unhappy about the circumstances and about getting no credit for all the work we were doing. I felt unappreciated and used. I made a decision to do something about the situation so I went to Nairobi without permission and remained there a whole week. I went to see a Mr. Collins, who was senior administration officer in the Ministry of Community Development and Rehabilitation Headquarters, and told him about the situation in Mwea and about the reasons for my unhappiness with my position. I was pleased that he agreed with my analysis and chose to post me to Kajiado. He sent a message to Gavaghan to effect the transfer.

On receiving the message, Gavaghan was furious. He left word in the camp that as soon as I came back, I was to go and see him. When I arrived in his office, we had a confrontation. Gavaghan probably thought he could fire me but I was ready for anything. He asked me where I had been and demanded to know who had given me permission to talk to superior officers in Nairobi.

I informed him that no one had given me permission and that even if I had asked for permission, I was sure it would not have been granted.

"Who do you think you are?" he asked me.

"My name is Jeremiah Gitau Kiereini."

"I have received a posting notice, but I'm telling you this, you will not go!"

I protested that I had been posted by headquarters but he stood his ground.

He then declared, "I've been in government for 13 years and I will use my 13 years' experience to ensure that you leave Mwea, not for Kajiado, but for your home!"

I stated, "You are a small-minded person. If you are going to use your position and power to finish a junior man like me, you must be a very small man, indeed."

He shouted at me, "Get out of my office!"

I went to my house and awaited developments.

The following morning, the Provincial Commissioner for Central Province, Dick Wilson, came for a tour and Gavaghan and I took him round to see the camp.

Before the PC left, he called me aside and said, "Jeremiah, Gavaghan has told me all about you. You are not going to be transferred to Kajiado after all."

He was very senior to me and all I could say was, "Yes, Sir!" and leave it at that, without knowing exactly what he meant by his cryptic words.

Three days later, I went to Gathigiriri camp, my new posting. When I got to the gate, I met a lorry loaded with luggage and saw a European rehabilitation officer sitting in front with the driver. Later, I learned that he had been fired and I was to take over from him. There was no formal handing over at all and I found an empty office.

Gavaghan introduced me to the British prison officer in charge of the camp. His name was William (Bill) Halsey. Gavaghan told him, "This is Jeremiah Kiereini. He is now the officer in charge of rehabilitation in this camp." His words were a surprise. I had been unceremoniously elevated from a Community Development Assistant to a full Community Development Officer in mid-1957. The Administration had decided to promote me.

Although Gavaghan and I quarrelled and disagreed on several points, I believe he may have been the person who recommended my promotion. He was the sort of man who thrived on controversy and believed that any individual who was tough enough to face him and stand up to him was indeed a good man. He was rough with everyone, Europeans included, and fought everywhere he went.

During the time Gavaghan was a District Officer in Kiambu, he was known as *Karuga ndua* (the crusher of gourds). According to Kikuyu culture, gourds or calabashes were special containers for liquids and breaking them intentionally was viewed as sacrilege. Such huge calabashes were normally used for traditional beer, which could not be brewed without permission from administrative officials. Therefore, as the administrator in charge of the law, Gavaghan would just smash everything into the ground if he found any sort of brewing equipment.

At Gathigiriri, William Halsey was in charge of the prison. He had a haughty manner and looked down on Africans. Not long after my transfer, we had our first major confrontation.

As I mentioned previously, prison warders would take the detainees to work during the morning hours and then later they would be handed over to me and my assistants for counselling, games and other events. One day, as I walked around the camp, I realised that the compound was very dirty. There was litter everywhere, long grass and bushes, and dilapidated equipment lying all over. Conditions for the detainees were poor, and this grime merely created even more depressing living conditions. I decided to do something about it. That afternoon, when the detainees were handed over to me, I took them round the camp, clearing the bushes and burying or burning the trash. In a few hours, the whole camp was clean and everybody was happy. Or so I thought.

Halsey had been away the whole day and he had not been around when the cleaning exercise took place. When he arrived at camp in the evening, he saw what we had done and he was furious. He was the sort of character who felt offended if someone else came up with a good idea and outshone him. The fact that this time round he had been upstaged by an African made it even worse.

He marched to my office and, without any formalities, charged furiously at me. "Mr. Kiereini, who do you think is in charge of this camp?"

"You are in charge," I answered. I had no idea why he was so angry.

"On whose authority was this exercise done?" he asked, pointing at the various places that had been cleaned up.

I was surprised. I would have thought that congratulations would be in order for such an initiative, and here was Halsey, livid and breathing fire just because I had decided to clean the camp. I was not shaken by his fury and I let him know as much.

"It was done under my authority, Mr. Halsey. I am here to clean the minds of these detainees and I cannot clean them in a dirty environment. I thought you would be pleased," I chided him.

Halsey stormed off and drove to Thiba camp where our boss, Gavaghan, was staying. Halsey gave him his version of the story, something about my insubordination, or a report to such effect. I was not concerned. I had never been worried about doing something right and I was not going to start at that point. Halsey's high-handedness did not impress me at all, and I did not care that he was British. Later, his wife, who was a good-natured woman, came up to me and told me that we should try to resolve the issue amicably.

When Gavaghan came to the camp the following morning, he called us both from our offices and told us, without beating about the bush, that there would be dire results if we did not start cooperating.

"You two will work together, or you will both get the sack," he told us.

With that, he walked away. Gavaghan did not favour any side or pass judgement. He just made sure we knew he regarded us as equal, and that he was the authority over us. Later, Halsey and I maintained a lukewarm relationship as we discharged our duties together in the camp.

I intensely disagreed with Gavaghan about the use of force to coerce the detainees to confess the oath. At one time, I tried to advise Gavaghan that using violence was counterproductive and would only create more bitterness among the detainees. As I have mentioned before, Gavaghan and other senior administrators were under pressure to release detainees and end the programme. Some of these administrators chose to use violence to hurry things along.

"These people are only human," I told Gavaghan. "They are bitter because of the discrimination they have faced."

In one way or another, Gavaghan recognised the justice of my remark. "I understand what you're saying," he once told me. "I'm Irish, and 300 years after being treated brutally by the English people, we still have never forgotten or forgiven them. However, we must get these people out of these camps."

I remained in the Mwea camps doing rehabilitation work with detainees for three years, from June 1955 to November 1958.

* * *

The two rehabilitation camps where I worked the longest, that is Thiba and Gathigiriri, had a similar set-up. Most of the camps in Mwea had a capacity of 800 prisoners. There were quite a lot of prison warders, although I cannot now recall the numbers.

The people involved in rehabilitation consisted of a very different group. There were elders from the local community or from the churches. They would screen the detainees and they usually consisted of two teams of five persons each. For the civic rehabilitation, we had a team of three or four in each camp.

The staff houses were located around the outside of the camp and those of us in rehabilitation were housed in little A-frames, meant purely for a bachelor existence, although a few individuals brought along their wives. The British Prison Officer in charge had his own family house within the premises. In Thiba, there was also a large house for the head of the rehabilitation in Mwea camps.

The detainees lived in long dormitory-like structures built of corrugated iron sheets and slept on mats on the ground. There were about a hundred detainees in each dorm and eight dorms in the compound. Initially bucket latrines were in use but later pit latrines were constructed. There were watering points for the detainees within the prison and, in the Mwea camps, the detainees were working on irrigation projects, so there was no problem with dehydration, such as occurred in some other camps.

Like any other prison, the detainees would stand in line in the morning to be counted and would then be divided into labour squads with a prison warder in charge, and go off to work. On the other hand, those of us involved in rehabilitation never went outside the camps, so we did not see the detainees until they returned in the afternoon.

* * *

In any group of humans, one is bound to find a few people who go to extremes. This was true of the rehabilitation system as well. There were many different personalities working within the camps and each individual brought his own character and proclivities into his method of dealing with the detainees.

Although I would say most of us were effective, sympathetic and humane in our treatment of the detainees, a few were outright sadists who seemed to take great pleasure in bullying, humiliating and even physically injuring the detainees.

I recall an incident that occurred when I went home on one month's leave. My replacement, an African staff member, started mistreating the detainees through a variety of cruel punishments. One day, he decided to force the detainees to carry *karai* (large metal basins) full of stones and ballast on their shaven heads, purely for punishment. The detainees were marched rapidly back and forth in the midday sun and several started bleeding from the abrasive metal on their heads but they were given no chance to rest. Before the day was over, one detainee was dead.

When this happened, I was urgently recalled from leave after only a week away and the guilty member of staff, who had replaced me, was immediately transferred.

I thought it unfortunate and disgusting that the medical examiner's report gave the cause of death as "natural causes" and that the individual concerned went on to perpetuate his cruelties in other camps.

Fate finally caught up with him. In his next posting, this man instructed a detainee to dig a deep pit. After the excavation was complete, he ordered the prisoner to enter the hole and then was buried in the earth up to his armpits. The detainee died shortly thereafter and the staff member was charged with murder. Justice was at last taking notice of this sadist in the system.

Ironically, some of the British officers were upset at the charge. They felt that the African staff member had loyally gone about his duties for the government. They apparently felt that such cruelty was justified in the name of keeping discipline. One of these British officers got together a team of senior chiefs and went to State House to see Governor Baring in order to plead with him, on the point that the man had been faithfully carrying out the responsibilities of his position and should never have been charged at all.

Baring advised the officer to be patient. He said the law must take its course and that they should wait for the case to go through the courts. He assured the officer that he would personally look into the case and would use his powers of clemency, if the case merited it.

According to the story I heard later, the officer then protested vigorously. He accused the governor of being a coward and said, "If I were in your position, I know what I would do." With that remark, he walked out on the Governor and led the chiefs out of the office.

The Governor took offence. This was pure insubordination and by the time the officer went back to the field, he found that he had been posted away and immediately demoted from a District Commissioner to an Assistant Secretary. As for the sadistic staff member, he was found guilty, but the charge of murder was reduced to manslaughter and he was sentenced to about two years in prison. I was pleased that he never again worked within the rehabilitation system.

* * *

Caroline Elkin's book, *The British Gulag: Brutal End of an Empire,* has interesting insights into the Mau Mau camps and the way they were handled. She talks mainly about the period after the formalisation of the 'Pipeline', and about the hardcore camps and indeed, there was violence in these camps. I understand she actually started her research and writing about the Mau Mau from the British point of view, but when she got the facts on the ground she changed her mind, and decided to write about the atrocities, the untold stories hidden by the British and western media.

However, she was carried away in trying to interpret the oral history she received in her interviews and used some unforgivable descriptive adjectives and superlatives including some that implicate me unfavourably. She refers to me twice as "the notorious Jeremiah Kiereini" and implies I was a very brutal man who tortured Mau Mau detainees in the Mwea detention camps.

In the nine years she says that she researched the book, she never even once sought an appointment with me to hear my side of the story.

It should be kept in mind that detainees felt that anyone working with the enemy was also their enemy. In this respect, rehabilitation staff were indiscriminately lumped together with the prisons staff, who were known to regularly use violence. Second, after undergoing tough conditions at the hardship detention camps, the detainees coming at the end of the 'pipeline' were supposed to be 'mellowed'. There was allegedly no more 'need for violence', and this was where rehabilitation took place.

* * *

The whole story of the State of Emergency and detention is much bigger than just the 'Pipeline'. When the State of Emergency was declared and British 'Johnnies' were brought in from the United Kingdom, the Africans in the native reserves and towns suffered horribly and conditions were terrible. These events are not fully recorded and if the full story were told, it would be shocking. For example, while searching for information about the Mau Mau, the arrogant 'Johnnies' would torture women by forcing bottles into their private parts. In addition, since Africans were supposed to take off their caps and hats in the presence of Europeans, many 'Johnnies' shot dead innocent people in the name of 'removing' their hats using bullets. These atrocities have not been documented comprehensively and the world has not yet understood the suffering Africans underwent, especially the Kikuyu, who suffered great torture at the hands of British soldiers and settlers.

From my point of view within the rehabilitation system, I concluded that if detainees were enabled to return to their homes without once more resorting to conflict, I had succeeded in my ultimate aim. My attitude was never to condemn those who fought for their rights, for their land, and opportunity, and for their own government. After all, I was one of them. These were our rights as Kenyans. The few of us who had adopted this approach tried to assure the detainees that confessing the oath would not destroy them. We attempted to convince them that the struggle for *Uhuru* (Independence) had already progressed and accelerated in favour of the Africans.

For example, before detention programmes had been established there were no elected black Members of Parliament but by 1957, there were already 12 African representatives. We informed the prisoners that Kenya had already made immense progress and it was now time to settle and get back to their ordinary lives once again. Nothing more could be achieved by continued fighting. After all, the Mau Mau movement had all but collapsed and there were few fighters remaining in the forests. The movement had disintegrated with the arrest of Field Marshall Dedan Kimathi in 1956 and his subsequent hanging in Kamiti Maximum Security Prison on 18 February 1957.

In June 1954, the colonial government decided to establish "Emergency Villages". This forced-resettlement affected Kiambu, Nyeri, Murang'a and Embu Districts and was intended to cut off Mau Mau's supply lines. By the end of 1955, over one million Kikuyu were held within 800 such villages.

By putting 'natives' into closed villages, the colonial authorities had, for the most part, sealed the routes used to deliver food and arms to the fighters in the forest. Their morale had fallen and, under-armed and starving, many of them had surrendered to the authorities. In short, we tried to make the detainees understand that there was no sense in fighting the Mau Mau war any longer and that progress was being made on the political and constitutional front.

There was also considerable pressure on the colonial authorities because the camps had become an embarrassment to the British Government. There were no trials, no legal proof and the incarceration of so many people was regarded as a scandal by the international community. For example, in July 1953, the Attorney General, Sir John Whyatt, had bragged that, in the previous two months, no fewer than 10,000 Mau Mau cases had been dispensed with. This effectively meant that each case was listened to and recommendations passed at an average speed of two minutes per case! The British opposition and some members of government felt that this kind of justice, which was being applied in the detention camps, was actually no justice at all.

International pressure increased after the Hola Massacre of March 1959 and as a result, the British were forced to accelerate the release of detainees. The British opposition was also up in arms because the detention programme was costing their government millions of pounds and was in operation for much longer than had been anticipated.

No matter how one looks at the situation, it is nevertheless obvious that the aim of rehabilitating the detainees was never successful. The detainees never gave up their goals. As soon as the detainees realised they could go home after coming clean, they did so. Most were not anxious about any repercussions. They confessed, but their statements were not genuine. They merely made up spurious declarations of guilt in order to leave detention. No one genuinely changed. Those of us in rehabilitation were well aware of the ruse, but ignored it and even condoned it. Detainees had endured too much hardship and misery and many of their colleagues had not lived to see the camps at the end of the 'pipeline.'

There is considerable disagreement regarding the total number of deaths occurring as a result of the Emergency. Caroline Elkins gives the figure as "tens of thousands, perhaps hundreds of thousands". However, the British demographer John Blacker disagrees. He explains that hundreds of thousands of fatalities "implies that perhaps half of the adult male population would have been wiped out – yet the censuses of 1962 and 1969 show no evidence of this – the age-sex pyramids for the Kikuyu districts do not even show indentations".

Other leading authorities on Africa have also criticised Elkins' mortality figures.

There were Detention Camps scattered throughout Kenya. They consisted of Fort Hall, comprising Kamaguta, Kandara, Kangema, Kigumo and Mariira; Embu comprising Dondueni, Gathigiriri, Kandongu, Karaba, Mwea and Thiba; Meru comprising Mbeu; Nyeri comprising Aguthi (Kangubiri), Karatina, Mukurweini, Mweru, Othaya, and Nyeri Showground; Kiambu comprising Gatundu, Githiga, Kiambu Transit, Ngenya and Waithaka; Rift Valley comprising Marigat; Coast comprising Hola, Mkoe and Takwa; Southern Province comprising Athi River, Kathonzweni, Mara River and Ngulot and various miscellaneous centres such as Lodwar, Kamiti, Mageta Island, Manyani, Nairobi Dispersal, Saiyusi Island, South Yatta, Fort Hall Prison, Meru Detention Camp, Kisumu Prison, Marsabit Prison, Nairobi New Prison, Kamiti Y Camp, Hindi, Mombasa Prison and Wamumu.

In my view, the so-called 'rehabilitation' was only successful in one sense, which was to get people out of camps. This, after all, had been my main focus when I joined rehabilitation. Detainees would otherwise have been there much longer. As it was, they went back to their families and, if they wanted to continue with politics after that, it was by their own choice.

As I explained, while I was working with the government as a Community Development Assistant, my former friends regarded me as a traitor, in the same way that anyone working with a hostile government would be regarded. However, the people who thought of me in this way misunderstood my motives completely. I had always supported the liberation of Kenya and, time and again, I was actively involved in both overt and clandestine activities promoting independence, with the Mau Mau while at Kiamwangi, with local political operatives, with British parliamentarians at the Indian High Commission and socially with individuals like Tom Mboya and Pinto, among others, in Nairobi. Therefore, I did not see any conflict in assisting in the rehabilitation and release of prisoners back into normal society nor did I see a conflict in my normal life as a Christian and in my work as an employee of the government.

Furthermore, I have always regarded myself as a man with strong religious principles, which have guided my life. Over many years, my concept of religion has changed, although my fundamental principles remain the same. I have adopted what I like to think of as a more universally spiritual concept of God, that is, not strictly the biblical view. I believe in a supreme creator, but whether this is a Christian, Islamic or a concept of God of other faiths is, to my mind, irrelevant. One's behaviour, guiding ethics and values are far more important than the faith to which one belongs.

As a Christian, my conscience was clear during the period of rehabilitation and I would not hesitate to perform such duties again. I considered myself different from the others working in rehab. Even Gavaghan's book, *Of Lions and Dung Beetles: A Man in the Middle of Colonial Administration in Kenya* points out that I was different. For one thing, it mentions that I was more political than Isaiah Mathenge. My philosophy was more humanitarian and I was never violent. I treated the detainees as real people, people from my community and not just as mere prisoners. I tried to appeal to their more humane side, to show them that they were still good people despite the treatment they had been subjected to by the warders in the hardship camps.

* * *

After I left the rehabilitation department, a particularly notorious event occurred in Hola camp, which I thought was very cruel. According to official records, Hola was then one of the few hardcore camps still operating. On 3 March 1959, eighty-five hardcore prisoners were marched out and directed to dig a trench. Suddenly, while they were working, there was an altercation and they refused to comply with any more instructions. A British officer in charge commanded the warders to use force to compel the prisoners to submit. Approximately 200 guards beat the prisoners and this was prolonged for two hours. When the assault was over 12 prisoners had been beaten to death and an estimated 60 others were seriously injured.

There was a conscious effort by prison officials to conceal the incident. They claimed that the dead prisoners had drunk contaminated water but an inquest by a member of the Colonial Judiciary, which was spearheaded by Barbara Castle of the House of Commons in London, revealed the truth. The pathologist who performed the post-mortem examination exposed the brutal savagery of the entire process and disclosed in his findings that the prisoners had been bludgeoned to death. As soon as the conclusions were made public, the opposition in England condemned Hola and the whole detention programme. The massacre and the events surrounding it were given a very high profile by the British and international press. Soon thereafter, the detention system was dismantled, camps were closed down throughout Kenya and detainees were freed. It was a truly horrible event.

There was no rehabilitation staff at Hola. It was purely a prison, and people were incarcerated there because they were seen as incorrigible. They were the people the colonialists had failed to break. None of those who went into these camps, wherever they were, was ever tried in any court of law, or their classification scrutinised by any legal system. There was never any intention to 'try' them. The law of detention was seen as sufficient to justify their imprisonment at the time.

When the number of detainees decreased and camps were about to close, we were given the choice of either to continue as Community Development Officers out in the districts or to assume general duties in the Provincial Administration.

In November 1958, I chose to take up general duties in Administration. I believe we were all weary of Community Development, especially in regard to dealing with the harsh conditions of detention. For those of my rank, we became, not DOs, but District Assistants. The older District Assistants were earning about 684 pounds per annum while I was earning over 732 pounds because I was transferred from the post of CDO, which was more highly paid.

Early portrait, 1961.

With my elder brother Zakayo Njoroge (right) and his son Stephen Kiereini.

With my friend Kagumu (right), 1961.

Early portrait, 1970s.

With John Malinda (left) at Oxford, 1961.

Early portrait.

With Kagumu Muhia.

Jackson Mulinge and I look on as President Kenyatta welcomes Group Captain of the Royal Air Force, Edwards, at State House, 1970.

With my wife Eunice Muringo at our wedding on 13 November 1971.

This is the group that went to London in 1962 for a course in administration. From left to right: Joseph Musembi, Sila Boit, myself, Peter Shiyuka, Peter Oranga, Daudi Wabera, an officer of the court, John Malinda, John Michuki and Sam Josiah outside the Nairobi High Court.

From left to right: Bernard Hinga, Kenyatta's ADC, Mzee Kenyatta, Moi and myself, 1970s.

Front row, from left to right: John Mburu, Paul Boit, Mbiyu Koinange, Mzee Kenyatta, Daniel arap Moi, Kariithi, Eliud Mahihu and Kamwithi Munyi. Back row, from left to right: Bill Martin, Isaiah Cheluget, Isaiah Mathenge, Charles Koinange, Simeon Nyachae and myself, 1969.

Presenting a trophy to one of the military units, as PS, Ministry of Defence. Looking on is General Mulinge, Chief of Defence Staff.

With Duncan Ndegwa, Tom Mboya, Paul Ngei and others.

With Charles Njonjo and Ben Gethi at a national function.

With James Gichuru and senior military officers among them J.M. Ndolo.

With Isaiah Mathenge and Barrack Osare.

With President Moi while receiving a gift from J.P. Mbugua.

With relatives and friends at my wedding, 1971.

With Grace (best maid) and Charles Njonjo (best man) at our wedding, 1971.

My daughters Caroline (extreme right) and Mumbi (third from left) at a school party, Thogoto Junior School, 1961.

In a pensive mood.

At Kabarnet Gardens, with wife Eunice and children Mburu (left) and Githae, around 1976.

Early family portrait.

My family:
Front row, from left to right: Saidimo, Douglas, Joyce, Gitau and Namaisa. Back row, from left to right: Njeri, Githae, Mumbi, Errol King, Rose Wambui and Mburu.

With my wife Eunice, son Douglas and his wife Joyce.

With Waruhiu Itote aka General China (centre) and GG Kariuki at a National Youth Service occasion, Gilgil.

Board of East African Breweries Limited:
Seated, from left to right: Richard Kemoli, myself and Isaiah Cheluget. Standing, from left to right: Gerald Mahinda (second), John Kagema Mwangi, David Hampshire, Michael Karanja among others.

With, from left to right: David Hampshire, Henya and the pro at a competition sponsored by Diageo – the Johnny Walker Classic. This was after a board meeting at Glen Eagles.

Golfing at Karen Country Club, 1990s.

With President Kibaki during a visit to the Breweries.

From left to right: Gerald Mahinda (Chairman of Diageo), Hauma, President Kibaki, myself and Nick Blazquez (President, Diageo Africa).

Mburu and his wife Wambui

With Charles Njonjo at my son's (Mburu and Wambui) wedding. At the back is Joseph Karuga Koinange.

Tending to our beautiful flower garden.

My son Mburu and Wambui at their wedding.

Our family home at Karen.

Composite picture celebrating my 80th birthday presented to me by my children.

Chapter 6

From Rehabilitator to Administrator

My posting to Meru as a District Assistant (DA) for Land Consolidation turned out to be a completely new life and I enjoyed it very much. Many of the people I met were the detainees whom I had released earlier on, while at Gathigiriri. They were partial to me, despite the fact that I did not speak Ki-Meru, their language. I would have had a difficult, not to say impossible time, if I had treated them as badly as Caroline Elkins insinuates in her book.

It is strange that even in the Provincial Administration of the time, petty political squabbles were going on. At the time of my transfer, John Cumber was the District Commissioner for Meru and Frank Lloyd was the Provincial Commissioner for Central Province. While I was in Meru, Lloyd was transferred to Government House and Dick Wilson took over as PC in Nyeri. Cumber had a grudge against the previous PC because although Cumber was more senior, Wilson was appointed PC over him. Furthermore, Cumber was of the opinion that I had been posted to Meru because Wilson favoured me. I found the job impossible under such circumstances in which perception and personal relationships between senior officers negatively affected the working conditions.

When I first reported for duty in Meru, I was called to Cumber's office and he started to criticise me, saying, "You have come here to do Land Consolidation. Please understand that you were not invited here and there is no way you are going to bully the Meru the way you did with the Kikuyu. You go out and do what you are told by the Meru Elders." I just stood there surprised and did not even know what he was talking about because, at the time, I was unaware of the bad blood between my superiors.

As may be noted, I have never hesitated to tell my superiors when I thought they were wrong. I have never feared any of them, even when some of them looked down on African officers. I had many work-related disagreements with Gavaghan, Bill Halsey and Cumber but in the end, we managed to work together.

I admit I was rather hot-headed, especially in my early years in the Civil Service, and I believe this is due to several factors.

First, my father taught me to be principled and to stand my ground if I knew I was right. Cowardice was not part of my upbringing. Second, I was educated and, with my level of education, I had no illusions about Europeans. In most cases they were senior to me, especially in my early years in the government, yet I had a better education than many of them, and understood the work better than they ever could, being foreigners. Many of the old African administrators regarded Europeans as supernatural beings who could not be questioned, but those of us who had been to Makerere and other universities could not condone such nonsense. Therefore, I did not tolerate rubbish from a senior officer simply because he was European.

Furthermore, political enlightenment was part of the exposure I received at Makerere and particularly while working at the Indian High Commission. India had achieved its independence from Britain just a few years earlier and the Indian Government and the High Commission in Nairobi enthusiastically supported Kenya's independence struggle. As such, many activities that took place within the confines of the Commission were anti-British and the High Commission was regarded as a sort of enemy platform by the British authorities.

With this insight, naturally, I was more aware of the despicable actions of Europeans against Africans and I could not tolerate their high-handedness. I knew my rights and knew the extent to which I could go, and most importantly, I always stood on my principles. On occasion, I may have run the risk of being sacked, but I was efficient, competent and thorough in my work, even if I say so myself, and I relied on that fact to make me indispensable. Highly educated Africans were hard to come by in those days.

I arrived in Meru when Land Consolidation and Adjudication was just beginning in the area. Land adjudication and registration was being carried out because, previously, the 'natives' did not have title deeds for their land. Our communities cultivated or made use of land otherwise, on either a family or clan basis, and although there were boundaries existing in some places, they were not clear and obviously not legally binding. To demonstrate to the people that they would indeed get the land for which they were agitating, something needed to be done to accentuate their legal rights to property.

It was on this basis that the Swynnerton Plan was put into effect. Roger Swynnerton was an official in the Department of Agriculture. His radical ideas for African agriculture first surfaced in a memorandum written in 1951 and formed the basis for his department's submission to the East African Royal Commission on Land early in 1953. It had been realised that there were as many acres of potential land for lucrative cash crops like coffee, tea, sisal and pyrethrum in African areas, as there were already under cultivation by European settlers. The objective was to create African family holdings, which would be large enough to keep the family self-sufficient in food and enable them to create a cash income. Thus, one can say that one of the Mau Mau's successes was the advent of land adjudication in Kenya.

As it was originally envisioned, the Swynnerton Plan was intended to be applied in many areas throughout Kenya. It was initially forced through in areas of Central Province and the surroundings and then spread outward. In most places, it had mixed results, some succeeded and others did not.

When it comes to the question of how many people were willing to go along with the recommendations, we should bear in mind the problems associated with bench terracing. Bench terracing was a government scheme put in force in the 1940s to curb soil erosion but which met great resistance from political leaders, particularly Jomo Kenyatta.

Although terracing came along prior to the Swynnerton Plan, it was opposed vehemently, because the approach and application were misconceived and badly implemented. It was forced upon people and if any individual refused to carry out terracing, he was punished. A chief in Murang'a District got into considerable trouble in this manner. Instead of educating people about the benefits of this practice in controlling soil erosion, he forced it upon them and some who refused were punished.

Unfortunately, the practice was that a chief would get a commendation if his area had implemented terracing, no matter what method he might use to coerce the people. Naturally, this led to abuse but I believe most chiefs tried to convince people without such punitive measures.

At this juncture, a great deal of blood had been shed because of confrontations over land and freedom. The Swynnerton Plan was one of the methods chosen to put a stop to this political agitation that had already claimed thousands of lives and cost millions of British taxpayers' pounds. The Plan intended to give the Kikuyu and their cousins – the Embu and Meru – rational land management through consolidation. Furthermore, through the incentive of being allowed to grow cash crops, it was hoped to turn African minds to farming, rather than protest. One weakness was that it did not address the issue of the 'stolen lands', which Europeans had expropriated from Africans.

Many Kikuyu were too intimidated to grow coffee but somewhat earlier, Senior Chief Koinange had got into trouble for breaking the law because he had deliberately planted coffee on his farm, just like the European across the road from him.

After the introduction of the Swynnerton Plan, Africans could legally plant up to 50 coffee plants. Before that, between 1900 and 1936, coffee was strictly grown by settlers only. It was alleged that if Africans were allowed to grow coffee, it would lead to lowering the quality and the spread of crop diseases. The ban was lifted later and Africans were allowed to grow a limited number of trees under government supervision. Even then, in Kikuyuland, only a few people were allowed to grow the crop. The Kikuyu in Central Kenya were only allowed to grow coffee freely in the early 1960s and after the demarcation of land in 1958 and 1959.

Later this limitation went up to 100 trees, which was still not much when one considers that an acre can hold about 500 trees. Afterwards other cash crops such as pyrethrum were introduced as well.

Under the colonial government, Africans had been banned from farming such crops for a number of reasons. The original concept was that the settlers needed labour on their own farms and in order to make this 'native' labour available, the colonial government denied Africans the right to grow cash crops. In addition, much of the traditional Kikuyu lands had been expropriated to make up the 'White Highlands'. This economic marginalisation forced the Africans to seek employment in European farms.

Land consolidation was a big challenge in Meru. It had already been carried out in Kiambu, Nyeri and other places that were hotbeds of Mau Mau activity and it was not popular. The general population suspected that land consolidation was just another ruse by which the Europeans hoped to get African land. Unfortunately, most of it was carried out and implemented while many people were in detention. It brought about considerable injustice because land was partitioned and, while the real owners were in detention, other people laid claim to it.

No land belonging to suspected Mau Mau adherents was ever confiscated by the government. This misconception (through popular rumour) held that when detainees were released, they found that all their land had been taken. The fact is that there was no legal method for the government to confiscate land belonging to the Mau Mau for one simple reason. No individual had land titles before the consolidation programme.

The land was owned communally by clans and people farmed and grazed their livestock on the vast tracts belonging to each clan. Of course, a whole clan could not belong to the Mau Mau and be arrested and detained, so those who remained behind were left to take care of the land. When consolidation came, some of those who were in detention were given a raw deal by their own relatives, unscrupulous land officials, or junior administrators. This was because they were not available to pronounce their declaration of ownership or to protect it from others and therefore the land went to whoever claimed it.

Furthermore, if an individual held a miniscule portion of land, his sons might be landless, as further subdivision would create portions that were no longer economically viable. In this way, land consolidation brought the increasing awareness that there was not actually enough land for everyone.

Land tribunals were established by the government to hear and adjudicate on the many grievances that arose from the consolidation. Furthermore, Europeans took land consolidation as an opportunity to create a wedge between the Meru and the Kikuyu. As farther back as 1933 during the Carter Land Commission, the colonialists had attempted to alienate the Kikuyu from their Embu and Mbeere cousins.

The initial solidarity of these communities presented difficulties for the colonial government, and it sought ways to discredit and isolate the Kikuyu. By drawing up new boundaries, the Embu and Meru, who had previously been in Central Province, were amalgamated into Eastern Province. This was an effort to demonstrate that they were not part of the Kikuyu, as the Kikuyu were the most aggressive and persistent community in their fight for freedom and land. These divide and rule tactics took place as can be seen by the following example.

Long before land consolidation, in the late 1930s, there had been a major disagreement between the Mbeere and the Kikuyu of Ndia over the jurisdiction of vast grazing lands in Mwea that cut across the two communities' territories. The Mbeere lived on one side of the Rupingazi River but both sides could graze freely in Mwea where there was good pasture. The two communities had always been friendly and had helped each other in times of war and peace, but due to population pressures, differences began appearing over the pasturage area.

Finally differences ensued which had the Mbeere, led by Chief Kombo Munyiri, pitted against the Kirinyaga Kikuyu (the Ndia) led by Njega wa Gioko.

The Carter Land Commission was set up to look into land grievances in the colony and at a sitting in Nyeri on 27 January 1933, Chief Kombo Munyiri accused the Ndia people of encroaching on land that had always belonged to the Mbeere people. He stated, "The Kikuyu of South Nyeri claim that Mwea belongs to them and not to the Mbeere ... Mwea originally belonged to the Mbeere." Countering the statement, Njega told the commission that, "... the Mbeere are lying. Mwea belongs to Ndia, and has belonged to them for many years. Our fathers were there when they were boys and our grandfathers were born in Mwea. Mwea has belonged to us since the time of our great-great-great-great grandfathers."

British administrators deliberately laid emphasis on such altercations to divide various communities because their unity would have meant stronger resistance. They increasingly sought to isolate the Kikuyu as the agitation for independence increased. There were many other cases in which the authorities fuelled tribal animosities among the indigenous communities to ensure that there was little unity. In general, the Mbeere were regarded as more peaceful than the Kikuyu. This may be because of the fact that they actually had nothing much to fight for, because their land had not been alienated by the British.

To show the Meru that the government recognised them as a community, a separate Meru Land Unit was set up for the consolidation exercise. The Meru elders had been attempting to carry out land consolidation and were marking boundaries using the naked eye. It was not only ridiculous but also chaotic. They used estimations that were often inaccurate and this led to arguments. They had no liking for the whole exercise and did not really understand it. They would ask questions such as, "How can you make sure no soil gets lost along the way?" when different parcels of land were consolidated.

Therefore, when I took up my new posting, I was quite preoccupied with explaining the process. I told them all about the procedure and took considerable time explaining the concept of consolidating small land parcels. I spent about six months in the bush and the results were not very satisfactory. Even with surveyors and equipment, it was a difficult task. The fact that I had a testy relationship with my boss did not help.

Meru was quite a big district. I worked with the assistance of some clerks who dealt with land cases. They did surveying, so we had survey instruments and could determine the size of plots and their locations. I recall I had quite a good team and although there were a few hiccups, I did not have any major problems with the staff. I completed one area in Upper Abothoguchi and did well, and after that, some adjacent areas saw the advantages and agreed to the process.

I used persuasion to convince the people. In every meeting, I explained the various advantages of consolidation. For example, when all the separate little land parcels were consolidated, the landowner would no longer have to travel from piece to piece, trying to manage them all. It would be much easier to grow coffee, or keep grade cattle, for instance, on one piece of land, because the farmer would easily be able to keep an eye on them. In addition, it would be simpler to get a title deed and a bank loan. There was a great economic advantage in having one piece instead of 10.

At this time, all milk in Meru town was supplied and packed by a European farmer in Timau. I told the farmers that if they could agree to consolidate their little parcels, they too could use their own initiative to develop themselves. I told them that if they could keep grade cattle and feed them well, the European farmers would no longer control the market.

I occupied the house that had been previously occupied by a British DO. At the time, people did not see much difference in these ranks. They called us all 'Bwana DO'. My official car was an old Land Rover. I can remember that the registration number was OHMS 6091 (OHMS, On Her Majesty's Service). Land Rovers were the favourite form of transportation for police and administration officials. These vehicles could get to the remotest corners of the country, even where the roads were very poor.

By this time, I already had my own private car. While I was still in Mwea, I had purchased a very old Vauxhall, for 900 shillings. It was so old that it required constant service and repairs. In order to keep it running I actually had two engines. I would use one while the other was being overhauled and constantly had to carry a bag of spanners in my trunk in case it broke down. Luckily, one of the detainees in Mwea, an excellent mechanic, not only taught me how to drive, but also taught me basic mechanics as well.

When I was transferred to Meru, I managed to sell the Vauxhall for 1,500 shillings as part exchange and purchased a Morris Minor 1000 van. I bought it mainly so I could carry a few commodities, such as *njahi* (beans), potatoes and cowpeas, from Meru to take home to sell. At the time, my wife, who was a teacher, and our children, were in Kibichoi, so I would visit regularly and each time I went I would take a bag or two of vegetables. I actually made enough profit to cover my petrol costs.

To get home I would drive up to Nanyuki, following the well-maintained route to the north. Although it would have been shorter to travel on the Embu-Meru road, at that time, it was a nightmare. It had 95 sharp corners, traversed several rivers and was not properly graded.

Getting back to my experiences with land consolidation in Meru, Cumber was later transferred and Donald Hodge took over. Donald Hodge was understanding, and had a good education. In our approach, we held discussions with the DO in charge of Land Consolidation, John St. Mathews, and the three of us developed a strategy that was surprisingly successful.

We called the people together in Kithirune area and informed them that we would try something temporary, just so that they could see what was meant by consolidation. At Kithirune, there was a neat straight ridge that could easily act as a straight boundary from the road to the river and would be fairly simple to divide. We informed the people that we would not actually divide the land but merely mark out the boundaries so that they could see the results and judge for themselves. We used qualified surveyors from Nyeri who measured up the plots and then put beacons on the pieces of land. After they had completed the work the people were called back to come and examine the result.

We asked them to confirm the consolidated pieces and see if they measured up to the same size as the scattered pieces they held. They went through the process of checking the area and became convinced that the procedure had been done accurately. They all agreed and said the boundaries should be permanent.

We were pleased with finally achieving this difficult phase and decided to invite the PC for Central to see the pilot scheme. When he eventually made his visit, the people told him they were very happy with the method that had been adopted. The PC then remarked that if other areas could be demarcated in a similar manner there would be no problem in completing the consolidation. Later the DC actually brought in people from other parts of Meru, who were suspicious of the process, to tour the demonstration area. That was the nucleus of land consolidation in Meru and afterwards, it was plain sailing.

I talked to a considerable number of people concerning the need for consolidation. I explained that adopting that course of action would give them a feeling of pride by creating individual ownership of land. On an individual piece, one had the choice to farm, graze livestock, or do whatever they wished without the constraints of communal ownership where individual decisions were not feasible. Secondly, with a title deed, it became possible to get a loan from banks and thereby develop the farm. Coffee and tea were quite profitable at that time, and with the help of a loan, farms could be developed to prime cash crop production. As for cattle rearing, I explained that vast tracts of land were no longer necessary because of the progression to zero grazing. Keeping grade cattle on a small piece of land could bring in a larger income than vast herds of traditional cattle. I believe I succeeded in eliminating a large part of their initial scepticism and I was proud of this accomplishment. Unfortunately, the Meru have, up to the time of writing this book, not completed land consolidation, and this is so in other parts of the country.

The Swynnerton Plan was an excellent concept, and, to a large extent, succeeded in its endeavours. Land consolidation in Meru was negotiated, not forced, and as such, the people accepted it. When a number of people began to make false claims and the level of dishonesty escalated, it became difficult to determine the facts. People began making claims on land that they had no rights to, or claiming larger pieces than they had originally occupied. Eventually, despite such predicaments, people found new satisfaction in their status as land owners, some long-standing arguments were settled, people began planting coffee and tea, and to improve their land parcels by terracing, and good husbandry.

I spent two years in Meru from December 1958 to December 1960, working in land consolidation. I met challenges, but no insurmountable difficulties. My time in Meru made up the most productive, enjoyable and satisfying years in my life, notwithstanding my relatively low standing in the administration. I believe there is nothing that gives greater joy than tackling a daunting challenge and being successful.

During this time of my life, I was known as Gitau, and some of the friends I made in Meru still speak of "the slender young DA called Gitau", who made land consolidation a success. I feel honoured and humbled by such appreciation.

From Meru, I was posted to Kandara as a District Assistant, General Duties, for three months and then went to Kangema Division. There were extensive complaints about land consolidation. In some parts of the Kikuyu area, consolidation had been done extremely unprofessionally. Falsification and fraud were so widespread that the exercise had to be completely redone. A great number of discrepancies were found in Murang'a and Dr Julius Gikonyo Kiano, who was the MP for the area, brought up the issue in Parliament and caused an uproar. Land consolidation clerks were selling non-existent land from land registers in their offices and as a result, there was more land in the registers than on the ground.

As late as 1961, I recall that when I went to Kandara Division, we were still trying to educate people on the benefits of protecting their top soil from erosion. We had to go very slowly because the original imposition of terracing had caused so much trouble.

I would go to places near the Chania River, which is the boundary between Kiambu and Murang'a, and hold *barazas* (public meetings) to talk to the people.

"You can see for yourselves. Just look at your land. It is very good, but you need to plant something other than wattle. Wattle is not economical and it damages your soil, so you should cut down these trees and then make bench terraces and plant coffee."

I would also tell them, "Just look across the river near Mang'u and see the little coffee plots. See how well they are doing!"

It was often difficult to effect a change in the farmers' attitudes. There was a little story I was told by the Murang'a people (by those who were ready for change) who understood my attempts to transform land usage practices.

Apparently, while the people in Kiambu and the people in Murang'a were working on their farms on opposite sides of the valley, the two groups would occasionally talk across the river that made the boundary.

The man in Kiambu would say, "Eh! You people in Murang'a, you hold on to your ways! We in Kiambu have been forced to make terraces, but you are a brave people. You be defiant! Continue to defy! You are brave, so stick to your ways and hold on. You keep that *shamba* unproductive!"

It was funny to us at the time and at least it showed that some of the Murang'a people realised their own weaknesses. Through jokes like these, I learned the attitude of the Murang'a people.

The majority were misled and continued planting wattle trees. They thought it was a sign of independence, a sign that they had not bowed down to government pressure. Yet the man across the valley in Kiambu had a beautiful coffee *shamba* and got a good income from his coffee but the man in Murang'a got a pittance for his wattle trees.

Whenever I had the opportunity to address the farmers, I said, "Now people, if you can joke about this and recognise your weakness, why can't you agree to change? If you see that terracing is good in Kiambu, surely it will be good in Murang'a, too. Prepare your *shamba* in the same way and you will benefit, instead of just talking about it."

Because the people were so unwilling to change, even land consolidation was badly executed. They just could not accept it and their lack of cooperation created a terrible mess.

One might say that the Swynerton plan helped the development of agriculture in central Kenya but I believe that, when it came to agriculture, the areas around Mount Kenya were ahead because the people there had been agriculturalists for a long time. I do not think there was any other significant reason.

* * *

When I was posted to Kangema Division, I took over from Peter Shiyuka, and lived in the District Officer's residence. I was the first African to live there, despite the fact that I was still a District Assistant in 1961. It was a red-roofed, spacious bungalow on top of a hill and had incredible panoramic views over the deep valleys of Murang'a. The sight of the lovely dales and meandering streams coming down from the Aberdares was something I enjoyed immensely.

As a point of interest, John Njoroge Michuki, a fellow administrator who later became a Permanent Secretary (PS) and Cabinet Minister in both the Moi and Kibaki eras, eventually bought the house I had stayed in while I was in Kangema. He made his home there. I was invited back many times and although Michuki renovated and expanded the residence, it was impossible not to feel a touch of nostalgia.

The view these days is nothing like it once was because the land is cultivated. One of the nicer parts of the view is the beautiful cover of grevillea trees that have been planted all over Murang'a.

Because of the dynamic nature of the work and the lack of sufficient staff on the ground, the life of an African District Assistant, or a District Officer, involved constant transfers after several months' stay. For this reason, I was unable to travel with my family and they continued to reside in Kibichoi. This problem was not shared by the colonial administrators because they used to be posted for much longer periods of two to three years, and were therefore often able to be accompanied by their families.

While in Kangema, after a period of intensively studying the law, especially the Indian Law of Evidence[1] and Local Acts, I underwent an examination, the Administrative Law Examination, which was for all administrative officers, and passed well. The exam itself was set in Nairobi, but I took it at the exam centre in Thika. This test was to assess

---

1 The Indian Law of evidence was widely used in all British colonies.

our capabilities of acting as First Class Magistrates. I was proud of passing this exam, because many officers took it, and quite a few failed. Along the way, we managed to pick up the usual Latin phrases and I found it intensely interesting.

When I acquired the power of First Class Magistrate, I had national jurisdiction and as a result, cases in Kangema no longer had to go all the way to Murang'a, as I could hear them myself. I was then able to hear many different types of cases, including murder but I did not get much of a chance to hear any outstandingly interesting legal actions because shortly thereafter I went on to Oxford for further training.

Chapter 7

Taking Over from the Colonialists

The Mau Mau achieved their objective of independence. I did not believe in their ideology of using violence, however, because they caused a lot of grief among the Kikuyu and the majority of their victims were their own tribesmen. At the end of the rebellion, the Mau Mau had killed 32 Europeans and thousands of their Kikuyu tribesmen. Nevertheless, all manner of peaceful means had been tried over many years, and I doubt independence could have been achieved by other means, such as constitutional change, alone. Under the circumstances, violence seemed the only way forward.

Although the Kikuyu Central Association was influential in making the colonialists give in to the demands of the Africans, I wonder if greater political activity on their part might have achieved more than militancy. To be realistic, the Mau Mau had no chance of winning a military war against the imperialists. They had little training and their arsenal was pathetic. One cannot fight a modern army with a few stolen guns, pangas and spears. Most importantly, military action by itself could not be successful until the hearts and minds of the people were won over to the cause.

Through increased political pressure, the country made an immense step forward and as the struggle went on, people acquired more education and had greater awareness of their rights. There was no turning back. People everywhere were bursting with political excitement and fervour.

Because the Kikuyu had suffered most under the colonial land policies and mistreatment by Europeans, the Mau Mau were greatly concerned with fighting for the benefit of their own communities. It should be understood, that they never saw themselves as a separate part of Kenya and the leadership was keen to encompass others in the cause. Yet, for the most part, others were not as responsive as they anticipated. It was primarily the Kikuyu (and their Meru and Embu cousins) who were fighting for their land and for the education of their children. It was natural that people from around Nairobi, including other tribes resident there, were more intensely involved in the struggle. As the major urban area, Nairobi was the site of most employment. Thus, modern ways of social analysis, political awareness and the fight for political rights also started in Nairobi and the ripples spread outwards to the rest of Kenya. Other tribes, even if they suffered under colonial oppression, had little opportunity to experience this awareness and therefore took little action.

One exception was William ole Ntimama who was employed as a DA. He was a nationalist who did things his own way, and when he thought he might be sacked, he wrote a letter of resignation and went back to Maasailand.

It is also interesting to note that Mau Mau militant leaders were generally from Nyeri and Murang'a, not from Kiambu, even though a great deal of land in Kiambu was expropriated by the settlers. Non-combatant support for the Mau Mau, and the source of weapons, was substantial and principally from Kiambu. Kiambu people themselves did not engage in the hostility directly. Murang'a, Nyeri, Embu and Meru had Mau Mau generals, but there was not one military general from Kiambu and the factors behind this anomaly are not clear. It is historically known that the Mau Mau oath was first taken in Olenguruone.

During the transition to independence, my colleagues and I spearheaded the management of government and the takeover from Europeans. As a result, those of us ready and willing to work were promoted rapidly. There were not many of us prepared to take up senior positions in the government and at one particular stage, we were running the country with over 50 vacant positions for District Officers. The country did not have anywhere near enough adequately educated and skilled personnel to fill the positions required in various sectors of the economy. We were elevated to eminent ranks and the Europeans in the country were forced to concede that independence was unavoidable and that Africans would hold vital government positions.

The year 1962 was to see the tail end of colonial rule. By this time, there were already the four African District Commissioners (DCs), Juxton Shako, Geoffrey Karekia Kariithi, Ezekiel Josiah and Isaac Okwiri.

By September 1962, I was DO 1 Machakos and the DC, my superior, was Bob Wilson. When the DC was away, I was in charge but it was not always smooth sailing. Many European settlers were unable to grasp the idea that Africans would one day make up the core of government administration. They maintained the belief that Africans were, by divine intention, subservient to Europeans and were bound to remain so. For seventy years, the concept of White superiority had been accepted.

We defied intimidation and exercised our authority as was required in carrying out our duties.

One day a European farmer came in to the office and found me seated at the District Commissioner's desk.

He said loudly, "I would like to see the DC."

"The DC is away today. May I help you?" I asked, anticipating some trouble.

"I don't want to see his clerk! I want to see the DC!" he replied rudely.

I informed him that I was the DO 1 and was in charge of the station at that moment in time. When he started creating a scene, I called in the administration policemen and had him physically thrown out of the office, to the amusement of the *askaris*.

In general, that was the attitude we came to expect from most Europeans. Few could envision an African officer being as competent as a European or measuring up to the intellectual level of the White race.

When Bob Wilson returned to the office, I reported the incident and he said, "Jeremiah, you have to treat these settlers with patience. I don't think they understand the changes that are taking place."

Just two days later, a farmers' meeting was scheduled in Lukenya Club, where the Small World Country Club is now situated. The DC requested me to accompany him to the meeting, which all European farmers in the area were expected to attend. This took place during the time Bruce Mackenzie held the office of Minister for Agriculture and the meeting had been organised so that the farmers could prepare and deliver a brief to the minister. When we arrived, the Europeans sullenly refused to deliberate on any of the issues because I, an African officer, was present.

The DC advised them. "Listen, ladies and gentlemen, you must learn to accept the situation as it evolves. You have to come down to earth and accept the reality of changing times."

The settlers were not happy about that, but the DC continued.

"This man might be your DC tomorrow," he stated.

They were adamant and the discussion stalled, so the DC and I departed and the meeting ended. Bob Wilson was on his way out at the time, on transfer to another station, so there was not a formal follow-up on the issue. I believe the farmers may have held a private conference elsewhere and then passed their views directly to the minister.

Paradoxically, it also took time for ordinary Africans to accept African DOs or DCs as equal to their former British administrators.

This was a significant indicator of how deeply colonial brainwashing and racial disparity had been ingrained. Some politicians were happy with a Black administration, but many others required a significant amount of time to accept the transition to an administration composed of Black DOs and DCs. Some felt the administrative officers had been indoctrinated for far too long under the British and were mere 'yes men'. Despite these factors, we soldiered on.

There were a number of problems we encountered as we understudied British district officers. Often, we were merely relegated to the field. Our proximity to office files, policy formulation and decision-making was severely restricted. I gradually became aware that a good number of 'sensitive' files were missing from our offices and that they had been removed before we arrived to take up our positions. I also noted that we were never allowed into security meetings, and the European officers were exceedingly reluctant to involve us in any of the more delicate administrative processes. Obviously, most had no trust in our managerial abilities and some of them were blatantly racist. In fact, when the British DCs were finally reassigned, in many cases we had to draw up our records and files from scratch, which made the process extremely complicated.

The chiefs had further problems in adjusting to the concept of political parties. By 1963, various parties had established offices in rural areas and, in the view of chiefs, the individuals in such offices were perceived as agitators and troublemakers. It was difficult for the chiefs to change to a new reality and to deal with the Kenya African National Union (KANU) and other political entities. Political parties were seen as the new kids on the block, keen on interfering with the general way of running things and not loyal to the established order.

It is important to keep in mind that historically, over 70 years since the formation of the colonial administration, the role of the 'chief' had been transformed from that of a traditional ruler-elder, responsible for the well-being of his people, into a government employee owing loyalty directly to the governor, and later to the president. It was only to be expected that chiefs would experience difficulties with politicians, who had their own agenda and certainly never regarded chiefs with any particular degree of deference. Indeed, it had taken nearly a generation for the colonial chiefs to realise that they actually occupied impotent positions with virtually no power of their own.

* * *

I have not yet explained how I came from being a District Assistant at Kandara and Kangema, to the position of District Officer. I was in Kangema for only three months and from there I went to the University of Oxford. There were 12 of us selected to proceed to Britain to pursue further studies. It should be remembered that even those of us who had gone to Makerere for two years were not recognised as university graduates because at the time, Makerere had not yet been accredited to confer degrees. Along with two others I cannot recall, those chosen to go to Oxford and Cambridge were John Michuki, Moses Mutiga, Peter Shiyuka, John Malinda, Sila Boit, Sam Josiah, Peter Oranga, Joseph Musembi, Daudi Wabera and myself. Daudi Wabera, who was the Isiolo DC, was shot and killed by the secessionist Shifta in Isiolo soon after returning from the course.

In Oxford, we went for what was known as the 'B Course', which lasted one academic year. These courses for administration officers were held at Oxford, Cambridge and London. We were allowed to select the focus of our studies and I chose federalism, which included local government. I chose this subject primarily because of my interest in the Nigerian experience.

Nigeria had attained its independence a few years earlier and had chosen a federal system with a central government overseeing semi-autonomous states. I was intrigued by the functioning of this method of administration and had misgivings about the structure, knowing that religious and ethnic differences and divisions were potentially explosive issues. Frankly, I never thought it would work. The northern part of Nigeria had the larger part of the population, and this majority was less-educated and were Muslims. The minority in the southern portion was more educated, had progressive leaders, and had more wealth but, since they would never be able to outvote the north, the situation seemed untenable. The nation later broke up into many internal states in order to attempt to redress the imbalance.

When I look at this impasse created by democracy and compare it to Kenya, I often feel, that although democracy worked for a while under Kenyatta and part of Moi's regime, it is probably not workable in Africa at this time. Looking back on it, I think that pure democracy is alien to Africans and that we would be better able to develop under a benevolent dictator, with one source of authority. The difficulty, of course, is to find such an incorruptible leader who would consistently operate with the good of the nation in mind. This is an impossible task.

To get back to our training, eight of us went to Oxford and four to Cambridge. It was intended that after this course, we would be able to handle higher responsibilities. The courses had previously been a tradition for all young British officers who joined higher ranks of the provincial administration.

Originally, British DOs had first undertaken studies referred to as the Devonshire Course (the 'A Course') and then later went back to university for the higher 'B Course'. Needless to say, these courses catered for the Empire-bound young British officers destined to administer, manage and expand the British Empire, whereas we were entering the civil service at the Empire's demise.

Most European administrators went through Cambridge and Oxford before the phenomenon of the Mau Mau. Before our group, the first three Africans to go to the UK were Geoffrey Kariithi from Central, Juxton Shako from the coast and one other, Ezekiel Josiah from Nyanza. It was obviously a British policy to keep the groups of students regionally balanced by including representatives from various areas.

Our course lasted one year and I believe most of us acquired a greater appreciation of the affairs of the world. There was no examination at the end of the 'B Course'. Our performances were evaluated by lecturers who observed the degree of our participation and general contribution in the form of papers we submitted on various subjects.

One of the reasons our studies were so enjoyable is that we had the chance to travel with our wives. In fact, many of the ladies had the opportunity to do various courses, such as secretarial studies, while we were there. Esther, my wife at the time, studied for a civics course, although she was in the UK for a brief while only. I was grateful that Esther's parents were able to take responsibility for the three older children, Douglas, Caroline and Rose Wambui. My friend Njiiri Karago and his wife looked after the youngest, Mumbi, who was only two months old at the time.

We arrived in the UK just before the winter of 1961. I recall that we stayed on Davis Street in a British Council Hostel for a day or so before going on to the university. We had been warned that the winters could be very harsh and luckily enough, we were given a 'warm clothing' allowance, which enabled us to purchase coats and sweaters to get through the winter comfortably. Our flight arrived in the evening and the following morning we went to purchase our winter clothing.

One colleague and his wife went shopping but they were not sure about what exactly to buy or where to buy it. When they found a rather expensive clothing shop near Oxford Street, they went in and were amazed to find a European lady, a shop assistant, who immediately greeted them with, "Good morning, sir! Good morning, madam! How can I help you?"

After the unfriendly colonial attitude of Europeans in Kenya, this courtesy was absolutely astonishing to them. They could not understand how a British woman would call them 'sir' and 'madam.' Nevertheless, they explained their problem – they were from Kenya and needed warm clothing – and the shop assistant welcomed them in heartily. They spent all the money they had and the gentleman bought a wonderfully warm and snug, thick winter overcoat. Unfortunately, this marvellous coat, made of such bulky material, was utterly useless in the rain. Once it was wet, it became so heavy and awkward that the sheer weight of it made it impossible to wear.

Another couple came back to the hostel with the momentous news that they had seen a Barclays Bank, just like the ones back home in Kenya. They had not realised that Barclays was an international financial institution.

As for me, one day as I was walking along the road, I was startled to see a road gang composed of British labourers. They had a compressor, picks and shovels, just like any other road gang, but I had never stopped to think or imagine that Europeans would do such labour.

By this time, I had mixed with Europeans a little in Kenya and Uganda, but I was surprised that I never encountered any sort of racial attitudes in Britain. At the university, there were people from all over the world and it was fascinating to see how curious and respectful the local people were.

We went to London many times, but I also went to work in Belfast for two weeks, on attachment to study local government as a minor part of my course. I found that Belfast had a carefree environment. When I happened to go to the bars, I found that the Irish people would stare at me, but instead of keeping away, they were actually attracted and would buy me drinks. They would come up and chat, perhaps because they had not seen many Blacks before. Frankly, I found their accents difficult to follow, but they were a warm and welcoming people.

We were pleased when, after the first term of study, we were all promoted to District Officers while still at Oxford in 1962 and then, when we returned to Kenya, we were each posted to various districts as DO 1. The intention was that we were to understudy the British DCs and then take over their positions after six months. The initial three months served as an induction period to understudy the DO 1 in the district, the next three months we were to act as District Commissioners and then finally receive promotion to the full District Commissioners.

The criteria for this series of promotions were based on reports from our seniors, yet on our return to Kenya, the procedure did not function as intended. When European officers realised that independence was inevitable, they began exploring other opportunities. Many abandoned their posts before our induction was complete and therefore our promotions were further accelerated.

The functions of DOs and DCs, at the time, were quite strenuous. The DC was expected to visit each division every week. Although the DO had a driver, when the DC arrived, the driver took a back seat and the Divisional DO drove the vehicle himself. The DC would sit in the front so that he and the DO could communicate freely. It was vital that the DOs be knowledgeable about each locale within their administrative jurisdiction. For example, if the DC noticed a respectable, progressive *shamba* (farm) while on these rounds, he would make enquiries and the DO would be obliged to have all the answers at the fingertips. Questions might include topics concerning the crops, the name of the farmer, or for that matter, the schools, the headmasters, or focus on any particular theme that would catch the DC's interest. On rare occasions, they might walk, in order to examine particular points of interest.

Aptitude for administration was judged on how much was accomplished in the district, by knowledge about the predicaments of agriculture in the area, the status of health, the roads and the attempts made to overcome the particular problems that were encountered.

The District Commissioner was the key person in the district. He had to know his district and his people thoroughly. He was responsible for the social and economic well-being of the inhabitants. He made proposals as far as his district was concerned, in regard to what he thought could be done, whether in health, agriculture, security or whatever field. His proposals, as a DC, were regarded as most important in the headquarters and carried a great deal of weight when it came to the allocation of funds from the ministries.

He had a district team composed of officers from other departments and they all met regularly so he was kept well-informed of progress or weaknesses. The DO and the DC in any particular district were thus fully in charge of all government activities and depending on the enthusiasm and dedication with which their duties were undertaken, this was where the differentiation was made between individuals who were capable of rising, or were just occupying a position. The effectiveness of a DC could be evaluated by how successfully he welded the district team together.

In September 1962, after returning from the UK, I was posted to Machakos as a District Officer. I was there for a short time as DO 1 in the district headquarters and while there, I met people like Joe Kibe, Simeon Nyachae, and Joseph Muliro, who were posted as DOs.

As I mentioned earlier, as DO 1 in Machakos, I served under Bob Wilson. He was quite a good man to work with and it was his conviction that educated Africans were entirely capable of taking over administrative functions.

While in Machakos, I finally had a chance to hear some interesting cases in my capacity as a First Class Magistrate. I presided over family cases, land cases and others. One, which I recall, involved a lady who had sued one of my colleagues for maintenance of her last-born child. At this time a law called 'The Affiliation Act' was in force, and this act provided that a man must pay for the maintenance of any children he fathered, whether within marriage, or without.

I felt rather embarrassed about the case, seeing that the respondent was a friend, but I tried my best to be careful, objective and fair. Luckily, it turned out that the evidence made it easy to make a decision and I threw out the case.

First of all, my colleague denied responsibility for the child, but what made the matter straightforward was that my friend managed to bring this lady's three other children to court. They were in rags and were malnourished, yet the lady was already collecting court-ordered maintenance for these children, from other men. With that evidence, it was obvious that the lady was actually making a living from claiming maintenance, yet she did not seem to care about the children at all. She was a professional litigant and used the Affiliation Act just to make money.

My friend, by the way, was afterwards transferred out of the station. Perhaps it was the best solution to such an embarrassing problem.

* * *

From 1 December 1962, I was posted to Embu as the District Commissioner. I was there until 13 April 1963. At that time, Embu had four divisions, Ndia, Embu, Mbeere and Gichugu. Three of these divisions stretched from Mount Kenya all the way down to the river Tana.

While I was the DC, I visited the various divisions every week. There was no way to fully understand the difficulties, needs and problems of an area if one merely sat in the office. All DCs held *barazas* (public meetings), listened to the people, saw progress with their own eyes, and discussed everything with the district officers. There were always different problems such as roads, schools and health facilities. People were fully able to express the issues and raise questions and the district officers could either answer, or discuss the matter.

I was promoted to DC at the age of 33. I was younger than most of the chiefs, but my age did not present much difficulty *per se*. If I had been a young European, I would have had no problem with regard to my status and respect due to my position, but since I was an African, some of the chiefs were sceptical and condescending. We had some particular problems with some of the chiefs in Ndia. First, the chiefs did not readily accept me because I was a Kikuyu. The colonialists had driven a wedge between our two communities and the Embu viewed the Kikuyu as cunning and wily people. Second, I believe there was a subconscious antipathy towards working with an African DC.

In Embu, there were four outstanding chiefs, Steven Machere in Mutira, Bernard Makanga in Baragwe, Jotham Nguri in Inoe and Chief Njagi in Embu. They no longer conformed with the ideals of the new political dispensation and KANU did not accept any of the old colonial chiefs. Three of them were sufficiently educated and the government decided to investigate the possibilities of promoting them to the positions of DOs so that they would not directly interact as much with politicians in their local areas.

As the DC, I had to approach each and see if they were ready to work outside of their local areas. Chief Njagi decided he would not fit in and opted to retire. Jotham Nguri also retired. He wanted to remain in his home area. Makanga agreed to be promoted to DO and he did well. He rose through the ranks and ended up as DC, Kitale.

Steven Machere was a distinct character. He came in to see me and I informed him of the government's plans. He merely gazed at me and drawled, "Bwana DC, just forget it. I'll see the PC, Frank Lloyd, and talk to him."

I found his attitude disrespectful. I told him, "You cannot see anybody else about this. I am the one dealing with it!" I felt his manner and intentions insubordinate.

Yet, it may be that Machere felt I was succumbing to pressure from KANU troublemakers and that I should have stood firm against political agitation. He found it difficult to accept the changes that accompanied independence and had little tolerance for the new political dispensation. Eventually he got into considerable controversy as a chief and was subsequently appointed to the position of Revenue Officer and was posted away from the district.

As for politicians, they had little sympathy for district commissioners and the administration in general. They were of the opinion that politicians formed the centre of power and the three arms of government that is the Legislature, the Judiciary and the Executive, were alien concepts to them, since they only understood the overriding role of the governor and his administrators.

When any sort of extreme political agitation arose, we were expected, as part of our mandate, to arrest the ringleaders. This naturally led to a great deal of friction and resentment from KANU officials who were enormously influential and formidable at the time. Two of the difficult and sometimes aggressive KANU officials who were active during this time in Embu were Gichoya, and Munene Kibuga. As administrators, we were fully aware of political agitation originating from local leaders but were often forced into the general position of unwilling acceptance. As representatives of the government, we would not always agree with the politicians.

I recall one such problem regarded the settlement in Mwea Rice Scheme. The people in the area never supported the scheme because they wanted the land reserved for their grazing. When the government took over and developed the place, it paid a certain amount to the County Council as compensation, but it seemed that the funds were regarded as insufficient and the people did not take it. Thus, from the beginning, the Council thought their land had been taken away unfairly and that they had not been properly compensated. Worse still, when the rice scheme was completed, the people from Ndia and Embu refused to take up any plots in Mwea because they said that the land was taken under circumstances that were not agreed between them and the government. Consequently, the government settled a few landless people from Murang'a, Nyeri and Kiambu on the land and finally the Ndia agreed to settle in the rice scheme.

We were few administrators, thin on the ground, but gradually the government concept of control changed from pure policing to one of development. Initially, under the colonial government, people would be forced to comply with any orders of the administration. In general, African politicians would support any project that helped the people, but in cases where the implementation was forced, it was the cause of much resentment and rebellion.

During the first few years of transition, administration was complicated and difficult. The provincial administration held the authority, which was monolithic and perhaps even dictatorial because the instructions always came from the top. Nevertheless, in order to effectively accomplish any goal in our districts, it was vital to consider and be aware of public opinion, and the system was thus more democratic. To a large extent, the people's voice and approval was regarded as most essential.

When the settlement schemes for the landless were inaugurated in 1962, it was a countrywide programme designed for the whole nation and as such was established all over Kenya. The colonial government set in place the Land Resettlement Plan in 1962. Britain gave the government money to buy land from settlers and resettle Africans on it. Bruce Roy McKenzie, the Minister for Agriculture, Lands and Settlement, was in charge of the programme. The first phase cost the British 2 million pounds. In the second phase in which 22,000 acres of land were involved, the British gave 5 million pounds.

The money allocated for settlement funds was granted for a specific purpose, which was to assist the government in acquiring land from departing Europeans. This served to purchase land for the landless in areas like Nyandarua, Laikipia, Kisii, Lugari, Nandi and elsewhere. Jomo Kenyatta was determined to source alternative land to settle the landless, but it was the duty of chiefs and DOs to identify who should settle on it. They were to select landless people who would benefit and it was expected that the DOs would know which particular families had no property. Naturally, there were a few instances where greedy individuals attempted to acquire land unjustly, but overall, the problems of the landless were largely eased. However, soon thereafter the rapid rise in population swiftly increased the demand for land once again, as families grew larger and larger.

Some may feel that the Kikuyu had greater benefit from such schemes. However, one must see it in the same light as education. If education was available, why didn't everyone go to school? My point is that when opportunities are available, there must be those ready to seize them. Overall, there might have been some sporadic favouritism but nationwide it was generally fair.

* * *

While I was engaged in such activities concerning land, early in 1963, a select group of African officers underwent Aptitude Testing at Jeanes

School. Our mental ability, analytical skills, numerical ability and others were assessed and evaluated. We were being tested for our leadership qualities.

Rather than regarding this with suspicion, we looked at it as a means of ascertaining whether we would be able to carry out all the required tasks of the positions to which we would be appointed.

* * *

In March 1963, the Boundaries Commission determined new regional boundaries for Kenya. The concept of Regional Government was seen by most Africans as a delaying tactic designed in favour of the remaining European settlers. The Commission created a short-lived endeavour to divide Kenya into seven regions namely Central, Rift Valley, Western, Nyanza, Eastern, North-Eastern and Coast with Nairobi as an extra district. At the time, the main population of European settlers was concentrated in or near Nairobi, with many also residing in the Rift Valley and a few in the Coast. The creation of regional governments, therefore, would establish 'fiefdoms' in which Europeans presumably felt they would be more protected from the larger, more politically active communities, and would have greater influence in the remaining regions containing more amenable Africans.

Toward this goal, Europeans attempted to befriend minority tribes, and persuade them that they would have little influence in a unified nation. They convinced the smaller tribes that they would be dominated by the Kikuyu and be without protection. Europeans argued that one central government would result in *de facto* Kikuyu rule and the Kikuyu were portrayed as the new colonisers. Therefore, adopting regional governments would limit this ascendancy and assure autonomy and greater self-control of the Rift Valley, the hub of the 'White Highlands', and the Coast region. Regional government was engineered on this basis and the Kenya African Democratic Union (KADU), led by Ronald Ngala, adopted *Majimbo* (Regionalism) as part of their party platform.

Those of us in the administration already viewed Kenya as a 'nation state' and the concept of regionalism seemed awkward and unmanageable. However, using the Rift Valley and Coast as their hub, the settlers were adept enough to impose *Majimbo* and the concept was accepted.

Kenyatta resisted *Majimbo*, but when it came into existence, he treated the concept with expediency. He would not let it block the path to independence. He and others who shared his viewpoint set their priorities on achieving self-government. Once that hurdle was surmounted, they would be able to shape the nation according to the Kenyan vision.

Ostensibly, *Majimbo* was created so that authority and privilege could be devolved to levels more accessible to the people. Yet this did not function as expected. In January 1963, Taita Towett and Narok's Justus K. ole Tipis threatened to throw out Kikuyu who did not respect the will of Rift Valley's permanent residents. "Unless malevolence like that brought about by the Land and Freedom Army ceases in the Rift Valley, a move to get all Kikuyu back to their region (of origin) will be embarked on," they were quoted as saying.

"Any troublemakers will be dealt with mercilessly by the permanent residents of the Rift Valley ... now that regional borders have been published, no nonsense will be tolerated from non-permanent residents of our region."

For example, in the Rift Valley, European farmers, who were quite wealthy, visualised themselves ruling as before, regardless of the fact that they were forced to act through African politicians.

Kenyatta reacted to this attitude saying: "We have no time for settlers who want to be *bwana mkubwa*. The white settlers have been trying to hide behind *Majimbo*. What benefits have you (the people of Eldoret) got now, as a result of regionalism?" Kenyatta is quoted to have said. "KADU leaders have been cheated, like (Moise) Tshombe of Katanga (in Congo) who has been following the advice of his foreign imperialistic masters."

At one meeting in Nairobi, Peter Brown, the Civil Secretary in the Rift Valley referred to the Rift Valley regional president as "My President, Mr. Moi". This caused an uproar and Duncan Ndegwa, who was in the process of taking over in the Office of the President, responded by telling him there was only one president in Kenya and that was President Kenyatta. Action was taken against Peter Brown and by the time he returned to the Rift Valley, he had already been replaced.

Civil servants were well aware of the weaknesses in the system, which could be exploited for the benefit of the Europeans. We quickly became acquainted with its complicated structure and the complex processes involved. For example, if a crime was committed in Central Province and the criminal crossed into Rift Valley, the police in Central could not follow him into the Rift because it was under a separate administration. Consequently, we were biased against this method of governance right from the start. We were not prepared to permit the Europeans to continue subjugation and exploitation of the Africans in the regions.

"The present constitution is based on profound mistrust, widespread suspicion and corrosive fear among the various groups and communities. Without faith in our fellow man, without mutual trust among us there can be no stability in this country no matter how cleverly the constitution is worded," Kenyatta is reported by the *Daily Nation* of 3 January 1963 as saying.

With the creation of regions, changes in staffing occurred and all titles were modified. The change in titles may prove confusing to the reader; however, the whole process only lasted a little over a year.

Embu District was divided into two, Embu and Kirinyaga. Embu District, in Eastern Province consisted of Embu and Mbeere divisions. Kirinyaga District, in Central Province, consisted of Ndia and Gichugu divisions and had its headquarters in Kerugoya. As a result, before they could appoint a DC for the new district, I became Assistant Regional Government Agent (ARGA), which was equivalent to a DC, for both districts. Neville Judge worked under me. He was very cooperative despite my being his boss, and seemed to have no issues with taking orders from an African.

Later, I became the Deputy Civil Secretary in Embu. Although I had been provided with an office and a house, I had to move out and release both to the Civil Secretary, Bill Rainor. I moved into smaller premises. Each of us moved down the line. However, we were few officers and it was not difficult to accommodate these changes. In mid April 1963, Moses Mutiga took over as ARGA, Embu, and Neville Judge became the ARGA, Kirinyaga, briefly and was soon after transferred to Wajir where he was unfortunately murdered by Shifta bandits.

Eastern Region encompassed a huge area. It included Machakos, Kitui, Embu, Meru, Isiolo, Moyale and Marsabit. Some of these areas had security problems with Shifta bandits in the Somali areas.

The Shifta (Somali word for bandit) war was partly influenced by the concept of *Majimbo*. The area concerned was the Northern Frontier District (NFD), and the ethnic Somalis, the majority within the region, felt they had little connection with Kenya. During colonial rule, the region was referred to as a 'closed district' and permits were required for movement in and out of the NFD. The people of the region were so unfamiliar with Kenya that, if a traveller was passing through the barrier at the border to the NFD, the *askaris* would ask him, "How is Kenya?"

The Shifta war was partially due to the fact that the people of the area wanted to be united with their kith and kin in Somalia. There was strong agitation for secession from Mogadishu. However, secession was not acceptable to a sovereign Kenya. National boundaries had been set out in the Berlin Conference in 1884-1885 and were accepted internationally by 1920 and reaffirmed by the OAU Charter in 1964.

In general, the reception of African officers posted to most areas of the country at independence was good. However, when African DOs were posted to areas like North Eastern, the population felt they were being colonised again, this time by Kenya, by the so called *nywele ngumu* (hard hair) as they referred to other communities whose hair was kinky, compared to theirs. This problem existed from quite early on in the Shifta struggle.

During the colonial days, the British army once held a military exercise in the NFD which annoyed the people of Somalia. The exercise was dubbed, "Sharp Panga". The Somalia government saw it as a sinister move by the British and Kenya authorities to emphasise NFD's being part of Kenya. "The British government could not have chosen a more significant and provocative time to carry out the military manoeuvres," said the Somalia Consul to Nairobi at the time. Two days later the Somalia ambassador to Britain was recalled home for "consultations". KANU Chief Executive Officer, Mwai Kibaki, demanded that Colonial Secretary Duncan Sandys gives a definite assurance that the British would not give NFD to Somalia. "Britain has no legal right to give away part of Kenya and the Somali have no right to claim parts of Kenya which have never belonged to them," he said.

Although most of us never ran into any problems with Shifta or bandits, the Assistant Regional Government Agent for Isiolo, Daudi Wabera, himself of Somali origin, was killed by Shifta while he was travelling on the road. He was a very useful man who loved his people. I recall that whenever he addressed a meeting, he would always turn the topic to water, a subject that was dear to his heart due to the scarcity of the commodity in that part of the country.

Wabera's death made the government reassess the situation and take the Shifta issue much more seriously. His killer was known to be a young man, an agitator who was pushing for the secession of northern parts of Kenya, which were occupied by ethnic Somalis, to Somalia.

* * *

After three months, in Eastern, in July 1963, I was appointed Under Secretary in charge of Provincial Administration in the Ministry of Home Affairs in Nairobi. Robin Wainright, the Chief Native Commissioner, had just retired and I took over from him.

Taking Over From the Colonialists

I came to Nairobi and my family and I moved into a large house in the Upper Hill area, at the junction of Elgon Road and Hospital Road. I was the first African to live in that house.

About a year later, in May 1964, I bought a small coffee farm in Ruiru from Alan Bockett. It had a nice two-bedroom house and there were 25 acres surrounding it, of which 20 were under coffee. I used to commute to Nairobi every day in my private car, and since the road was tarmac up to Ruiru, and the traffic was not too heavy in those days, the trip would not take me long, perhaps only half an hour. Even the little narrow coffee farm roads were tarmac at the time and there were no potholes. It is a pity that these roads have deteriorated.

By this time, my family consisted of my wife and our four children, our son Douglas, who attended Alliance High School, and our three daughters, Caroline, who attended Loreto Convent Msongari, and Rose Wambui and Mumbi, who both attended Alliance Girls. Mumbi was baptised at the age of 12 and, since she had retained the name 'Mumbi' for so long, it just stuck with her rather than getting a Christian name. My wife, Esther, gave up teaching and decided that it would be more profitable to manage our coffee farm. I generally travelled home every week to look after things, as well.

Psychologically, being promoted to Nairobi was rather an adjustment because, when one is in the rural areas as a DC or DO, one is regarded as a prominent person. However, in Nairobi, one almost disappears among the many other, even more important people.

As I mentioned, the position I held was previously designated 'Chief Native Commissioner (CNC),' but under self-rule, that position had been abolished, as was to be expected. Kenya was already running its own affairs and independence was only months away. Most of the British administrators were leaving or were already gone. I reported to Jaramogi Oginga Odinga, who was then the Minister for Home Affairs.

As administrators, we accepted any political changes that occurred and, in the main, the actions of politicians agitating for independence worked in favour of pioneer senior African administrators such as ourselves. Thus, we generally benefited from the pressure they exerted on the British.

After that, the first three African permanent secretaries were appointed: Duncan Ndegwa (Office of the President), Kitili Mwendwa (Home Affairs) and Kenneth Matiba (Education).

Even if our advancement had been rushed to a little extent, it was imperative to do so because the British were leaving rapidly. British officers had to exercise their options within a specified time limit if they wished to take up various benefits or to proceed to positions in other colonies. Consequently, many left their posts hurriedly and Kenya had to act quickly in order to maintain the structure of all sectors of the government.

In order to fill the vacancies, we were under pressure to recruit teachers and chiefs. They may not have been specifically qualified for these positions but the Kenya Government had no alternative but to appoint them, despite their lack of experience.

Later, there was also an effort to recruit Kenyan students from abroad. I often felt that many of those students who came back to Kenya were completely misled. They had grandiose ideas of their own importance, demanded that they be given jobs as a right and felt that they should immediately be promoted to the topmost positions. They had bloated ideas and looked upon the rest of us as the relics of colonialism, or as sycophants. Quite a few of them had never even managed to go to secondary school and it was strange and doubtful to see them returning with university degrees after just four years of study.

However, in light of the shortage of officers it was often difficult to carry out our duties. We had no choice but to progress as expeditiously as possible, working long hours and making personal sacrifices. Our patriotism carried us through.

The general population definitely did not deem themselves rushed. They had, at long last, achieved victory in their struggle for independence. They now had lofty expectations and were ecstatic to see Africans in charge. As African administrators, we were capable of understanding the problems the common people encountered, because they could communicate more freely and openly with us.

This transition led to some amusing incidents. I recall a colleague in the Ministry of Commerce and Industry had a particularly sly sense of humour. He had suddenly been promoted to the position of Permanent Secretary but the European who held the post had not been informed of the change. Early one morning, my colleague entered the office and relaxed on the PS's chair behind the executive desk. Then the European came in and was shocked and dumbfounded to see someone else sitting on his chair.

"Good morning! What can I do for you?" my colleague asked.

This was a bit cheeky, and the European officer must have become flustered beyond words, but then my colleague explained the matter. He had been promoted to take over the post. At the time, there were many other such cases of sudden changes, long anticipated by Africans, but too abrupt for the Europeans.

As Deputy Secretary, in July 1963, I had European assistant secretaries under me. When they were replaced by Africans, they did not quibble over the change. One of these was Keith Foot. He had been my DO in Meru while I had been subordinate to him as a DA. At that time, I called him "Sir" but now, on the verge of independence in Nairobi, he called me "Sir". In such incidents, one is forced to find life unpredictable and even comical at times.

However, if we examine our readiness for independence a little more critically, on the basis of whether everything was *in situ*, we must conclude that we were not, in actuality, prepared for flying solo. We were certainly far ahead of some other African countries, such as the Belgian Congo, where Europeans were unceremoniously booted out and destroyed almost all they left behind in the form of physical or governmental infrastructure. In any event, Kenya had well-trained personnel capable of taking over from the colonialists. It was not so in the Congo.

Certain deficiencies were to be expected at independence, yet even today, there are a few areas of the country where it could be considered that we have insufficient infrastructure in place to boost development. For example, in central Kenya, individuals are capable of achieving a considerable amount of development without the need to involve the government. People have managed to establish health centres, schools, transportation facilities and many others, and these projects have largely been envisioned and spearheaded by individuals, committees and the private sector. In certain other areas of the country, however, the citizens do not have either the funds or skills to organise such enterprises.

One of the changes that accompanied independence was strikingly obvious and the source of much delight – the elimination of the colour bar. In 1953, while I was working in Nairobi in the Indian High Commission, many restaurants, bars and hotels were divided by racial classification. By 1963, this segregation quietly disappeared and was no longer permitted. On occasion, it might have proved difficult to get service in some establishments and waiters would quietly tell us that they were not allowed to serve Africans. However, we pushed ourselves in quite boldly anyway. After all, this was our country.

At Three Bells Restaurant on Victoria Street (today's Tom Mboya Street), Jaramogi Odinga and Tom Mboya were once ejected and, unsurprisingly, they raised hell. Similar situations occurred at Hallian's Night Club and at Lavarini's Restaurant on Government Road. To the chagrin of hardcore racist Europeans, it all died out incredibly fast. Once Africans started getting into high positions, it was impossible to maintain the colour bar. In fact, I recall that some of us went into such establishments just for the fun of it, to break the colour barrier and snub our noses at the racists.

Chapter 8

The New World of Independence

Kenyatta's charisma, eloquence and his fiery utterances had so frightened and transfixed the Europeans and the colonial government, that releasing him when security in the colony was most fragile, was unthinkable. I have no evidence but I imagine that, assured term of prison or not, the colonial authorities were not about to release him so quickly after mayhem had broken out throughout Kikuyuland.

Jomo was sentenced to seven years in prison in 1953. He was jailed in Kapenguria, but when the rest of the Kapenguria Six were released in 1960, he continued being held. He was under virtual house arrest in Maralal for close to three months before he was eventually released in August 1961.

At the time, I was just planning to start up at Oxford and those of us going to undertake the course were overjoyed at his freedom. We did not actually celebrate, but we were supremely happy and looking forward to our coming independence.

Previously, the Registrar of Parties, J. D. Coward, had rejected Jomo's election as Chairman of KANU *in absentia*. Therefore, in May 1960, James Gichuru assumed the chairmanship of the party. However, immediately upon Kenyatta's release in August 1961, Gichuru stood down in favour of Jomo. Subsequently, Kenyatta led the KANU team to the second Lancaster House Conference in London in February 1962 and this paved the way for the second General Election in May 1963.

KANU was victorious and formed the *Majimbo* Government on 1 June 1963, with Kenyatta as Minister for Planning and Ronald Ngala as Minister for Home Affairs in charge of the Administration. On 12 December 1963, Kenyatta became the Prime Minister and Kenya achieved independence under the recognised sovereignty of the Queen. The Union Jack was lowered for the last time, and an air of excitement was palpable throughout the nation. Finally, the dream that Africans had cherished had been realised. It was a new dawn and a new beginning. The celebrations were incredible.

I was still stationed in Embu during Madaraka Day and my family and I drove down from Embu to Uhuru Gardens in Nairobi, where the ground was soaked with heavy rain. There were massive crowds and we were all proud and happy that, after so many years of struggle, we were finally free. Our happiness was difficult to explain, as it was so overwhelming. After the celebrations, very many people were stuck in the mud. Thank goodness, I never got stuck myself, but I was in the queue for a very long time and it was almost 2 am when we got home to Embu. In those days, we had no fear of travelling at night. There was peace.

Those of us in the civil service were overwhelmed with the sense of victory and vindication at independence. We had wanted to control our destiny and now the opportunity was irrevocably ours.

Changes inevitably occurred in November 1964, KADU dissolved itself voluntarily and joined KANU.

KADU's leaders, namely Daniel arap Moi, Ronald Ngala, Masinde Muliro and Justus ole Tippis were assimilated by KANU. This brought Kenyatta's dream of the unity of all political parties sharing common goals and a committed leadership structure to fruition and the following month, on 12 December 1964, Kenya became a republic *(Jamhuri)*. That was the end of any official opposition until March 1966, when Oginga Odinga formed the opposition left-wing Kenya People's Party (KPU). The party was banned in October 1969, thus making Kenya a *de facto* one party state.

The notion of national unity was new and important to Kenyans, and possibly, it was a bizarre concept to Kenyans in the more remote corners of the country where modernisation had not yet made an impact, such as in Turkana or the Northern Frontier District. Certainly, Europeans never attempted to foster any form of unity among Africans or to promote national cohesion. Not realising that they were on their way out, some British administrators still did not want to involve other races in affairs of the colony. During a cocktail party in Government House, to welcome incoming Governor MacDonald in January 1963, Lawyer Fitz de Souza (Kenyatta's legal counsel in Kapenguria) remarked, "I was shocked to find only about 50 non-British guests out of the 800 to 900 people in the function. These people must be very naïve".

It was never part of their agenda and, on the contrary, they used the theory of divide and rule. Europeans exploited tribal loyalties to create disharmony among various communities. The more detached and isolated the 'natives' were, the easier it was to manipulate and dominate them.

The new leaders of independent Kenya faced the gargantuan task of uniting the country into one people with a common vision. This is not to say that the different identities of tribal groups were to be ignored or eliminated. For example, although the United Kingdom is very much one nation, people are proud of being identified as Welsh, Scottish, Irish and English. A national outlook can withstand and incorporate a certain amount of ethnic identity.

For the new Kenya, national unity was an intensely realistic necessity. Kenyatta emphasised the need to examine the long-term scenario for national unity. Yet he was nonetheless cognisant of the cultural diversity and economic disparity between distinct communities. There were extremely persuasive measures established in order to encourage the concept of national unity. Primarily, every year development plans, goals, and programmes were created which encompassed, at all times, a national outlook. Although there were discrepancies in implementation and short-sighted parochial politics that occasionally diverted national targets and objectives, the government's efforts aimed for a united community of Kenyans.

Despite these attempts to unite the country through administrative means, there were great weaknesses that hindered the development of a truly national spirit.

In my opinion, the concept of nationalism was unfortunately never sufficiently fostered after independence, and consequently we still witness considerable strife between various communities. For example, no clearly spelt out political indoctrination, such as that carried out in Tanzania and elsewhere, was ever put in place in Kenya to foster national unity.

Kenyans were extraordinarily united in their struggle against the British prior to independence. Everyone, stretching from Mombasa to Kisumu, spoke with one voice, demanding the transfer of power to a sovereign Kenya. However, it seems that despite the general desire for independence, the various ethnic groups maintained diverse perspectives. There were no modalities of instituting a united purpose after successfully removing the common enemy.

Prior to independence, European settlers and administrators were well aware of tribal tensions and weaknesses and, through KADU, used this vulnerability to induce small communities from the Rift Valley and the coast to accept *Majimbo,* the regional system of government. As explained elsewhere, the settlers did not want to leave the 'White Highlands' and thus exploited the suspicions dividing Kenya's communities. Tribal sentiments were played up and nationalism became the victim.

Because *Majimbo* is still regarded as a controversial issue, I would like to elucidate my views on the topic a little further. As I stated earlier, while in Oxford we were each able to choose a subject of specialisation. Because federalism was my choice, I became increasingly convinced that the *Majimbo* system was cumbersome and impracticable.

In terms of Kenya, I asked myself how the different regions could possibly be self-sustaining under a *Majimbo* system. I do not believe anyone had given serious thought to the practicalities like funding the eight regions. What then would be the most equitable way of sharing resources? Would areas with a hard-working and ambitious population be willing to subsidise areas where the population was not as well-educated or were less willing to work, or had less resources?

In the *Majimbo* system, the police only had jurisdiction and authority in each separate region and it was as though they were working for different governments. Furthermore, the political and administrative will to cooperate simply did not exist. I thought it was a disaster and must admit my colleagues and I did little to advance the *Majimbo* policy.

Kenyatta was always a practical and realistic leader. In my opinion, Kenyatta handled the imposition of *Majimbo* exceptionally well, despite the fact that he knew it was unworkable. Both *Majimbo* and the coastal strip were unwieldy, awkward issues but KANU felt they should not hold back independence. An independent Kenya would be free to choose its own future and alter the system.

In addition, there were also intra-tribal uncertainties and distrust just below the surface, particularly in the case of the Kikuyu. Those from Kiambu believed themselves superior to those from Murang'a and Nyeri, and frequently referred to the latter in a derogatory manner. This arrogance among the people of Kiambu probably originated from the fact that education and western influences infiltrated their community earlier than the others.

Kiambu people snidely referred to their Murang'a counterparts as *Metumi* (meaning those who do not talk much or are secretive) and those from Nyeri as *Tumundu twa Nyiri* (meaning 'those little people from Nyeri'). Such prejudices were mutual and the Kiambu people were termed *Thweri cia Kabete* (meaning those unreliable people from Kabete or the 'Kabete Swahili'). The Kikuyu perceived the early Swahili traders and the guides and porters of European travellers to be cunning and sly.

In the opinions of people from Nyeri and Murang'a, the Kiambu Kikuyu were devious, wily and crooked and could not be trusted.

The haughtiness of the Kikuyu also created suspicion among other communities. In view of the fact that the Kikuyu were advanced in education and more exposed to modern ways, they routinely considered other communities as inferior. Much of this sentiment was due to differences in culture. For example, among the Kikuyu, women did weeding whereas Luo men had no issues with carrying out this task.

It is depressing that the same sentiments of tribal suspicion and hatred continue to be exploited by politicians in order to incite people to violence to this day. Due to the failure of our leaders to address such challenges during the early days of Kenya's statehood, this atmosphere of distrust will linger on as a thorn in the flesh of the nation for a long time to come. Naïve and unscrupulous politicians continue to be the scourge of this country. It seems that they have no shame soliciting votes through the promotion of tribal bigotry and animosity. Such selfishness by politicians, in addition to the politicisation of public affairs, has been the undoing of our nationhood.

I believe Kenyatta was a strong nationalist at heart. I had the opportunity to work for him, as I shall explain later, and I am well aware that he envisaged a united country. He intended to achieve this ambition, but a number of factors hindered the successful accomplishment of this goal.

Jaramogi Odinga was also a nationalist, notwithstanding the fact that he disagreed with Kenyatta. These were two people with widely differing views on a number of issues affecting the nation, and at that time, the 'Cold War' power blocs had considerable influence. The factors of the Cold War were the strongest influences that came between Odinga and Kenyatta. Odinga was a friend of socialist Russia and Kenyatta was closer to Western capitalism, so the two simply could not work together. Odinga was also motivated to gain the 'top seat', as well. After all, who did not want it?

During this period, the functions of the Vice President's office included Immigration, Provincial Administration, Police, Prisons and others. There were increasing disagreements on the running of government. Odinga thought he should have more power. He took certain decisions that bothered the Cabinet and made visits to the Socialist bloc. He also made certain appointments without clearing them through the system. Later, there were stories about Odinga bringing in guns through Tanzania but that was something that was never properly verified.

Another basis for the failure of Kenyatta's aspirations toward national unity was the unfortunate truth that, like a great many African leaders, he remained in command for a prolonged period. I believe that if Kenyatta had relinquished his power earlier, he could have come close to attaining the admiration and stature of Nelson Mandela. However, his nationalistic zeal was gradually eroded by evolving politics, by his increasing age and debility.

Kenyatta did encourage a number of policies that were of benefit to the nation. He was especially concerned about the increasing pressure on the land. For example, he persistently emphasised the slogan *"turudi mashambani"* (return to the land), pleading with people to perceive agriculture as a crucial national economic resource. At that time, there was considerable land available and numerous activities were implemented concerning agriculture. With only seven million Kenyans at independence, population pressure had not yet exerted a significant impact. DCs, DOs and chiefs ensured and encouraged proper farming techniques and thus enabled people to stay on the land.

Despite these services, it was felt that rural–urban migration was too high. Therefore, Jomo also attempted to decentralise certain facilities, locating them out of Nairobi. He promoted the establishment of industries in Thika, Nakuru and Kisumu. On the whole, he also had faith in the criteria of merit and, therefore, did not interfere with ministries.

The relationship between the civil service and Kenyan politicians has rarely been comfortable or uncomplicated. As civil servants, we were well aware that politicians ultimately controlled us. Parliament formulated policies, and our responsibility was to implement them. At the time, we were a well-structured, highly motivated and orderly civil service. A minister would state a policy and request the PS to formulate a paper articulating the decision and thereafter seek approval from the Cabinet. On occasion, the PS also played the role of policy initiator. To this day, ministers continually depend on the civil service to accomplish the inclusive activities and factors that are incorporated in the ministries' policies.

In the civil service, we were aware that we were unequivocally accountable for our own performances. The President and other politicians might discuss and manipulate politics all they wished, yet our place was to convert these policies into actions and carry them out to achieve optimal results.

Kenyatta did not undertake any radical ideological or nationalistic changes after independence. He placed all his emphasis on development as defined in African Socialism 'Sessional Paper No. 10 of 1965'. This basically affirmed our economic aspirations and our culture. Kenyatta felt that nationalism for its own sake had nothing to recommend it. For example, in Nakuru in 1964, he urged the settlers to stay. His aim was to continue with things as they were and not to disrupt economic productivity. He was acutely aware of the political divergence between a number of his cabinet colleagues and those of the European settlers and initially decided to maintain the *status quo*.

For that reason, he took only James Gichuru with him to the difficult meeting in Nakuru. James Gichuru was a realist and moderate. At this time, some of his colleagues were extreme radicals to whom even the thought of Europeans remaining in Kenya seemed anathema. Kenyatta was wiser and more pragmatic. He knew the contribution that the farmers would make to the new economy and sought to encourage the Europeans to maintain their farming activities, with the proviso that they respect the laws of the land and refrain from abusive behaviour towards Africans. There was also a lot of discussion in the papers at the time, of the 'scorched earth policy', which meant that the Europeans might destroy all their assets and leave nothing behind once independence came. This would have been disastrous to the economy and it was an issue that required acute discretion. Furthermore, Kenyatta was aware that most Africans had not yet developed the capacity to handle large commercial farms and ranches.

In perspective, one could say that Kenyatta had the foresight to avoid the errors that Robert Mugabe made in Zimbabwe decades later. Mugabe allocated large European-owned farms to freedom fighters and sundry supporters. Total chaos resulted from Mugabe's decision since the new owners were unable to farm in any viable manner, as they lacked the equipment, resources and expertise.

In Kenya, farming was doing well, agriculture was doing well, and, for Jomo, that was what mattered. There was no need for Kenyans to adopt radical concepts. In addition, a great deal was being done to facilitate the small farmers in rural areas such as stationing agricultural officers at the grassroots and the establishment of farmer training centres. Unfortunately many these structures collapsed later due to corruption, ineptitude and gross mismanagement.

* * *

One of the important courses of action that the government adopted at independence, to improve the position of Africans in the economy, was the policy of Africanisation. Africanisation – also going under the term "Kenyanisation" and "Indigenisation" – was the equivalent of the Black Economic Empowerment initiative in South Africa, meant to redress the inequalities of the Apartheid era. The aim was to give those who were previously disadvantaged, economic opportunities which had not been available to them. Thus, the move was characterised by deliberate efforts to nurture and support indigenous entrepreneurs in manufacturing, financial services, agriculture, and other economic sectors through specialised programmes. Africanisation was implemented in four stages, the first being the indigenisation of the civil service; the second, buying out settlers from their agricultural lands; the third, replacing the Asian commercial bourgeoisie and the European managers of multinational firms; and the fourth, competing eventually with international capital through new investment and the purchase of firms. The latter resulted in the setting up of the Industrial and Commercial Development Corporation (ICDC), in the early 1960s to provide capital for start-ups. In the pursuit of its mandate, the state corporation set up an investment arm – ICDC Investment (now Centum) – to help "Africanise" companies that were previously owned by the white settler community.

The Africanisation of the upper levels of the civil service took place extremely rapidly. It was essentially completed by 1965, save for professional and technical positions, which took a few years longer. The speed was remarkable, as there were very few Africans in the senior civil service in the late 1950s. Those with plausible qualifications were promoted with great rapidity and quickly found themselves at the top. Recruitment and promotion of Africans in the lower and middle ranks of the senior civil service were based on qualifications and performance. Capture of the very top positions, however, tended to depend on having the confidence of the President or someone close to him, particularly for the generalist positions.

Initially the policy was very effective. For example, take Bazaar Street (now called Biashara Street) where Asians owned all the shops. If there had been no legislation, I do not believe the situation would have changed and no African would have ever had a shop there. These businesses had to be licensed and thus, by enforcing the law, a few Africans started to come in. Africanisation was basically rectifying this historical anomaly.

Quietly, but deliberately, the policy ensured that Africans were also able to take up such businesses, especially through ICDC and the Kenya National Trading Corporation (KNTC). These policies were quite successful, but eventually many of the Africans had difficulty in running the businesses. They simply did not have the expertise or the capital to run such shops.

Managing these enterprises was not as simple as running a general store. One had to know how to import material, the sources to import from, where and how to get clothing made, the banking systems abroad, how to interact with such banking systems, how to obtain letters of credit and a great many other details. Generally, Africans had no knowledge of these systems and thus encountered many obstacles. The supply of goods became uncertain and this led to the rapid decline of these businesses in African hands. The consequence was that Asians either bought up the businesses once again, or acted as partners. Occasionally, such partnerships were only on paper.

When the government noticed that Africans were being hampered by a lack of experience, it established a company called KNTC, which carried out the 'middleman' import work and ICDC was the umbrella under which they operated. They helped to finance the traders and imported material on their behalf.

The measures, which were put into place at the beginning, were right, but it was a pity that they were never sufficiently supported. We knew what should have been done, we knew where we intended to go, but we never worked out the details, we never had a clear strategy, nor were the specifics ever pursued.

It was necessary to redress the imbalance; however, the implementation process was difficult. In fact, some people came to be associated with bribery over the policy. Many were accused, but whether this was true or not, I cannot say. One has to be very careful over such accusations and not take things at face value.

Africanisation is no longer an issue. Although manufacturing industries still have many foreigners, particularly those from the Indian subcontinent dominating these areas, there are many African industrialists. It just happens that Asians in general have been better businessmen and this is a product of their culture, which emphasises the particular set of skills that make them successful in commerce.

When one compares Kenya to other African countries, I believe we are farther ahead than many. If we had only managed to keep up the same pace, the same direction and the same behaviour that we had up to 10 years after the Europeans left – if we had kept on that course – we would be one of the three most successful countries in Africa, that is Kenya, Egypt and South Africa (perhaps followed by Nigeria). I have heard similar opinions from Diageo, Standard Bank and others, that in terms of manpower and people who work hard, Kenya would be in the lead if corruption had not interfered with its progress. The misfortunes we have had are all of our own making, our carelessness and our corruption.

An additional insight on other racial issues was that after independence, Africans treated Indians with more disdain and prejudice than they did the Europeans, despite the despicable and brutal treatment Europeans had meted out to the 'natives'. The first reason behind this may be that many Asians sided with the Europeans during the colonial days. The term "Asian" is used indiscriminately in Kenya, mostly to refer to persons whose origin is in the Indian sub-continent but can include others from outside that region. Few Kenyan Africans are aware of the many different communities within that classification.

Because they were in contact with the local people on a day-to-day basis, Asians were seen to hold the economy in their hands and thus appeared to be more exploitative than Europeans. Despite the support of some extraordinary Indian nationalists and support by India itself, this prejudice held. Many more Asians, in comparison to Europeans, remained in Kenya after independence, which made them seem like relics of colonialism to many Africans. The bigotry against Asians seems to continue to this day, though it is gradually disappearing with each new generation.

* * *

The zeal and enthusiasm with which we undertook our jobs right after independence was remarkable. Civil servants were genuinely happy to be working for an independent government and they put their hearts into the tasks they were assigned. Corruption in the civil service was virtually non-existent. Jomo Kenyatta did not take kindly to anyone who made use of his name to cover up dishonesty or mismanagement. He may have been a 'godfather' to certain individuals but he would abandon or dismiss them if they exceeded their limits. Looting public property and impunity were not tolerated and all employees were expected to accomplish their assignments in a suitable, efficient manner. We were imbued with the idea that we were serving our country and we did so with pride.

It was not quite as easy as it sounds.

Duncan Ndegwa, as Head of Civil Service, had the unenviable task of creating an almost new civil service from scratch. Some posts had been scrapped, others had been established. Very new departments came into being. Ndegwa was working for a president who had never administered elsewhere. He was Secretary to a Cabinet of ministers, some of whom were under the impression that they were demi-gods due to their influence in political parties or due to their contribution in the struggle for independence. All these affairs and disparities had to be streamlined by a very strong and sober mind, and Ndegwa proved to be up to the task. Although plagued by some inevitable teething problems, the government and the civil service functioned quite well.

Those of us in the front row were almost overwhelmed by the new tasks that confronted us, but we believed in our abilities and this carried us through. Many senior staff in the civil service went for refresher courses or higher studies. In 1966, for example, I led a team of administrators to a six-week course at the University of Wisconsin. With me were PC Eliud Mahihu and five District Commissioners.

We attended lectures on general administration, government and politics. The university atmosphere led to broader discussions, not just the Kenyan perspective. For example, we talked about the differences between the position of a Provincial Commissioner and a governor, and the positions of district commissioners and counties.

By 1968, the civil service still lacked sufficient qualified staff. As a result, I went on a recruitment mission to universities in the USA. My team identified Kenyan students who had graduated or would soon complete their courses of study, and tried to interest them in careers in the civil service. I travelled with John Malinda and Habel Nyamu of the Directorate of Personnel Management and the Educational Attaché in Washington, Archie Mbogo, and some others. We travelled to New York, Cleveland, Boston, Denver, Chicago, Seattle, San Francisco, Minneapolis, Atlanta, Puerto Rico and many other places, talking to Kenyan students in the surrounding areas and ended up recruiting hundreds of them. I assigned them various positions in the administration even before they came back, and the government paid for their air tickets home. It was quite exciting to see our young civil service growing with professionals.

A few of these newly returned graduates had a difficult time adjusting to a role in administration. Some of them felt highly nationalistic to the extent that they resented the fact that their superiors, or bosses, had risen through the ranks during the few years before independence. They felt that the government was still implementing the same system that the Europeans had left behind. Others felt that the education they had received in the USA placed them a cut above the existing civil service structure. Some went for short courses in respected institutions like Harvard, and then called themselves alumni of the university.

These were difficult attitudes to deal with, but most of them settled down after they worked in the field for some time. Disciplinary matters were a concern, just as always in management. Every organisation had its special needs and problems but regulations were developed in order to achieve certain targets in provincial administration.

A number of the new recruits failed to do their jobs satisfactorily. It was as though they were waiting to be promoted, without doing the fieldwork properly, just because they were university graduates.

New recruits were expected to learn their jobs on the ground, and courses were also offered at Kenya Institute of Administration to instil some of the skills needed in the field. These courses included training in police discipline, the use of firearms and in commanding and training armed Administration Police (AP). The latter was useful in some of the more insecure areas of the country and during official functions such as taking the salute or inspecting a guard of honour. After all, the district commissioner and the district officer were the commanders of the APs under them, and in order to command them, they had to have the skills themselves.

In those days, it was interesting to observe actual development taking place. Services to the people were delivered and carried out with dignity and delight. People were patriotic and enjoyed the fruits of liberation. However, it makes me and many others of those early civil servants extremely unhappy to realise that now, the ordinary man has to part with a bribe in order to be served in a government office. This was completely unheard of in the years immediately following independence. I do not understand how we have stooped so low as to loot from ourselves.

* * *

I am aware that senior civil servants were, and still are, accused of looting public coffers and grabbing vast tracts of land, but in the majority of cases this was not so. It must be understood that, among the African population, civil servants were just about the only people with guaranteed incomes. They had regular pay and could therefore save and invest. They were, furthermore, educated and thus were familiar, to a certain extent, with commerce and the banking system. Consequently, many took advantage of this knowledge and took loans in order to invest. They purchased land and property and invested in businesses for their spouses or families. Many farmers and rural people, on the other hand, believed it was unwise and imprudent to use a land title as collateral for a loan. They imagined such loans were an elaborate scheme to dispossess them of their land and they wanted nothing to do with financial institutions.

When my civil service colleagues and I wished to take loans to buy farms, most of us found it convenient and we did not find any conflict of interest. Our families and farm employees managed the farms we bought while we went on with our official duties. In fact, some individuals even engaged professional managers to run their newly acquired farms. Through this arrangement, we ensured that we would be able to carry out our duties as efficiently and promptly as before, for our employer, the government. We were not insatiable or covetous and certainly looting from government coffers was never an option. The structures and proscriptions were so strict and exacting that there was no possibility of exploiting the system on any significant scale.

Looting came later, along with land grabbing. I sometimes wonder how this deterioration came about and I cannot pinpoint the exact cause, but somewhere along the way, our leaders lost or abandoned their vision of a united and prosperous Kenya. Politicians hijacked the administration and the civil service was relegated to the periphery of decision-making and management of public affairs. It seems to me that some politicians became too formidable and eventually wielded such weighty influence that even committed and dedicated civil servants were intimidated. Those in the civil service were virtually forced to seek protection and favours from such dominant politicians. This 'godfather' culture insidiously infiltrated the government, thus the integrity and efficiency of the civil service and other government bodies began to erode. As a result, many people lost their idealism and allegiance to the country, with ugly materialism taking the place of these virtuous qualities. The sleaze in the civil service and in the government, nepotism, favouritism and grand corruption continued to grow unchecked and became overwhelming during the last five years of Kenyatta's reign. Later, it grew to stratospheric heights under Moi.

* * *

As for my own position, I had four acres, which I inherited from my father, and then, after Land Consolidation in Kibichoi, I purchased bits of land totalling six acres, four of which are now under coffee.

In early 1964, a friend of mine, Douglas Njiiri Karago, had persuaded me to buy another farm. Douglas was interested in buying a coffee farm but he knew nothing about coffee farming, therefore he asked me to accompany him while he went in search of an available piece of land. We went to look at farms around Kiambu and then he told me there was another farm available near my original home that he wanted to look at. In fact, when we got there, I saw it was the actual farm where I used to pick coffee in 1936 and 1937.

I went to see the owner, a European called Alan Bockett. I was against taking a loan because I was nervous about repaying it. The farm was going for 140,000 shillings and I had nowhere near that kind of money. At that time, one could get loans from the Land Bank, which is now the Agricultural Finance Corporation. In fact, I was so much against getting a loan that I even refused to pay the one shilling that was required to buy the application form. However, Douglas was very determined. He went and bought two application forms, filled one for himself and then, when I refused, he filled the other one for me. That evening he asked me to append my signature and then, the next day he took them to the Board of the Land Bank. Amazingly, my loan application went through and his failed. Douglas was a good friend and was my best man in my first marriage and godfather to two of my children. I have never forgotten how kind he was to me.

Much later, he got another farm. Nevertheless, I still do not know why my application was approved and his declined. He was a senior manager with a big company and was earning a lot more money than I.

The bank said they could only loan me 100,000 shillings, so I had to look for an additional 40,000 shillings. After some consideration, I decided to see Bockett. He was a nice old man and he told me not to worry about the matter. He said he would let me have the farm and after I had harvested and sold the crop, he would take 50 per cent as the balance of the payment, while I could take the other half to run the farm. I managed to pay off the remaining 40,000 shillings within the first season and then moved into the house in May 1964.

Part of my reluctance to take a loan may have been because, much earlier, Africans would simply not be loaned any money because they had no security. In fact, no African was allowed to open a bank account or to operate a chequebook. At that time, the Post Office was the only facility available to Africans who wished to save their money and I had opened an account there while I was still in the Indian High Commission.

* * *

The year 1964 proved to be an interesting one for me. We were all struggling incredibly hard to prove that we deserved to be in our positions and that we could administer Kenya just as well as, or even better than, the Europeans.

I had come to Nairobi in July 1963 and taken over as Under Secretary in charge of Provincial Administration. In this position, and later as deputy secretary in charge of Provincial Administration, I was in charge of all the day-to-day affairs within the Provincial Administrative Department. There were only very few matters that I had to refer to the Head of Civil Service. Everything, including internal security and intelligence, came to me. Staff matters, under the Directorate of Personnel Management, such as appointments, and discipline, were handled without recourse to consultation with my superior.

Maintaining discipline was the most difficult aspect of provincial administration. There are laid down regulations and it is necessary to ensure that they are followed in order to achieve certain targets and set objectives. Divisions and districts all had certain unique needs and problems, which were different in every area.

In 1964, when the President and the Vice President started to see things from different points of view, a rift opened up between them. As a result, the Provincial Administration was transferred from the Ministry of Home Affairs to the Office of the President. I became, therefore, the Deputy Secretary to Duncan Ndegwa, who was the Head of Civil Service. Duncan and I became quite close and established a harmonious working relationship that facilitated the smooth handling of day-to-day tasks.

However, this façade of business as usual concealed a number of crucial and intricate issues. As is common when a sizeable team is involved in a gargantuan task, especially when it involves something as complex and intricate as running a country, there were opposing forces contradicting each other, or attempting to outshine others for personal reasons. Egos were bound to clash. This was the situation in the civil service and government, even in those early days. There were individuals who vied for ascendancy and pre-eminence while others were hostile rivals for whom each encounter resulted in confrontation. Certain senior civil servants viewed themselves as experts and maintained a patronising and supercilious attitude towards the rest, who, on many occasions, found it incredible that these persons were their superiors. Nearly everyone coveted positions that would place them in close proximity to Kenyatta. I vividly recall an incident where I was caught in the middle of a significant clash. I was the Under Secretary in charge of Provincial Administration and Duncan Ndegwa had just ascended to the post of Head of Civil Service after Jeff Ellerton left. The clash I refer to involved my superior, Duncan Ndegwa, and Charles Njonjo who had recently taken over from Griffiths Jones as Attorney General. Njonjo had previously been a State Crown Counsel in the AG's Chambers.

Njonjo and Ndegwa clashed over a divergence of tactics and leadership on various issues and suddenly their dispute became a power struggle, with the two of them at loggerheads, intent on outmanoeuvring each other.

Njonjo believed that his position as Attorney General placed him in an exclusive, singular rank, superior to that of the Head of Civil Service, and as such he believed that he was not accountable to Ndegwa. Ndegwa, on the other hand, insisted that Njonjo was indeed a civil servant and thus answerable to him. Factually, of course, Njonjo was, by virtue of being Attorney General, a civil servant but in a class of his own vested with authority such that he did not have to report directly to the Head of Civil Service.

In addition to this disagreement, there was persistent distrust between the two, who were both Kikuyu, on the trivial grounds that Ndegwa had his roots in Nyeri whereas Njonjo came from Kiambu. Separately, each of the two was markedly friendly with Kenyatta and each struggled to outdo the other in escalating his personal and confidential status with the old man.

Furthermore, Ndegwa considered it improper for Njonjo to attend Cabinet meetings, while Njonjo insisted it was his right and privilege. The two quarrelled and differed over such protocol issues and other matters, consequently developing into an extreme antipathy.

Since I was Ndegwa's deputy, Njonjo considered me in the same light as my boss. I doubt if he knew that my origins were in Kiambu District. Kenyatta sided with Njonjo, because he also had the impression that I was from Nyeri. This misconception arose because Ndegwa frequently spoke on my behalf and gave me his support and backing when Waira Kamau, a founder member of the Githunguri Teachers' Training College, continued to disparage me.

On one particular day, I believe it was in early 1966, Njonjo called on Kenyatta at Gatundu. He found a delegation of elders with him. They were seeking permission to perform a cleansing and thanksgiving ceremony in Githunguri, Kiambu, where the Githunguri Teachers' Training College had once stood. This ceremony, referred to as *kigongona* in Kikuyu, was to be attended by Mau Mau veterans and their supporters. The elders wished to cleanse Githunguri in view of the fact that, during the State of Emergency, a Court of Assize was established in that area in order to try the Mau Mau and their supporters, who included the Lari Massacre suspects. Unlike an ordinary court, a Court of Assize is constituted periodically to handle a specific issue before it is disbanded.

The Githunguri Court of Assizes convicted many Mau Mau adherents and some were hanged on the spot in the same compound.

The elders believed that it was necessary to cleanse the area because the blood of freedom fighters had been shed there. After hearing the delegation's wishes, Kenyatta informed them that he had no problems with the ceremony. He remarked that, as Attorney General, Njonjo would liaise with them on the arrangements since he was the 'head of the law' and Njonjo effectively gave them permission to proceed. However, either deliberately or by chance, he did not inform Ndegwa of the arrangements. Thus the Kiambu DC, Charles Murgor, also remained ignorant of the preparations.

As a result, when thousands of former Mau Mau adherents gathered in Githunguri for the *kigongona*, the provincial administration was caught by surprise. The DC, the DO, the police officer in charge and the intelligence officer had no clue about the purpose or intention of the gathering. Alarmed, Murgor telephoned me, as his superior, and enquired whether our office was aware of the Mau Mau gathering. He informed me that the organisers claimed to have received verbal authorisation from the President in the presence of Charles Njonjo. I replied that I knew nothing of the matter and immediately called my superior, Ndegwa. He, in turn, said that he had no knowledge of the ceremonies taking place in Githunguri.

Ndegwa was not amused and felt that, since the procedure for authorising such a gathering was not followed, the assembly could not be permitted to continue. There was the vital matter of public security to be taken into consideration, among other factors. I then telephoned the Kiambu DC, Murgor, and told him to instruct the police to dismiss the gathering.

The meeting was disrupted and the elders were notified that the assembly was illegal. Immediately thereafter, four of the organisers proceeded to Njonjo's office and acquainted him with the developments. Njonjo then wrote a terse note to the Kiambu DC informing him that the President had indeed authorised the meeting. The elders conveyed the memo to the bewildered DC, who telephoned me again for further advice. I concluded that the situation was getting out of hand, and asked the DC to bring the note to my office in Harambee House without further delay.

Upon receiving the memo, which was written in green ink (a colour that was used in correspondence by only three individuals at that time, that is, President Kenyatta, Charles Njonjo and Daniel arap Moi, both while he was Vice President and later as President) – I showed it to Ndegwa. He was infuriated and instructed me to ensure the meeting did not continue. Straight away, he departed for State House in order to protest to the President. Njonjo set off to see Kenyatta with the same intention and found Ndegwa had arrived before him.

Kenyatta gave both of them audience and listened intently to each of them. Ndegwa complained that Njonjo had gone behind his back and given informal permission for the gathering without informing his office. Njonjo, on the other hand, stated that he did not see the necessity of involving Ndegwa's office in such a matter. Kenyatta made it a practice never to take sides when his lieutenants disagreed unless it was completely obvious which side was in the wrong. After Ndegwa and Njonjo ended their quarrel, he directed them to resolve the issue themselves, as he had no time for their petty squabbles.

Ndegwa returned to his office, but was agitated to such a degree that he was unable to concentrate. He decided that he had had more than enough of Njonjo's interference and that it was time the AG was put in his place. He abruptly left his desk and marched in a temper from Harambee House to Njonjo's office in Sheria House. He stormed into the AG's office and, with a few curt, outraged syllables, an argument started. Ndegwa accused Njonjo of creating detrimental distractions and thus attempting to belittle him before his subordinates and even before the President.

According to Ndegwa, Njonjo was aware that in this particular incident he had no leg to stand on, and decided to beat a retreat. Njonjo informed Ndegwa that the event was merely a simple issue, which had been blown out of proportion by me and Murgor, the DC. Ndegwa wished to clarify the matter immediately. He used Njonjo's phone to call me. He requested that I repeat exactly what I had told him about the whole affair. I did so, and he, in turn, conveyed my words to Njonjo. However, Njonjo claimed I was not being honest or straightforward. Ndegwa phoned me once more and asked me to speak directly to Njonjo and reiterate precisely what I had told him on that particular morning.

"What did the DC tell you?" Njonjo asked me.

"He told me that you had given those people permission to hold a gathering in Githunguri. He even brought a letter, in your own handwriting, giving the elders permission to hold the meeting," I answered.

"Kiereini, you and your DC are liars," he told me.

My mind snapped.

"If there is any liar in this whole mess, sir, it is you!" I retorted and banged down the receiver.

As the intended gathering never took place, it was soon forgotten.

My relationship with Njonjo also remained frosty but as time went by, he and I slowly became better acquainted and gradually began to understand one another. He discovered that my character was neither underhanded nor devious, merely that I took my professional and business life exceedingly seriously, as did he. We eventually became good friends and business partners, a situation that continues to this day. In fact, we became very close that Njonjo was my best man when I remarried in 1971.

Nevertheless, it was not always easy being Njonjo's friend. I remember an instance that occurred at Mayfair Hotel. I almost killed someone, merely to defend my friendship with Njonjo.

On that particular day, I met Edward Kariuki wa Kimani, who was then Njenga Karume's business associate. Kariuki and Karume had purchased the Agip Motel (now Jacaranda Hotel) and the adjoining Pizza Garden. I and other senior civil servants often met at the Pizza Garden on Saturdays afternoon, sitting out on the verandah, having snacks and drinks. Such meetings would often stretch into the evening as some people left and others came in. On this Saturday afternoon, only Kariuki and I happened to be present.

I asked Kariuki, "Are we going to sit here, just the two of us, as though we are outcasts?" I suggested that we look for a different venue, where the two of us could sit with friends and talk, and we ended up at Mayfair, which usually had a good crowd, and had excellent steaks.

Kariuki did not like it. He always thought of the Agip Motel as his home. He complained that he was going to be forced to mix with unfamiliar people and he was right. At Mayfair we found Bernard Hinga, the Commissioner of Police, Ignatius Iriga Nderi, head of the Criminal Investigations Department, Ben Gethi, head of the General Service Unit, and Harun Muturi, a businessman. None of these people were Kariuki's friends and all of us chatted, but Kariuki remained silent.

It so happened that during the previous week, members of Parliament had been severely critical of Charles Njonjo over the allegation that he had land in Surrey, England, and therefore he was not regarded as a true, patriotic Kenyan. There was generally the feeling that Njonjo did not respect Africans. He grew up in special circumstances as the eldest son of a chief and somehow felt himself superior to others. This was one of the topics we began to discuss. Because Njonjo was my friend, I stood up for him.

Now, Harun Muturi was often careless with his talk and did not stop to weigh the consequences of his words.

Muturi looked at me and said, "You and your friend Njonjo should be kicked out of Kenya. You should go and live in Surrey. Go tell your 'husband' Njonjo that I have said so!" *(Thiĩ ũkeere mũrũmegwo Njonjo niguo ndoiga!)*

He was extremely abusive and insulting towards me and I became very angry.

At this point Kariuki, who had been quiet throughout our conversation, finally got his voice back. He started abusing me as well and said resentfully, "Now you suffer! After all, you were the one who brought me here!"

I was so enraged at Muturi's foul and vulgar insult that I decided I would shoot him. I went to my car in an overwhelming rage, to get my gun. I realised that none of the group knew I had a weapon, and, for a second, in a red blaze of fury, I even considered shooting them all! But as I walked out into the fresh air over to the parking lot and looked around at the everyday world surrounding me, I came to my senses.

I told myself that what I was contemplating was stupid. Seated at the table that I'd left behind me when I stormed out was the Commissioner of Police, the Head of the GSU, the head of the CID, and the Special Branch. If I actually let my rage get the better of me and committed the act, one or another of these people would be called as witnesses. There was no way I would escape punishment. So I tried to think rationally.

As I calmed down, I finally decided just to get away from the place. I quietly put my gun back and drove away. I went straight home and slept that night, but I continued to feel terrible.

For a long time, I was never able to forgive Muturi. He tried hard to make up with me and I decided not to continue quarreling, but at heart I still remembered his insults and I hurt badly.

In addition to developing a friendship with Njonjo, when I was posted to the Ministry of Defence, in 1970, I was appointed Permanent Secretary and had the opportunity to meet James Gichuru, who was my minister and one of the greatest Kenyan patriots I have ever known.

James Gichuru was Minister for Defence, a post he had taken over after being transferred from the Ministry of Finance in 1970. Together with Mbiyu Koinange, Gichuru was one of Kenyatta's most trusted friends. Gichuru was sincerely loved and valued by Kenyatta because he had constantly and consistently had faith in Jomo's leadership, and had never questioned any of his actions. As far back as 1949, Gichuru had surrendered the chairmanship of the Kenya African Union (KAU) – the leading African political party agitating for independence – to Kenyatta. He believed that Kenyatta was more experienced and better placed to lead the party and the nation. Later, after the Kapenguria trial, Kenyatta was imprisoned and subsequently KAU evolved into the Kenya African National Union (KANU), with Gichuru as chairman. However, on Kenyatta's release from prison in August 1961, Gichuru again stepped down for Kenyatta.

Gichuru, who was the MP for Limuru, was exceptionally respected by Kenyatta. Those desiring Mzee's favour knew better than to speak ill of Gichuru. In private moments, Kenyatta would refer to Gichuru as *"Muthuri wa Kanitha"* (the Church Elder) while Gichuru would warmly refer to the President as *"Muthee"* (the Elder). So great was Kenyatta's fondness for Gichuru that when election results were being announced at night, Kenyatta would not retire to bed until he was informed that Gichuru had been victorious, as always.

Gichuru was astoundingly intelligent and a selfless, devoted and honest servant of the nation. He held the position of minister in the powerful and demanding Ministry of Finance after independence. However, due to his deteriorating health, Kenyatta transferred him to the less-demanding Ministry of Defence.

I was appointed Permanent Secretary in the Ministry of Defence as a result of a bit of a crisis. I was on leave at the time but was recalled by Geoffrey Kariithi, who was then Head of Civil Service. The previous

Permanent Secretary had a few personal problems and as a result, he became a notorious drinker. The PS wrote a letter to Kenyatta requesting to be allowed to retire, but his letter was rejected. The PS wrote a second letter, later on, again requesting retirement and apparently Kenyatta became angry and asked, "Who does this man think he is!" At any rate, he was retired.

Later on, he was arrested for driving while intoxicated. One time, the traffic police asked him to give a urine specimen, in order to investigate his alcohol level. Instead of handing over the bottle, he said "Cheers!" and threw the liquid at the officer behind the counter. He was then charged and sentenced to one month in prison. He did not serve the full sentence, however.

In James Gichuru, I found a cordial and humane individual that any PS would have enjoyed working with. He allowed me a liberal atmosphere in which to formulate the policies of the ministry, and we consulted extensively before arriving at our conclusions. However, Gichuru was ill and could not perform arduous duties. Kenyatta therefore summoned me to State House and instructed me to assist Gichuru as far as possible. In addition, Kenyatta charged me to consult him personally if I ever experienced difficulties. Furthermore, he recommended that I work very closely with Moi, who as Vice President was the Chairman of the National Security Committee.

Gichuru's constituency was Limuru, and it remained so until his death. His people believed in him. Kariuki Thande tried to stand against him at one time, making a statement at one public meeting that since Gichuru had a problem with his leg, he was unable to walk properly and therefore was unable to represent the constituency. However, Gichuru quickly refuted the statement by saying that although he did indeed have a limp, he was in Parliament to represent the people, not to play football! Thande was, therefore, unable to go far.

Although Gichuru was born in Kikuyu, and lived in Sigona, there was no problem with standing in Limuru, which was next to Kikuyu, anyway.

Unlike many of his colleagues, Gichuru found no attraction in the trappings of power. While most of his compatriots were assiduously amassing personal wealth, Gichuru concentrated on working for the betterment of Kenya. He was one of those rare politicians who are born to serve their motherland, and he accomplished this with zeal. I spent a good number of years with him in the Ministry of Defence, and felt extremely distressed when Gichuru died in 1982.

* * *

The site at Githunguri has never been cleansed as the elders had intended. The structures, for example the gallows, were dismantled and there is no monument or marker. I believe the people around the area would hate to see a reminder of something that they hated so much.

In fact, considering the perceptions of the people, it is clear that, even now, there are hardly any monuments either pro or anti Mau Mau, except Kimathi's statue on Kimathi Street. This is the character of our people and not many even want to talk about Mau Mau or the camps. It is not regarded as a polite subject of conversation. We saw people suffering on both sides and had no control over these things. Such emotions will probably still remain in the generation to come. In general, when we talk about civil strife or civil war, one must remember that society and even families were divided. Such monuments may be considered in the future, but everything has its own time.

However, because of this incident over the cleansing of the site, and because I worked for the colonial government as a DC, I was always looked upon with suspicion. People like Waira Kamau felt that I was a traitor since I had left the Mau Mau movement to take up employment with the colonial government. He went around spreading lies about me to everyone and especially to the leading personalities of the day. Thus, I found it very difficult at times to work in the civil service, because people doubted my sincerity. I am sure they were asking themselves how I could have worked for the colonial government yet now 'pretend' to be loyal to the independent Kenya government.

Unfortunately, that stigma remained with me. There might be people who still label me a collaborator. Although I was senior to other younger officers, it took me a long time to be promoted to the position of Permanent Secretary. Initially, Kenyatta would not even shake my hand, despite the fact that I was head of the Provincial Administration.

My progress was hampered for a long while. Waira did everything in his power to damage my name. He wanted me sacked.

Waira once gathered a delegation and took them to see Kenyatta to demand my dismissal. When they met Kenyatta and he asked them why they had come, Waira stood up to speak. He said that they had come to make a special request, and, from what I heard later, he accused me of being a disloyal traitor. He also accused me of having fought against the Mau Mau and all those who struggled for independence. Waira went on to say that I was allied with the Europeans while the Kikuyu were suffering. Finally, he remarked that it was sacrilege to keep me in the Office of the President.

However, by the time this meeting took place, Kenyatta had apparently known my character well and my background a little better and had changed his opinion about my loyalties.

Mzee told Waira that I had been one of the first African DCs. He wanted to know what it was that I had done wrong.

In response, Waira just said that I was a bad man and that I had been a home guard.

Kenyatta was generally opposed to these kinds of long-standing personal grudges and repeatedly emphasised the fact that Kenya needed people who would work together to develop the nation and move from dependence on the Europeans, to self-reliance.

Therefore, Kenyatta's response to Waira was predictably sarcastic. "Would your brother Babu be able to do the work?" he asked Waira. Mzee then went on to say that he knew I did my work well and that I had never harmed anyone.

When the people in the delegation heard Kenyatta's ironic response, they began to wonder what exactly Waira had got them into. It appeared that they had not been fully briefed on the reason for the visit to Kenyatta and many of them left Gatundu quickly thereafter. Three of those people, who knew me well, came straight from Gatundu to my office in Harambee House to relate the events.

However, from that day onward, I never heard of anyone else talking ill of me. Apparently, Kenyatta decided to promote me, although I do not know what prompted him to finally do so.

Chapter 9

Running the Defence Docket

I was promoted to Permanent Secretary in the Ministry of Defence in July 1970. The Ministry of Defence oversees the country's Armed Forces, which is the Kenya Army, Kenya Navy and Kenya Air Force. Since many people ask me what the duties a PS in the ministry are, I will try to elucidate this role, somewhat.

The Minister is the political head of a ministry. The Permanent Secretary, on the other hand, is the executive head of that ministry. The PS is fully responsible for all functions and for the initiation and implementation of the ministry's policies. He is also the Accounting Officer of the Ministry.

For example, when the military required some equipment or wished to replace obsolete equipment, they would evaluate their needs and constraints, recommend the type of equipment, cost the requirements and then come to me as the PS. I would examine the issues raised and once satisfied that the need was genuine, the matter would be presented to the equipment policy committee of the Armed Forces and thereafter to the Cabinet.

I would provide the explanation of the requirements, the quantity required and such relevant background information together with all the financial implications. Although I would have a certain amount of technical information, based on a thorough briefing provided by military officers, I was responsible for preparing all the paper work for the Minister to present to the Cabinet.

Of course, one of the complexities of the Ministry of Defence is that, issues of procurement must be strictly confidential as they directly affect the security of the nation. One would not want other countries or potential enemies to be aware of the exact logistics and equipment to be purchased.

Thereafter, I would draft the proposal for Cabinet appraisal, and if approved, the Treasury would then be requested to release the funds. As PS, I would subsequently account for the expenditure, and in case anything questionable arose, such as the money being diverted from its original purposes, I would ultimately be held personally responsible.

I felt lucky and enjoyed my job tremendously. Time passed quickly; I was never bored and there were many changes. While I was in the Ministry of Defence, President Kenyatta seemed quite pleased with me.

At the time I was in the Ministry of Defence, the Chief of Defence Staff, as the position was then known, was Major-General J. M. Ndolo. He was in charge of all the branches of the Armed Forces, which were, in turn, headed by Service Commanders.

Ndolo was a career soldier who had risen through the ranks. He had been recruited during colonial times and had a great deal of military experience but lacked formal education. He had been promoted by the colonial government, not so much due to his ability as a soldier, but rather for his unquestioning loyalty to his superior officers. He was the first Kenyan to rise to the position of Major-General.

Officials in the ministry had many problems with Ndolo and the clique of military staff surrounding him. Ndolo believed that matters of national security should be left to the military, and he viewed me and other civil servants in the ministry as meddlers in the affairs of the Armed Forces. The PS in the Ministry of Defence before me had a similar history of difficulties with the services. Ndolo, for example, would refer to him in derogatory terms as 'my clerk', implying that he was nothing but a subservient pen pusher.

Ndolo would have to come to me with all his requirements, be they for remuneration of soldiers, procurement of arms and equipment or whatever matter that needed funding from the Treasury. We would discuss the merits or demerits of whatever guns, tanks, aircraft or other equipment that the military needed and we would then consult the suppliers. This arrangement did not please Ndolo at all.

Either because of his strong belief in the superiority of military might, or because of his poor educational background, he was never able to fully understand the relationship between the military and the civilian government. He felt that the military should have a much greater role in running the country's affairs and believed that the Armed Forces should be more autonomous and free of interference from civil servants.

The late 1970s and early 80s were turbulent periods for many nations in Africa. Governments were being overthrown left, right and centre, and new, inexperienced and naïve individuals, either idealistic or demagogic, installed themselves as Heads of State. Most of these coups d'état were instigated by military leaders, on the basis of grievances either genuine or perceived against the rulers. The new presidents embraced various political and economic ideologies. Some favoured communism, others capitalism, and others had more obscure, untried ideologies such as Pan-Africanism. Still others were manifest ruffians who were hungry for power and had no perceptible ideology or justifiable cause to overthrow their countries' regimes. The western capitalist powers and their eastern communist nemesis both funded many of these revolutions in order to safeguard their interests in Africa and to add allies to their respective axis.

One such example was General Idi Amin Dada, a despot who overthrew Milton Obote's government in 1972 and started a systematic bloodbath in Uganda.

This coup d'état was a major security interest to the Kenya government for two reasons. First, Amin, Mulinge and Ndolo had been in the Kenya African Rifles together, in the same battalion, and it was thought that his actions might influence the military forces in Kenya. Secondly, Amin threatened Kenya's borders. He stated that the Kenyan–Uganda border should lie around Naivasha area, where it had once been, way back at the beginning of the colonial era. Most of us considered him a clown but we treated him with care, as we were never sure whether he was serious or not. He was a difficult man to deal with.

I first met Amin when he came to one of the Nairobi Trade Fairs on an unannounced stopover. Later on, I met him again when he came to see Kenyatta at Lanet, near Nakuru, where a passing out parade was in progress, and he had lunch with us. My impression at the time was that he was polite and acted like a gentleman. He spoke in Kiswahili and seemed pleasant. However, all of us knew that he was the type of man who could smile on the outside, yet plot death in his heart.

In Kenya, however, there had never been a coup d'état. For the most part, the military maintained an apolitical stance. There had been a number of attempts, which were, fortunately, nipped in the bud through early detection by intelligence sources.

The first attempt was at the end of January 1964 when soldiers mutinied at Gilgil. Soldiers in Tanganyika, Uganda, and Kenya mutinied in rapid succession during the last week of January 1964 because their governments could no longer maintain the delicate balance of coercion and concessions that had kept the colonial soldiers in check.

In 1947, Amin had been transferred to Kenya for infantry service as a private and served in the infantry battalion at Gilgil, Kenya, until 1949. That year, his unit was deployed to Northern Kenya to fight against

Somali insurgents. In 1952, his brigade was deployed against Mau Mau rebels in Kenya and Amin shot and captured General Kaleba in the battle of Rui Ruiru. He was promoted to corporal the same year, then to sergeant in 1953.

Amin and Major-General Ndolo had undergone military training together in Lanet during the 1950s. Amin was not a particularly intelligent person but he was a forceful and ruthless military commander and exercised full control over his men. However, being a good soldier and a good president are two separate things. He was later to oversee a brutal bloodbath in Uganda and his actions led to Uganda's retrogression to depths from which it took a long time to recover.

In 1971, there were rumours in Kenya about traitors and KANU called for a meeting to denounce those who were planning to overthrow the legitimate Government. There was a loyalty demonstration at Uhuru Park and when Kenyatta spoke, there were some placards raised in the crowd, with the names of Major-General Ndolo and Chief Justice Kitili Mwendwa, who later had to resign. Other suspects were dealt with administratively.

It may be that Amin's mutiny and ascension to power gave Ndolo the idea for actions that would later lead to his disgrace and expulsion from the military. Intelligence reports later in 1971 indicated that Ndolo and a few others were in the process of planning a military coup in order to overthrow Jomo Kenyatta. The scheme never went beyond the initial stages. Because of his actions, Ndolo was forced to retire and Kitili Mwendwa, the Chief Justice, also lost his position.

President Kenyatta thereafter disbanded the Eleventh Battalion of the Kenya Rifles, and 170 men were dismissed after the mutiny was quelled while soldiers who were found to be loyal to the government were retained. The reasons behind the rebellion were never made clear, although soldiers grumbled about their pay and 'not being involved in government'. There were no casualties. When Ndolo was removed, the Army Commander Brigadier Jackson Mulinge, took over and was promoted to the rank of Major-General. The title for his position was changed from 'Chief of Defence Staff' to 'Chief of General Staff'. Although the titles are basically the same, this was changed to erase connections with Ndolo. Mulinge had a slightly better standard of education and was less self-righteous than Ndolo. Consequently, we had a cordial working relationship. Mulinge was understanding and clear-headed. He had no problem accompanying me on routine visits to see

President Kenyatta in order to explain the state of military affairs and requirements.

Both Ndolo and Mulinge came from the same community, that is, the Kamba. The main reason behind this was that, from early on, colonial opinion held that the Kamba made better soldiers. Therefore, colonial forces recruited soldiers mainly from the Kamba and Somali communities, in addition to pastoralist communities such as the Turkana and Samburu. As a result, after independence, when the British soldiers left, the senior-most African soldiers were predominantly from the Kamba community. Naturally, they took over the officers' positions since they were the most experienced and qualified.

The colonial government held assorted nonsensical stereotypes regarding different communities. The Somalis and others such as the Turkana were enlisted due to the preconceived notion that they were fearless fighters and, therefore, would make courageous soldiers, while the Kamba were believed to be loyal, obedient, and therefore amenable to discipline. The Luo, for whatever reason, were not considered good 'military material' and coastal peoples did not often qualify because they were, on average, too short. The Kikuyu were seen as recalcitrant and argumentative, mainly due to the fact that they had consistently agitated for freedom and had created difficulties for Europeans since the beginning of colonisation in the 1890s. After all, the Kikuyu had produced troublemakers such as Waiyaki wa Hinga, Harry Thuku and Jomo Kenyatta and, in the 1950s, had created the Mau Mau movement. They were only recruited during the first and second World Wars due to shortage of manpower.

That was how Ndolo, Mulinge and other Kamba came to hold such high positions in the military. After independence, however, Kenyatta's government – with its commitment to equality and balance – laid down quotas for military recruitment in order to ensure that all communities were well-represented in the armed forces. Through this system, the Kamba and Somali communities eventually lost their dominance in the military.

An interesting issue here was that Ndolo had been living in a spacious government house in Woodley Estate near the Royal Nairobi Golf Course. After his dismissal, he left the quarters and Mulinge, as his successor, should have assumed occupancy but he did not want it, nor did any other senior military officers. Some military circles spread the rumour that the house was haunted by Ndolo's spirit and hence it remained vacant.

Soldiers believed that the house was jinxed and that anyone residing in it would come to a bad end.

In 1971, due to difficulties in commuting to and from my farm in Ruiru, I happily moved into the house with my family. I can assure you that I never experienced the existence of any spirits, whether left behind by Ndolo or anyone else. I lived there with my family until I finally moved into my own house in Karen on 20 December 1980.

We had a comfortable dwelling there in Woodley and I fondly remember our stay as most enjoyable. My immediate neighbour was Vice President Daniel arap Moi, and we became close friends. Our houses were on a road called Kabarnet Gardens. I would often stop in for a cup of tea. The Vice President would come over to my house as well, and share a meal with my family. We would sometimes spend our spare time together, talking about various issues concerning the country. He was senior to me, but he had a humble attitude with no pretentious illusions about his status. Along with other grounds, this was just one reason we became close.

* * *

I joined the Ministry of Defence at a time when it was modernising its arsenal and equipment. The equipment inherited from the colonial military was of poor quality and much of it was nearly obsolete. Therefore, during my early years as PS, we oversaw the complete overhaul of military hardware to that befitting a modern army. It was an extremely expensive exercise but vital to national security.

At that time, Kenya's relations with a number of neighbouring countries were not at their best. Many wars were going on in various parts of the continent, and the government had to exercise utmost caution. There was Uganda, our neighbour to the west, which had just been taken over by Idi Amin. Amin quickly proved to be a sadistic brute whose course of action and reasoning were arbitrary. He could not be trusted to follow careful logical processes. The moment he assumed power, he expelled all Asians from the country on the grounds that they were controlling the economy, which should have been in the hands of Ugandans. He gave all their businesses away to the local people. The businesses, buildings and residential houses belonging to Asians were distributed to Amin's military cronies. This was the beginning of Uganda's freefall into an economic meltdown and the beginning of the darkest chapter in that country's history.

While most of those expelled from Uganda went to the United Kingdom, a sizeable number settled in Kenya and this heightened the mistrust between the two countries. The Kenya government was highly suspicious of Amin's actions. He made senseless and inane decisions on a daily basis. He expelled foreign diplomats and dictated economically suicidal decisions to Uganda's Central Bank. People he perceived as his enemies started disappearing without trace while his army executed others. He gave himself grandiose titles, which made him a subject of scorn and ridicule. In short, he was not a person whom a neighbouring government would dare trust.

As stated previously, one day, Amin demanded that Kenya cede all the land from Naivasha westward to Uganda. According to Amin, Naivasha and the Rift Valley wherein it was situated, delineated the true boundary between the two countries. His demand was utterly ludicrous but the basis of his assertion was founded on a historical premise.

After the Berlin Conference of 1884-1885 where European countries decided to divide and colonise Africa, the boundaries were roughly drawn up without any reference to the local population. African geography was not well known to the Europeans as they relied on sketchy reports from explorers, traders and missionaries. The British wanted to control Uganda since Lake Victoria was the source of the Nile, which they considered a strategic resource at par with the Suez Canal.

Originally, Kenya was only envisioned as a passage to Uganda – it was not important to the imperialists. Therefore, the early maps were drawn placing the boundary between the two colonies in the Rift Valley. Later, the British changed the boundaries to their present location after making Kenya a protectorate in the 1890s.

Amin's claim outraged the Kenyan public. Jomo Kenyatta, too, was outraged. Without mincing words, he said that Kenya would not give up even one inch of soil and that Kenya was ready to fight should Amin make the foolish attempt to alienate any bit of the country's land. This was Kenyatta's nature. He was a brave man and when challenged, he was fiercely direct and hard. The Kenyan Armed Forces were placed on red alert, but nothing came out of Amin's tirades. However, everyone knew he was an unreasonable person – someone to be wary of.

Kenya's relations with Tanzania were not rosy either. Tanzania grumbled that Kenya was benefiting unfairly from the establishment of the East African Community.

The East African Community was set up by the colonial government in 1940s to ease the economic transactions, infrastructure, movement and other aspects in the East African region of Uganda, Kenya and Tanzania (then Tanganyika). After the countries got their independence, the system continued up to 1977 when it broke up after irreconcilable differences. The three countries have been trying to recreate a similar system recently and are well on the way to success.

Although the East African Community worked while Britain was in charge, the association was doomed to fail at independence. The three countries went different ways because of following widely diverse ideologies. Kenyatta was a capitalist, having spent a good number of years in Britain. Julius Nyerere of Tanzania was convinced that *'ujamaa'* (socialism) was the best way to ensure development, while in Uganda, Milton Obote's ideology was not well defined. There was bound to be conflict.

The common currency changed after independence and each country minted its own coin. Common interests such as East African Railways and Harbours and East African Airways continued to function but there were many disagreements and Uganda and Tanzania constantly accused Kenya of reaping most of the benefits.

Once Idi Amin came to power, the situation between Tanzania and Uganda deteriorated rapidly. Nyerere never saw eye to eye with Amin. In fact, Nyerere hated Amin to such a degree that he would not sign any document with Amin's signature on it. The East African Community Secretary General, Charles Maina, had a hard time dealing with these two leaders. Any document requiring all three leaders' signatures had to undergo special protocol. Maina would first take the document to Nyerere to sign. Then it would come to Kenyatta, and finally it would go to Amin.[1]

The last nail in the coffin of the fragile East African Community concerned East African Airways. The airline had borrowed money from foreign sources in order to buy aeroplanes. All the three countries signed the contract on a 'jointly and severally' basis, meaning that if any of the other two partners defaulted on the loan, a single country would pay for the rest. The planes were bought, but the partners dithered on fulfilling their part of the deal. Uganda had no money since Amin had wrecked the economy, and Tanzania was unwilling to pay because it saw Kenya as being the major beneficiary of the coalition. As a result, the lenders required Kenya to pay up.

---

1   Amin was later expelled from Uganda after a short war with Tanzania.

Kenya's Attorney General, Charles Njonjo, opposed this position and freely aired his views on the matter, which then led to the worsening of his relationship with Nyerere, which had never been cordial in the first place.

It was said that President Julius Nyerere of Tanzania was opposed to certain personalities in Kenya, mainly those fronted by the Attorney General Charles Njonjo. For their own reasons, Njonjo and his group were hostile to the idea of the East African Community and made every effort to frustrate its operations. There was considerable distrust between the two countries over the issue.

Njonjo pointed out that, under the terms of the loan, if any of the aircraft travelled outside the country, they could be grounded and seized at any time. He, therefore, advised that the planes in Kenya be grounded immediately.

This brought the East African Community to a halt in 1977 and each of the three countries went its own way. Kenya created Kenya Airways and the grounded planes were sold off.

When Nyerere retired, he came to State House in Nairobi to say goodbye. I sat with him during a lunch hosted by President Moi. Talking over a cup of coffee later, I asked him about his *ujamaa* policy. He admitted that he had failed Tanzania. The ideology itself had been sound, he said, and he still believed in it. But if he were to do it over again, he would implement it differently. Unlike many African leaders, Nyerere was ready to admit when he was wrong.

* * *

On Kenya's east, there was Somalia. There was little love lost between the Kenyan and Somali governments. The majority of the population in North Eastern Province consisted of ethnic Somalis and again this anomaly was due to the arbitrary maps drawn up by the colonialists in 1885. After independence, Somalia had claimed that the province should be given up by Kenya in order to become part of its territory. In its expansionist vision, the Somalia government had created a blue flag with the emblem of a six-pointed star as its motif. Five of the stars symbolised the five states of Somalia and the sixth star represented the area in the North Eastern Province of Kenya. However, Somalia never realised its dream. The province remains in Kenya, but it has not been as peaceful and stable as the rest of the country.

Somalia funded and gave logistical support to rebel forces, called 'Shifta', who roamed northeastern Kenya causing chaos and mayhem. The Kenya government fought bitter battles with the Shifta, and by the time they were finally crushed in the 1970s many Kenyan civilians, police and soldiers had lost their lives.

I have great respect for Kenya's Armed Forces. Although, thankfully, they never had to fight an external war, they have shown bravery and commitment in UN missions, and I can proudly say that our military is one of the strongest and most disciplined in Africa. It has an excellent leadership and other than a few minor incidents, it has always been patriotic and has given full support to the government. There have been no serious attempts to overthrow the government, something that cannot be said of many other African countries. The 1982 coup attempt, which I will go into later, was an immature fiasco, and one can say the same of others such as Major-General Ndolo's plot. The government has maintained a generally excellent relationship with the Armed Forces.

There are people who complain that the military just sit idle in their barracks. They do not understand the larger picture. By their very nature, the Armed Forces are trained to fight. They must constantly exercise vigilance and upgrade their skills and proficiency in order to defend the country. Their presence and fitness ensure our country's continued existence. Requiring them to be involved in nation building activities such as constructing roads is too simplistic. The military is trained to attack and defend, and not for civilian duties it can only undertake in times of national disasters or emergencies. They are only involved in constructing roads or performing other duties that have a direct impact on the security of the country.

Chapter 10

Fear and Uncertainty

Earlier, in 1969, the *Chai* (tea) oath took place after the murder of Tom Mboya. He was felled by an assassin's bullet along Government Road (later renamed Moi Avenue) on 5 July 1969. After his assassination, there was great hostility towards the Kikuyu – especially among the Luo community. The *Chai* oath was intended to bind the Kikuyu to defend themselves against possible violence from the Luo and other tribes.

I was tricked by my superiors into taking the oath and this made me very angry, but it would have been defeatist for me to resign over such a thing. After all, I had many other more significant problems at the time, which could have led to my resignation. Nevertheless, I was annoyed and resented the fact.

I had been informed that the Presidential Escort guard had gone on strike over their salaries and I rushed to Gatundu to settle the problem. On arrival, I was first given a cup of tea in the main house and then I was invited to see the guards, supposedly waiting for me in the staff quarters outside the compound. Once I opened the door to the outer building, I was confronted with guns and a sight I immediately recognised as an oath administration ritual.

The rationalisation for the *Chai* oath was considered a way of 'self-preservation' for the Kikuyu. This period in Kenya's history was extremely sensitive. In some quarters, the general rumour was that an individual or possibly a group from the Kikuyu community had organised the killing of Mboya. Disaffection was high.

Among the Kikuyu, there was a perception that the other tribes were rising against them and I believe this was the basic motivation behind the oath. Those who organised the oath attempted to recreate the galvanising effect that the Mau Mau oath had once had on Kikuyu society. They believed the *Chai* oath would mobilise the community in the face of this crisis and show them that there was an urgent need to unite. On the contrary, for many Kikuyu, it had the opposite effect because of the force and violence employed.

By the mid-1970s, the local political scene was undergoing a metamorphosis. Given the age and frail health of Kenyatta, talk of his succession was rife. Such talk did arise, although at first it was conducted in whispers. Politicians close to Kenyatta were laying strategies on how to usurp power. The so-called 'Kiambu Mafia', all of whom were close to the President, contained individuals with ambitions to succeed Kenyatta. There was infighting and backstabbing among them as they jostled to be the chosen one closest to Jomo.

However, everyone who had aspirations for the top seat was aware of the one major obstacle that blocked their road ahead and that was the Kenya Constitution. The Constitution stated, quite clearly, what actions were to be taken, should the sitting President die in office or be incapacitated. In the event of such an occurrence, the Constitution allowed only one course of events: that the Vice President automatically took over and acted as the Head of State for no longer than 90 days, within which period a fresh General Election had to be held. Whoever won the election then took over as the new President.

There were many people who were not comfortable with this scenario. Moi was from the Kalenjin tribe, but the majority of Kenya's rich and powerful were Kikuyu, including the politicians holding powerful ministries, and they abhorred the notion of being led by a non-Kikuyu. Most of those with considerable wealth and powerful positions had taken advantage of their proximity to the President, and they would no longer be assured of protection if a non-Kikuyu took over from Kenyatta. There were others who, for various reasons of their own, did not think Moi was fit to govern. With the entry of Moi into State House, they had little doubt that their privileges would no longer exist.

In the mid 1970s, a scheme was created by the anti-Moi elements in Kenyatta's government. They realised that the surest way to prevent Moi from ascending to the position was to change the constitution so that the Vice President did not automatically take over as acting President in the event of the President's death. By changing this stipulation, they hoped to make it difficult for Moi to become President and therefore create an alternate power base. They knew that the 90-day period a Vice President would sit as acting President would give him sufficient time to entrench himself and position him to win the presidency when the elections were called. If this part of the constitution had been altered, Moi would have had a little chance in the race for the presidency.

However, Kenyatta would hear none of it. Kenyatta genuinely liked and trusted Moi, who had proved himself a loyal second-in-command.

Among his many lieutenants, Kenyatta viewed Moi as the most able to unite the country. He felt that, although Moi was not a Kikuyu, he was capable of keeping the nation united. Much as he liked his Kikuyu cronies, Kenyatta did not want to front any of them. He believed that the country was bigger than the interests of one community. However, he neither told off any of his ambitious friends nor, on the other hand, did he directly tackle the issue of Moi.

At this point, in 1971, the Gikuyu, Embu and Meru Association (GEMA) was formed to ostensibly look into the welfare of member communities who shared kinship ties and lived in proximity to one another around Mount Kenya. Originally, it was meant for economic empowerment, but it soon became influential politically. It had the support of the communities it represented, which made it powerful because those communities formed the largest voting bloc.

Other tribes already had associations of their own, such as the Akamba Union and the Luo Union. However, GEMA became most effective among them all because its leaders were close to Kenyatta and were his chief advisors. Hiding behind the façade of GEMA, they were able to push forward their own agenda.

At its initial formation, senior Kikuyu civil servants led by Duncan Ndegwa, John Michuki, and a few others established GEMA. Duncan was Head of Civil Service and Michuki was Permanent Secretary at the Treasury; thus they were the most senior civil servants among us.

When the idea was conceived, Duncan and the founders thought they should inform Kenyatta of their intentions, since they did not want to start the association without his knowledge. They also realised that others might interpret the alliance as a political union. Therefore, they asked for an appointment to meet Kenyatta and entertain him at his home in Gatundu. Paul Kihara, then an Assistant Secretary, was a sociable fellow who knew many entertaining songs and dances. He could keep people amused throughout an evening and thus he oversaw the event.

I did not go to Gatundu myself, but I was later told that when the proposal for GEMA's formation was tabled before Kenyatta, he did not disagree with it. On the contrary, he said it was a good idea; however he was opposed to civil servants taking leadership positions within the association.

Kenyatta told the founders that the public might see GEMA as a political organisation, and an indication that civil servants were getting into politics. He advised them to join the organisation as members, rather than leaders, and to look for someone else, perhaps someone in business, to be the head of the organisation. In this way, it would be detached from politics.

At the time, Kikuyu politicians, particularly the ministers, were not working together harmoniously. They seemed obsessed with infighting and arguing about how close each was to Kenyatta. None of them would have been capable of leading the others, and this was especially true of politicians from Kiambu.

Kenyatta was therefore shrewd in giving this advice. Other than Mbiyu Koinange, Kenyatta's constant companion and close friend, politicians were not involved in many of the decisions that the President made. Even Mbiyu, despite his favourable position, was on the periphery in matters outside the sphere of their personal friendship.

With Kenyatta's blessing the civil servants returned to Nairobi and began to look for an ideal candidate to head GEMA. As the President advised, they decided to select a prominent businessman who was not committed to politics and this is how Njenga Karume was brought into GEMA and became the chairman. At this time, Njenga had a reputation as a sharp-witted businessman who was quiet, friendly, and generous. He was apparently the only individual people felt they could trust. Despite the fact that Njenga Karume became the chairman, the officials of GEMA who were registered in the Office of the Registrar were Duncan Ndegwa, John Michuki and George Waruhiu. That did not change until later when they were taken to court, by the Attorney General for failing to file official returns.

Later, GEMA was politicised. It attempted to block the Vice President from automatically assuming the presidency for ninety days, should the president become incapacitated. Hiding behind the façade of GEMA, the leaders formed a movement to change the constitution after Kenyatta refused to support them openly.

Their idea was to campaign in parts of the country where members of GEMA had strongholds. With the support of the people, they would then mobilise their fellow legislators to change the offending clause of the constitution. They were seeking the legitimacy of public support in order to push for the implementation of their hidden motives in Parliament. They put forward the idea that, in case the President died, it would be too much of a risk to let a single person take over power in an acting capacity. That person might easily refuse to relinquish power or even refuse to call an election and continue ruling without legitimate right. They suggested it was therefore safer for three persons to be in charge of running the country for the 90 days until the election was held. The three people they proposed were the Speaker of the National Assembly (who was then Fred Mati, a Kamba), the Chief Justice (then Sir James Wicks) and the Head of Civil Service (Geoffrey Kariithi, a Kikuyu). No one individual would be able to consolidate the power of the presidency.

The anti-Moi group held many public meetings presenting their agenda to the people. However, in retrospect, it seems to me that the people were being used to legitimise an initiative they did not understand. The entire issue was based on tribal emotions rather than as a reaction to the personality of Moi or his ability to govern.

I was among the few Kikuyu senior government officials who stood by Moi during this trying period. I had never been close to GEMA leaders and I did not approve of their motives for rejecting Moi. Their rationale was merely selfish and not for the benefit of the country. In my view, actions inspired by ethnicity have but one result – ethnic hatred, which is a major problem currently affecting this nation. Furthermore, I did not see anything objectionable with that part of the constitution concerning the presidential succession.

It was despicable that some of those who wished to change the constitution showed open disrespect for the Vice President. On one or two occasions, the police went so far as to stop Moi on the highway to Nakuru and humiliated him by searching his car. It was said that this was done on the orders of the Rift Valley Provincial Police Officer.

I was a friend of Moi's and I knew him quite well. He was my neighbour for many years and my senior. I knew him as a humble man who had given unswerving support to Kenyatta in his efforts to build the nation. In addition, in my capacity as the PS for Defence, I had worked with Moi and got to know his values and ethics when he was the Chairman of the National Security Committee. Moi was a staunch Christian, a generally good person and our friendship had never been influenced or affected by the fact that we were from different tribes. Therefore, given this background, I decided to stick by him and support him. I decided that I would rather trust Moi to run the country than many of those others who were agitating for change. While Moi took his work seriously and was dedicated to serving the country, this could not be said of some of those who were now opposing his ascension to power.

GG Kariuki also supported Moi during this period. Kariuki, the MP for Laikipia, was popular and, as a Kikuyu, his support for Moi in Parliament was vital. Another senior official who stood by Moi was the Attorney General, Charles Njonjo. Njonjo was not close to many members of the Kikuyu elite that surrounded Kenyatta. With a viewpoint similar to my own, he also had never supported the idea of GEMA.

When GEMA became adamant about changing the constitution, Njonjo sprang a surprise on them. He found a way to restrain and obstruct their plans by accusing them of treason by 'imagining the death of the President', an illegal and subversive concept.

Someone told me later that Njonjo cleverly went to Nakuru early one morning to see Kenyatta about the matter. After some inconsequential small talk, Njonjo brought up the reason for his visit.

Njonjo told Kenyatta that people were holding public meetings to discuss his death. They were openly asking who would succeed Kenyatta. These meetings were being held everywhere and Njonjo revealed that the next such meeting was to be held in Meru over the weekend. The main topic of discussion was to be what the Kikuyu would do after Mzee's death. He told Kenyatta that such speculation was illegal, since it was banned in the Penal Code.

Kenyatta asked to see the particular law and Njonjo, having carried a copy along with him, showed the President the relevant section. Section 40 of the Penal Code provided that:

> (1) Any person who, owing allegiance to the Republic, in Kenya or elsewhere – (*a*) compasses, imagines, invents, devises or intends, the death, maiming or wounding, or the imprisonment or restraint, of the President; or the deposing by unlawful means of the President from his position as President or from the style, honour and name of Head of State and Commander-in-Chief of the Armed Forces of the Republic of Kenya; or the overthrow by unlawful means of the Government; and (*b*) expresses, utters or declares any such compassings, imaginations, inventions, devices or intentions by publishing any printing or writing or by any overt act or deed, is guilty of the offence of treason. The offence carries the death sentence.

Njonjo explained that people had been discussing the matter over the previous two months, and that it appeared the discussions were sanctioned by the President himself.

Mzee then insisted that such meetings be stopped. He instructed Njonjo to draft an announcement about the matter, which should be broadcast on the 1 o'clock news that day.

Njonjo prepared the announcement and gave it to Kenyatta to review and approve. After that, the President called his Presidential Press Officer to deal with the broadcast.

That was the end of Njonjo's audience and he then flew back to Nairobi aboard a Kenya Police Airwing aircraft.

Later the same day, a few of us met for lunch at the Red Bull in Nairobi, in our usual group of senior civil servants. As we sat at our regular table, Njonjo told us that he had been in Nakuru that morning, and while we were eating, the announcement was made.

Most people were happy that Kenyatta's decision had finally dealt with the matter and stopped the speculation.

* * *

Kenyatta's death finally came, on 22 August 1978, while he was in Mombasa.

I was in Mauritius with my family on holiday.

While I was taking my children to the hotel swimming pool, I passed by the bar, around 3pm. One of the hotel guests having a drink there, called and asked me, "Didn't you say you come from Kenya?"

I said I did, and then he told me that the BBC had reported that Kenyatta had died.

With great difficulty, I managed to call a friend in Nairobi and he confirmed the news. However, I could not fly out of Mauritius immediately, as there were only a limited number of direct flights to Kenya at that time. Otherwise I would have had to fly to Bombay or Johannesburg first, and then on to Nairobi.

I managed to get a flight about three days later. As I flew back to Nairobi, I was worried and many thoughts were running through my head. It was a complicated situation and I knew that the procedures to be followed immediately after the death of a president while in office were not clearly understood. However, by the time I returned, it was all over and Moi had already been sworn in as acting President. After that, we were fully involved in planning the funeral.

During the next 90 days, Moi consolidated his position by courting various KANU branch leaders and winning them to his side. At the end of the period, there was not a single candidate who came out to vie for the presidency. Moi was elected unopposed.

Chapter 11

At the Helm of the Civil Service

As was widely anticipated, there were many changes in government and in the civil service with the entry of the new Moi regime. Personnel were laid off and new ones appointed. This was to be expected as many of Kenyatta's people had to be retired so that Moi could create his own structures within the administration.

One of the tasks Moi had to undertake was the selection of a Vice President and this presented a dilemma for him. He was aware that many powerful Kikuyu were not comfortable with his presidency, therefore, in order to appease them, Moi felt he had to choose a Kikuyu as his deputy. He had promised Kenyans that he would follow Kenyatta's footsteps (*Nyayo*), although he never explained precisely what he meant by this statement.

Moi first used the word '*Nyayo*' during the memorial service that was held before the burial of Kenyatta. He praised Kenyatta and said that, in honour of the first President, and in the interest of the nation, he would follow the footsteps of the departed. He wanted people to know that he was not going to make any radical changes and that there would be continuity and stability. He may have been reassuring the Kikuyu, but the main point was that he wished to assure everyone that the change at the top would not interfere with the running of the government.

There were two people being considered for the post of Vice President, Julius Gikonyo Kiano and Mwai Kibaki. It was Moi's prerogative to select whoever he wished as his deputy, but he conferred with a group of his many and varied friends, myself included, over the matter. After some consultation, it was concluded that Kibaki was the better choice. Kiano was somewhat too political and partisan but Kibaki was a moderate who removed himself from political intrigue and avoided controversy. Since Moi needed a Vice President who would be loyal to him, Kibaki was considered the better of the two.

I enjoyed working with Kibaki while he was in the Ministry of Finance, and later as Vice President. He avoided controversies, intrigue and petty squabbles. He had no interest in recognition just for the sake of it, nor was he greedy for power. If he ever had such ambition, it was not apparent. This made him an exceptional legislator, in fact, virtually the antithesis of the common politician, and made him a most interesting man.

Moi's election was another turning point in my long life in the civil service.

On 25 September 1979, slightly over a year after Kenyatta's death, President Moi appointed me as Head of Civil Service.

Moi knew me well and we were friends and neighbours, but this was not what brought about my promotion. This fact is quite simply verified by looking at my record. Firstly, I had vast experience in the Civil Service, having risen through the ranks from 1955 onward. Secondly, I was already holding a senior position when I was appointed, and finally I had already worked in an acting capacity as deputy to Duncan Ndegwa and Geoffrey Kariithi, the previous holders of the office. If the selection was done in terms of merit, then I can say I truly did deserve it. Furthermore, Moi and I had been working together in the National Security Committee and therefore he knew my strengths and weaknesses when he promoted me.

There was another somewhat intriguing factor of history repeating itself as concerns my promotion. Ndegwa, who had been the first head of the Civil Service, had been two years ahead of me at Alliance High School. Kariithi, his successor, had been one year ahead of me. We had followed each other through high school and the same happened in Makerere. After all these coincidences, it did not sound farfetched to say that I was a natural successor to the position after Kariithi's retirement.

A most embarrassing thing happened on my appointment and I still flinch when I remember it. The day was 25 September 1979. President Moi had called me and informed me that the announcement of my appointment to the post would be made at 1 o'clock on the Voice of Kenya.

Kariithi was a level-headed and decent man and had been my mentor in school, in the university and in the civil service, but for some time Moi had been under pressure to appoint his own Head of Civil Service, and everyone, including Kariithi himself, knew it was just a matter of time before he was shown the door. Kariithi had already put in a letter requesting permission to retire, prior to this episode, but Moi had not accepted it.

Therefore, in order to avoid the embarrassment that would result when the announcement of my promotion was made, I decided to take off for an early lunch.

In those days, many senior government officials in Nairobi, especially those in the civil service, used to take their meals either at Bacchus Restaurant in the New Stanley or at Red Bull. I made my way out of my office in Ulinzi House, drove into the city centre and then went to the office of my friend, Deputy Public Prosecutor James Karugu in Sheria House, where I parked my car. We usually had lunch together on weekdays. It was a sunny afternoon and I had a feeling of excitement in my heart, knowing that in a short time I would be the Head of Civil Service. It was a great surprise, and I had not yet told anyone, not even Karugu who was at my side as we walked towards Red Bull.

Under such circumstances, fate has a way of playing tricks on us. As we sat down at our table in Red Bull, we were joined by Joe Koinange, then Dean of Students at Kenyatta University, and by Kariithi, who was the last person I wanted to see at the time. He normally did not have lunch with us so it was purely coincidental that he changed his routine that day and came to the restaurant, instead. He looked quite happy and relaxed as he joined us.

We ordered and ate our meal and chatted idly. After we had finished our lunch, we started on our way back to our offices and my embarrassment began. As soon as we stepped onto the street outside the restaurant, people who knew me, started coming over to shake my hand.

"Congratulations," one of them said.

Pretending not to know what he was talking about I asked, "Congratulations for what?"

"Haven't you heard? You have been appointed Head of Civil Service!"

The news seemed to stun Kariithi, who stood not more than a foot away, and I knew how he must have felt. Having served diligently for all those years, he had not even been made aware that he was about to be retrenched and replaced by his former deputy.

The situation became more difficult as we walked back to Sheria House. Everyone congratulated me. I was intensely embarrassed and it felt like the longest walk of my life. Of course, it was much worse for Kariithi, I am sure.

When Kariithi and I finally got back to our respective offices, I did not know what to say to him. I sat at my desk in a daze.

After some few minutes, he called me into his office and congratulated me. He was gracious and clearly understood my mortification.

"Do not worry, Jerry. These things can happen to anybody," he said.

I could only thank him. He had been a good boss and mentor, and I hoped I could accomplish the tasks ahead of me as well as he had. Later, I occasionally met Kariithi at board meetings, but we did not see each other often.

When he officially handed over to me, I started my tenure as the third African Head of the Kenya Civil Service. There was little new in my duties in that post. Since I had often deputised for the two previous Heads, I was well-aware of what was expected of me. My first years in the post were enjoyable, and I took pleasure in what I was doing.

Naturally enough, not everybody in government or politics was happy with my promotion. Much of this resentment was based on ethnic bigotry. Some politicians went to Moi and hinted that he had made a mistake by appointing a Kikuyu to such a senior position. They informed Moi that Kenyatta had always had a Kikuyu in the position of Head of Civil Service and therefore Moi should appoint a person from his own community as well. They wondered why he had appointed a Kikuyu, yet it had been the Kikuyu who had tried so hard to keep him out of the presidency. Nevertheless, Moi did not change his mind and, after some time, those who were not pleased at my selection had to live with the fact.

When I was appointed, Moi instructed me to create a job of Deputy Head of Civil Service, and thereafter Simeon Nyachae became my deputy. In turn, he became the Head of Civil Service after my retirement in 1984, but he was replaced after serving for about 18 months. I understand that this short period of service was due to the same type of political interference that plagued my time in office.

To get back to Moi, however, it was necessary for him to create his own personal stamp of authority as a president if he expected to govern well. Kenyatta, fortunately, had not needed to do so because, at independence, he was already well known and recognised by Kenyans as their leader and liberator. Kenyatta had been almost revered by Kenyans (although this admiration gradually started to erode towards the end of his reign) and he was respected by those who worked under him. Moi did not have any of these advantages, and had to demonstrate that he could come out from behind Kenyatta's shadow and be his own man. He was surrounded by sceptics and therefore had to prove that he had the ability to rule.

He was kind but somewhat unforgiving man. There are a great many examples of moments when he abruptly hardened his attitude towards his friends. One only needs to look at the case of Charles Njonjo. Njonjo had made immense sacrifices in his support of Moi, but he was later labelled a traitor, *'Msaliti'*, for no apparent reason. I do not know whether Njonjo had underhand motives for his actions or not, but it seemed as though Moi may have used him merely to consolidate his power.

* * *

There are questions that I am frequently asked, by people who would like to know more about the functions of the Head of Civil Service. What does he do on a daily basis? Who is he answerable to, and what exactly is his mandate?

Briefly, civil servants are employed in various ministries and in each particular ministry, they are all answerable to the Permanent Secretary. In turn, all permanent secretaries are answerable to the Head of Civil Service.

Through this structure, the Head of Civil Service supervises all the work done by the ministries through the permanent secretaries. They, in turn, formulate policies on the needs of their ministries and these reports are reviewed with the Head of Civil Service, in order to assure harmony in policy formulation.

I had the brief of updating the Head of State on all matters concerning the civil service and I was responsible for all matters pertaining to discipline, welfare, remuneration and other general issues.

It is the prerogative of the President to appoint the permanent secretaries. The President might consult the Head of Civil Service on the suitability of various candidates, and at other times, he might act on his own.

The Head of Civil Service initiates the action and going by merit and experience, evaluates and gives suggestions to the President. As such, I would be consulted on appointments to various state corporations and parastatals. However, the President would make all final decisions. For more junior positions, the permanent secretaries would propose the names for appointment to the posts under them.

The Head of Civil Service is also Secretary to the Cabinet. He is the one who is charged with the task of preparing an agenda and setting out the papers to be discussed in every Cabinet meeting after receiving them from the various permanent secretaries. Before a Cabinet meeting, the Secretary to the Cabinet has to sit with the President and explain the contents of each paper so that the President will go to the meeting fully prepared and with an understanding of the issues. The Head of Civil Service prepares the agenda and ensures that all the ministers have it in reasonable time prior to the meeting. In simple terms, the Head of Civil

Service does the duties that any secretary would do when there is a board meeting, that is, notify the board of the meeting, prepare the paperwork, liaise with the chairman of the board and ensure that the meeting goes on in an orderly manner.

After the Cabinet meeting, he will then liaise with the permanent secretaries of all ministries in order to ensure that the policies decided on by the Cabinet are implemented.

The Head of Civil Service briefs the President on how the ministries are running. If there is famine in a certain part of the country, he will receive suggestions from the administrators on what action should be taken and will discuss this with the President. If the Cabinet approves, the Head of Civil Service will work with the concerned ministries, say the Ministry of Agriculture and the Ministry of Special Programmes, to ensure that food reaches the people affected. If a certain PS does not measure up to the task, the President will sack him and the Head of Civil Service will sign the sacking letter.

The post of Head of Civil Service is vital, and the conduct and decisions taken as a result of his advice can have far-reaching consequences. Some ministers were not comfortable with this centre of influence, but they were powerless to do anything about it. I had my fair share of tiffs with ministers, but I always tried to resolve them amicably. On occasion, politicians did not fully appreciate that every position in the civil service had a job description and that one had to stick to the rules.

I once clashed with politicians on the completion of a government building. A particular ministry had just finished the construction of its headquarters on Haile Selassie Avenue in Nairobi. An Israeli company had been contracted to do the construction and, when the building was complete, some elements in the ministry connived with its officials so that the company would be granted the lucrative tender to furnish all the new offices.

Some ministry officials informed me that the deal to furnish the offices reeked of corruption. First, the company's quotation was not the lowest and second, it was a construction company and did not deal with furniture.

I went to the President and explained the danger of granting the furniture tender to the Israeli company without going through the normal procedures. Moi shared my view, and the decision to award the tender to the company was overruled. The minister involved knew that I had influenced this decision and he was infuriated. During the following Cabinet meeting, he made the offhand remark that if anyone wanted to know the details of what had been discussed in a particular Cabinet meeting, all he had to do was to have a drink at the Public Service Club in the evening.

At that time, in addition to my government post, I was also the Chairman of the Public Service Club. It did not take a nuclear scientist to understand that I was being accused of leaking secrets. I was furious. I knew he was inferring that I was the one who leaked the minutes of Cabinet meetings. This was an outrageous allegation and a serious one because no member of the Cabinet was supposed to announce the deliberations of meetings.

I demanded that the minister substantiate the allegation or withdraw. He did not do so and there was a standoff. Although the minister did not withdraw formally, the President played it down and no such allegation was ever repeated. Afterwards another minister told me, "Sometimes you get too angry."

Perhaps the person who made the accusation was just joking, or perhaps he tried to turn it into a joke when he realised I was upset about it, but I felt it was too serious a matter to just ignore.

However, had Moi chosen to do so, he could have sacked anyone revealing details of Cabinet meetings because such revelation would have been in breach of our oath.

Owing to the nature of my position, I had to keep in touch with the President at all times. I was always within reach, either in my office or at home. In those days, there were no car phones or mobile phones so I had a large radiophone in the boot of my car, which meant I could call or receive phone calls from the President, even when I was on the road. Wherever he was travelling, say to America or Europe, I would be able to discuss matters with him using that cumbersome radiophone. I also had direct telephone lines to the President's office in State House and to his homes in Kabarak and Nairobi so that I could contact him at any time during a crisis or an emergency.

I travelled out of the country with the President several times. However, after a few security issues cropped up back home when we were abroad together, we decided that this was a risk that was not worth taking. In the event of an emergency, the Vice President would manage the political angle of things, but if we travelled together, due to the nature of our positions, there would be no one to look after the civil service, that is, the executive side. The President and I then decided that it was inadvisable to travel out of the country together.

Those were the days when coup attempts were the order of the day on the continent and by remaining behind, I ensured that everything was in order, despite the absence of the President. This arrangement worked well and, when the President was away, the smooth administration of the government never faltered. Moi knew that I had no political ambitions and, therefore, he trusted me.

There was one interesting story surrounding one of the trips that we made together. The President, accompanied by a large delegation, went to Washington DC, to seek donor funds. When we arrived, the President went to stay in Blair House, where senior state guests are accommodated. The rest of us stayed in hotels in the city. Everything seemed fine that evening, but when we woke up the following morning, the *Washington Post* had huge headlines, "Beggars Arrive in Concorde!"

We were terribly embarrassed and the President was appalled. Nonetheless, everyone we met was tactful and none of the American officials mentioned the matter to us. It was as though it had never happened.

I think we were wrong to make such an entrance. Perhaps the choice of Concorde and the large size of the delegation were not well advised. It should be remembered, however, that the government is not a one-person organisation. The President had his own group of people with whom he liked to travel. He did not require anyone's advice on who he should or should not take. For many in the entourage, it was prestigious just to be seen with the President. The President, in turn, gained considerable support from different parts of the country, depending on whom he had taken.

Unfortunately, some of the delegates did not have enough background or experience to contribute to the discussions. A number of them did not even grasp the significance of arriving in a Concorde.

The size of the entourage itself would not have been so embarrassing if each individual had been capable of fully participating. For example, if 60 delegates went to Washington to talk to their business counterparts and exchange contacts, that would have been most useful. On the other hand, taking 60 people who do not even own a kiosk, was a total waste.

Nevertheless, if anyone had tried to go to the President to advise him not to take so and so, he would have been treading on dangerous ground and, of course, the President would know immediately that the person did not know or understand anything about politics.

The President blamed our ambassador for the embarrassing headlines in the newspaper. Moi felt that the ambassador should have had enough information in advance and advised the *Washington Post* not to print such a story. He was obviously unaware of the way the Press operated in America.

* * *

In 1980, the Cabinet and the President decided to change the long-standing title of Permanent Secretary, Head of Civil Service and Secretary to the Cabinet, which is the one I held, to Chief Secretary. The mandate of the position meant that the person holding the post was similar to a Minister and the President could allocate certain departments to him.

Some Members of Parliament (MPs) felt that it was excessively influential. For example, Hon. Peter Habenga Okondo queried the change of the title. He informed MPs that they were creating a powerful monster that held the powers of a Prime Minister.

"We are lucky that Kiereini is not a power hungry man. Just think of what would happen if this post was given to someone with greed for power," Okondo said in Parliament.

Chapter 12

Crushing the 1982 Coup Attempt

The most daring attempt to overthrow the Kenya government occurred in 1982. The government was well aware that a few Kenya Air Force men were disaffected and were planning a coup d'état. Apparently, a number of airmen from the Luo community were discontented and complained that they were being overlooked while their colleagues from the Kikuyu community were promoted simply because the Air Force Commander, General Peter Mwagiru Kariuki, was a Kikuyu.

They complained that the Luo were discriminated against and decided, rather naïvely, that the best way to rectify the situation was to overthrow Moi's government. They reasoned that by taking over the government, the Luo community would take its 'rightful' place in governing the country.

Unfortunately for them, they made quite a number of strategic errors in their conspiracy. The first error was that the rebellion was planned at a low level and not a single senior officer in the Air Force was directly involved. The plotters were virtually powerless because they did not have the necessary resources, either material or intellectual, nor sufficiently wide support within the Armed Forces to stage a successful mutiny.

The chief architects of the coup were, among other junior officers, Senior Private Hezekiah Ochuka and Sergeant Pancras Oteyo Okumu. However, Joseph Ogidi Obuon was the one who was first known to intelligence sources as the main organiser of the affair. The manner in which they carried out the recruitment of sympathisers among their colleagues was so sloppy that by early 1982, the Kenyan intelligence services, including the Special Branch and military intelligence, knew precisely what the perpetrators were planning. They used the Kenya Air Force to infiltrate the plotters.

After some time, intelligence sources informed the authorities that the plotters had moved forward the date of their attempt and that the time had come for the government to step in and stop further activities. It was felt that the rebels had little chance of succeeding due to their lack of sufficient support. A decision was therefore made to arrest the rebels and charge them in a civilian court.

Military authorities felt that handing over the plotters to civilian authorities like the CID and Special Branch would be scandalous as it would cast an unacceptably bad image on the loyalty of the Armed Forces. Such an action would portray the Armed Forces as lax or disloyal to the Commander in Chief. Military intelligence advised their Chief of General Staff that they had the power to charge these plotters in a court martial and the President accepted this advice.

A decision was made that the Commander of the Air Force would convene a court martial to try the rebels.

In order to convene a court martial, military authorities were required to have a complete dossier on the crimes. The task of compiling this dossier was given to Air Force Commander General Kariuki, since the rebels were among his men. However, there was a certain amount of delay in compiling the dossier, perhaps because it was believed that the coup planners would not launch their attack any time soon.

While I was away on official duty in London, an Agricultural Society of Kenya (ASK) show was held in Nyeri. At the showgrounds, General Kariuki was called aside by Chief of General Staff Jackson Mulinge, who inquired why he had not yet arrested the coup plotters and arraigned them before a court martial as planned. Kariuki replied that he had not yet received sufficient information from General Mulinge's Intelligence services or the Special Branch to compile a watertight dossier. Mulinge then informed him that the court martial should proceed anyway, based on the information already at hand, and Kariuki stated that he would initiate the process the following Monday.

Later that day, Kariuki headed for Nanyuki, where he had some farming interests. He stopped off at Nanyuki Air Base Officers' Mess and was talking with other senior officers when an intelligence official entered. He asked if he could have a word with General Kariuki, but was not well received. Kariuki resented being disturbed during his weekend break and was terse and impatient with the young officer.

When Kariuki asked the officer what he wanted, he was told that 'it' would happen that night. Kariuki then dismissed him, telling the officer that he was already aware of the fact.

Only General Kariuki can explain what he meant.

I learned about this conversation much later. I was supposed to return to Kenya on a Sunday, but I completed my duties in the USA earlier than expected and decided to fly back on Saturday instead. After I arrived home and rested, I briefly went to the Public Service Club, to catch up with the latest news. A while later I returned home.

The coup attempt took place that night.

At exactly 1 am, I received a call from Special Branch Chief James Kanyotu. He informed me that there was some trouble at Embakasi Air Force Barracks and that the coup attempt seemed to have kicked off. He further told me that the rebels were on their way to Nairobi city centre. He kept phoning, alerting me of the latest events as they occurred, although the information available was still scanty. The first person I attempted to phone was President Moi. I was aware he was in Kabarak, but I could not get through to him. I tried phoning General Mulinge but I could not get him either. Neither could I get through to Army Commander General John Sawe or the Air Force Commander General Kariuki.

As we later discovered, the rebels had disconnected most of the phone lines at the telephone exchange and thus no telephone calls or faxes could be made outside Nairobi. Some areas within the city were affected as well.

Fortunately, I finally managed to get in touch with the Police Commissioner, Ben Gethi, who was at his home on Limuru Road. The rebellion was shocking but we could not afford to panic. At around 4 am, after some consideration, I phoned both Gethi and Kanyotu and informed them that we should move to a central location at Nairobi Police Headquarters, so that we could be together to coordinate the government's decisions and actions.

I therefore left Karen in an attempt to rendezvous with the others. I took my wife's small car, a Datsun 120 Y, and dressed in ordinary clothes in order to remain inconspicuous. I said goodbye to my wife and decided to make my way to whatever fate awaited me. I then instructed my driver, an ex-Administration Policeman called Njeru, to carry my gun and informed him that I would drive. I had no alternative but to follow my instincts on where to turn or when to stop because I had no idea what I would find on the way.

I could have chosen to stay at home and hide, finding one excuse or another to explain my absence from the scene. However, I felt it was my duty as a servant of the country to do my part in protecting the government I had vowed to serve. I was the highest placed member of the government in Nairobi at the time and it was my responsibility to take charge. Therefore, I put my trust in God and began to drive to Nairobi city centre.

I drove without incident all the way to Nairobi Club where I noticed that there were only a few vehicles still moving along, so I stopped to assess the situation. Many cars were abandoned on the kerb on both sides of the road. From the hill where I was, I could see ruddy beams of light glowing above the city centre, which obviously originated from the gunfire I heard below me. My intention had been to join Haile Selassie Avenue and then look for a short route to Vigilance House on Harambee Avenue, but now I saw that such actions would be foolhardy.

I turned on a lane near Mara Road and drove to the Public Service Club. At that time of night, the Club House was closed, however I knew there was a phone booth just outside it. Fortunately the phone was in order but I nearly despaired when I realised I did not have a 50-cent coin to put in the slot. I approached the guard at the gate and asked him if he would give me 50 cents and fortunately, he had that vital coin and handed it over. At the time, that 50-cent piece felt like a million shillings.

I placed a call to Vigilance House, and I got Gethi who had already arrived. I believe he had been escorted there by the GSU. I informed him of my situation and he warned me not to attempt the drive to town. Instead, he advised me to drive to the Traffic Police Headquarters, which was located in a building next to Kenyatta National Hospital, and wait there for a police escort.

When I arrived at the Traffic Headquarters, I found Munene Muhindi, who was the Provincial Police Officer in charge of Nairobi, together with the Provincial Commissioner, Fred Waiganjo.

I waited at the Traffic Headquarters until a platoon of GSU officers arrived in three Land Rovers. We confirmed that they had been sent by Gethi, and thereafter I climbed into the second of the three vehicles, while Muhindi and Waiganjo remained behind. I got into the front seat and sat in the middle. All three Land Rovers then drove slowly to Haile Selassie Avenue roundabout, where we were flagged down by a contingent of armed insurgents.

I looked around and for the first time actually saw what was going on. There were dead bodies on the road and naked people being herded around by uniformed Air Force soldiers. I noticed that many of the mutineers looked and acted as though they were drunk. There was pandemonium, a great amount of shouting and the sound of gunfire from many directions. The Air Force rebels were shooting at random. One of the mutineers approached our vehicle and stopped at the driver's door, glaring at us.

"Who is this?" the soldier asked the driver, pointing at me.

At this juncture, I had little hope that I could escape. I was the Head of Civil Service in the government they wished to overthrow, and I was aware of the fate of senior government officials when military coups occurred. It had happened in Liberia and other places. I feared summary execution, or worse.

Confidently, the GSU driver evaded the question and answered, "We are on duty."

Despite my state, I was impressed and somewhat amazed by his courage.

"On duty?" asked the soldier, as my heart pounded.

The driver nodded, and the soldier grinned. He gave us thumbs up and flagged us off. I have to confess that this was the most frightening moment of my life and I would never wish anyone to go through the scare I had that night. I was a hair's breadth from death and I was shaken, but I had to go on.

From there we managed to drive to Vigilance House, where the Police Headquarters are located, without further questioning. We remained exceedingly alert and wary of the gunfire and chaos all around us.

It was then around 5 am on Sunday morning, and on arrival, I met Police Commissioner Ben Gethi, and Harrison Musau, who was a Senior Deputy Commissioner of Police. We knew that the Air Force rebels were scattered all over the city. They had been arriving from their base at Embakasi where the action had started. I was still trying to get the President on the phone and at last, around 6.30 am, I managed to get through, at which point he informed me that he was already in a safe place. I briefed him on what was happening and what we were doing and thereafter we kept in close touch.

We later learnt that at dawn, Air Force jets had flown in from Nanyuki, had dropped several bombs on Nairobi and then immediately returned.

The bombs were dropped on sections of Muthaiga, near the residences of Vice President Mwai Kibaki and Attorney General Charles Njonjo. We never knew whether it was the two individuals who were targeted or whether the mutineers were acting at random. All the same, these were very senior members of government and it would not be farfetched to speculate that they might have been targets of the rebels. Neither of them was hurt, though, nor was any other civilian injured by these particular bombs.

At the Police headquarters, we were facing a difficult predicament. Many of the officers in the Kenya Army were away. They had been training in Turkana, and, although they were now on their way back to Nairobi, most of them had not yet arrived. If they had been in the city, we knew we could depend on them to overcome the Air Force rebels. Nonetheless, we had to make an immediate decision on what actions had to be taken and therefore decided to utilise the GSU as our major force of attack. By this time, we had already phoned Army Commander General Sawe in his house.

We were fortunate that there were also a few loyal Army soldiers who had been left behind in Lang'ata and Kahawa, either because of illness or to maintain the station and we managed to muster this group to join the GSU force. We also managed to contact Major-General Mahmood Mohammed, and he led the few remaining army soldiers.

The Air Force insurgents had occupied Broadcasting House, where the Voice of Kenya (VoK) station was located along Harry Thuku Road. They were broadcasting propaganda announcements. The rebels had captured VoK at 4.30 am and at 6.10 am, their leader, Hezekiah Ochuka, forced broadcaster Leonard Mambo Mbotela to announce that the military was now in charge of the government, that Parliament had been disbanded and that all Cabinet Ministers were relieved of their duties. Through Mbotela, Ochuka and Okumu instructed the police to regard themselves as civilians and stay in their stations.

Speaking in Kiswahili, Mbotela said, "... a curfew is on and movement from one area to another is forbidden, for at this time the government is in the hands of the Armed Forces. The police are informed that they are to assume the roles of civilians until they are informed otherwise."

Okumu himself added, in a voice that was not very clear, "... a curfew has been declared and people are advised to stay indoors. All the borders with our neighbouring countries have been closed until further notice. Thank you."

The rebels simultaneously incited University of Nairobi students to demonstrate on the streets to show their solidarity and support for the removal of the 'corrupt' government, and the students did exactly that. The rebels actually went so far as to commandeer city buses and used them to bring in more students and looters.

In those days, student awareness and activism was at an exceptional pinnacle and they would take to the streets to protest against almost anything, no matter how trivial. On the morning of 1 August, the streets of Nairobi were teeming with Air Force mutineers, students and looters all shouting, "Power! Power!"

"Power!" was the slogan that Ochuka's men used as they created pandemonium throughout the city and it is regrettable that, apart from the rebels, the majority of the looters were students. Luckily, not many people had come to the city centre that Sunday morning.

We conferred with the Ministry of Defence headquarters and came to the decision that the best-placed troops to attack the rebels at VoK were the available army soldiers. Therefore, under the command of Mohammed, they surrounded the station. Quickly and efficiently, the mutineers were either killed or captured, and VoK was returned to government hands by 10 am on Sunday. In the battle for VoK, 70 Air Force rebels were killed, but there were no army casualties. The Nakuru-based 3rd Battalion also arrived in Nairobi around that time and quickly took over Eastleigh Airbase, while the Gilgil-based Support Battalion and Nanyuki's 1st Battalion took over Nanyuki Airbase.

The rapid recovery that followed clearly demonstrates the extremely weak and ineffectual organisation the rebels had attempted to put in place. The *Daily Nation*, in an editorial a few days after the coup, summed up the hopelessness and incompetence of the mutineers by stating, "... the coup plotters were amateurish to the extreme, ideologically and politically naïve ... wild and undisciplined gangsters." Nearly everyone agreed with this assessment.

The massive looting in Nairobi led to losses, which were later estimated to be over one billion shillings. For a few hours, Nairobi had been under siege, and anarchy reigned. Fortunately, the uprising was incredibly brief.

Ochuka had called his initiative 'The August One Revolution' supposedly spearheaded by the Kenya's People's 'Redemption Council'. Ochuka was 29 years old, a private in the Air Force, while Okumu was 33. Neither was highly educated, and both had limited military experience. The inspiration for their juvenile attempt remains unknown but they may have been motivated by the actions of Liberian soldier Samuel Doe, who took power through a similar coup at the age of 27. Whatever the case, the coup's failure was predetermined due to inadequate planning, immature leadership, pitiable preparation, and a host of other catastrophes. It later brought about significant ramifications, especially in the manner in which Moi ran his government in the years to come.

Where the rebels got the conviction that the army would join them, it is not known.

Using the intelligence we had gathered, we determined that the coup attempt had been quashed and, therefore, we could securely pronounce to the public that the President was safe and in charge and that everything was being done to restore the normal order of things. This was about midday and already the phone lines had quickly been reconnected. I drafted my announcement on a sheet of paper while at police headquarters and since it was only about a paragraph, I then called the President and read it to him for his approval. After he had listened, he told me to make it public, so we then called VoK and arranged for the broadcast. I was able to make the announcement over the phone while still at the Police headquarters.

The Army organised an escort for President Moi on his journey from Nakuru to Nairobi. He finally arrived at around 5pm that same day, and we all met in State House. He seemed quite shocked. We briefed him on the events and on the information we had gathered up to that point. He then made an official announcement over national radio and television at 7 pm in which he urged people to be calm and assured them that order had been restored. He also declared a dusk to dawn curfew in Nairobi and Nanyuki.

That must have been the longest day of my life. For more than 24 hours, Ben Gethi, Kanyotu, myself and others who were coordinating the battle did not eat a single morsel of food. Who among us would have found time to be hungry? I felt that we had all made a supreme effort and personal sacrifice to save our country from sliding into anarchy. I regard the endeavour we put in that day to restore stability in Kenya, high on the list of my achievements in the civil service.

However, President Moi's statement assuring the nation that order had been restored had some comical results. A number of people took his statement quite literally, concluding that everything was normal and decided to return to their usual routines the next day. One of my friends, Mutu wa Gethoi, actually decided to drive his wife to work and then proceeded to his own office in the industrial area. On the way, they decided to pass through town first, to see the after-effects of the coup. Imagine his surprise when he saw soldiers everywhere, people with their hands up, and showing their identification cards. He was shocked but continued driving as though everything was normal.

Another friend of mine, Joe Koinange, heard my announcement that the government was in control and decided to drive from Limuru into Nairobi, with his wife, again to see what all the fuss had been about. At Roysambu, they were alarmed to find the road blocked by fierce looking soldiers with guns. When they were challenged, they just turned and frantically drove away in a panic.

Then there was David Namu, a Deputy Secretary, who decided to return to work in Harambee House. The first thing he saw as he entered the gate was a dead body of a soldier with a gun still in his hands. He and his wife just ran away and he did not return to work until we called him.

At any rate, for about two weeks, the army was in charge of Nairobi. The military have a different attitude from the police. Whereas the police are trained in how to handle the public, the army tends to be more action-oriented, and perhaps they are not quite as patient with civilians.

The GSU deserve extraordinary mention in the history books for their actions to repel the Air Force mutineers that day. They fought valiantly under the command of Ben Gethi and managed to overcome the rebels speedily and with minimum civilian casualties, while they waited for the army to return to Nairobi.

Later investigations showed that most of the civilian casualties that occurred were caused by the Air Force insurgents, who in a drunken stupor, shot indiscriminately in the havoc they had started. Within those hours, the Air Force rebels had been overcome and dispersed while only some minor sporadic fighting continued.

After that, we were made aware that Ochuka and Okumu had commandeered an Air Force plane and fled to Tanzania, where they were arrested on arrival. When they were charged in a Tanzanian court with hijacking, the duo did not concern themselves with a defence. Instead, they utilised the courtroom as a platform to boast about their attempt to overthrow the Kenya Government. Ochuka went so far as to disclose that, for some hours, he had been referred to as 'Your Excellency' by Air Force mutineers wherever he encountered them.

Ochuka and Okumu were extradited to Kenya about a year later and were tried on the grounds of treason and sentenced to hang. Ogidi was jailed for 20 years. In 1985, Ochuka and Okumu were hanged at Kamiti Maximum Security Prison.

As for General Kariuki, he was subsequently arrested and charged in court with negligence of duty and complicity in the attempted coup. He was jailed for four years.

I have explained the events surrounding the attempted 1982 coup d'état in detail because it was the most stressful and challenging moment in my life in the Civil Service. I will never forget the tension, the turmoil, the uncertainty, the fear and, ultimately, the triumph that surrounded those of us who were involved in the effort to obstruct and overcome the insurgents. This rebellion was to have a profound effect on the nation, and in my life.

* * *

Were it not for the fatalities and losses, the 1982 coup attempt could be seen as a farcical venture; however, it had profound implications for the future of this country. Overnight, the lives of many Kenyans changed, some with almost insignificant details and others with major consequences. Those in the Air Force and those in high-ranking positions in government felt the most profound effects. The Air Force rebels were prosecuted and sentenced to jail terms and the Kenya Air Force was renamed the "82 Air Force". Up to date, the Air Force has not regained its second position in the military; it now comes third, after the Army and Navy.

A committee to review the salaries of the Armed Forces was appointed. Moi wished to prevent a recurrence of such an incident and we strongly supported him in this endeavour.

However, the deepest and most noteworthy transformation was in Moi's personality and this change had an avalanche effect on all those in senior government positions.

Moi had believed that the affairs of the nation had been going well and that people liked him. The attempted coup, therefore, made it difficult for him to understand how or why the Air Force had been plotting to take over. He had been quite tolerant of differing opinions and had visions for the future of the Kenya nation, but after this incident, his character changed to become almost unrecognisable. Suddenly, he began imagining enemies everywhere. He became paranoid and suspected any person whom he felt might have a motive to act against his presidency.

I believe he may have started questioning himself, as well. Perhaps he wondered if he had been misinformed or misunderstood, and he took it extremely seriously. I had never seen him in that mood before. All along, Moi had believed he was doing the right thing for the country. After all, he had taken over in 1978 and run the government for about four years, and everything he did was for the nation and for the people. Therefore, when the rebellion came up, contradicting his own beliefs, he had great difficulty accepting it. He just could not see anything he might have done, which could have resulted in a coup attempt. The fact that the rebels had been joined by civilians was especially difficult for him to understand. He became reticent and distrustful.

The coup attempt was followed by stories and rumours. The non-Kikuyu believed that Njonjo and Ben Gethi, among others, were to blame. Communication became less open. There was a great deal of misinformation going around the country and as a result, although I was never mentioned, it seemed that Moi was no longer comfortable to discuss matters with me. I am fairly sure he never doubted my loyalty but things were never the same between us.

Moi stopped relying on official channels and there was clear evidence that he started listening to diverse sources. I recall that later, around 1985, when Hezekiah Oyugi was in charge of internal security, he formed his own security forces and special DOs were posted all over the country. The Special Branch was renamed the National Security Intelligence Service. Many other institutions were re-named, for example Voice of Kenya (VoK), became Kenya Broadcasting Corporation (KBC), and the Air Force, as mentioned earlier, became the '82 Air Force'.

A few days after the coup attempt, Koigi Wamwere, the fiery former legislator for Subukia, Raila Odinga and George Anyona among others who had voiced discontent with Moi's leadership, were detained. Moi was not taking any chances. Other discontents like James Orengo, the radical legislator for Ugenya, and other individuals had their passports confiscated. Those who had previously differed with Moi were now prime targets for detention and prosecution. More than ever before, the Public Security Act, which permitted detention without trial, was applied.

Poor Ben Gethi! The Police Commissioner who coordinated the counter-attack in Vigilance House on the night of the coup was 'retired' two weeks after the event. His position was taken over by Bernard Kiarie Njinu. I have no idea why Moi sacked Gethi, but the speculation was that Gethi's enemies alleged he was the mastermind of the coup attempt.

In my opinion, Gethi had acted in a most commendable and praiseworthy manner and it was a pity he became a casualty of the coup attempt. I knew Gethi as a friend and as a loyal public servant. He had served under me and I can vouch for his patriotism.

The manner in which he determinedly handled the counter-attack was highly professional. He never behaved in any way like a traitor. The way he conducted himself that night and the following day impressed me as the behaviour of a patriot reacting to threats to national security. I was disheartened and dumbstruck when Moi sacked Gethi and subsequently had him held in prison.

Since Gethi had staff that was loyal to him personally, it was felt that he should not be arrested at Vigilance House. Instead, I was ordered to invite him to my office and, when he left, James Kanyotu was under instructions to arrest him. This was devastating and painful, since the three of us had always been good friends. I felt very hurt. It felt like betrayal, but there was nothing I could do about it, and I believe Gethi understood that neither James nor I had an alternative.

Gethi's sacking and detention shook senior public servants to the core. We woke up to a new Moi, a Moi who could capriciously sack and detain loyal servants and friends. Gethi's detention was a warning that no one was safe, no matter how close they were to Moi. If the President could erratically penalise the man who had effectively and loyally protected his power and the nation, who was safe? I was traumatised! Like everyone else, I discovered that Moi was now operating on another tack in which anyone in authority was viewed as a potential threat or enemy.

Politicians know how to manoeuvre and cover their backs. Within days of the coup attempt, they organised mass marches all over the country to demonstrate solidarity with Moi. KANU branch leaders made a beeline for State House with hundreds of delegates to pledge and prove their loyalty. Left and right, politicians competed in this unsavoury and toadying show of allegiance. Unfortunately, these overt displays entrenched the culture of sycophancy, which stretched on into the final years of Moi's rule. Moi's obsessive and virtually psychopathic mistrust now encompassed nearly everyone and he was arbitrarily suspicious of every action taken by politicians and senior civil servants.

This state of distrust and uncertainty had an incredibly negative effect on the morale of civil servants. The axe could fall on anyone at any time. People were relieved of their positions at random, and most times, for no logical or apparent reasons. The atmosphere of fear pervaded government offices and people began looking for protection by relying on 'godfathers', even when they had perfect records.

This issue of 'protection' arose due to a number of factors. Prime among these was that Moi started dismissing people from service and detaining them at whim. When he sacked people who he imagined were disloyal, he would replace them, without rhyme or reason, with individuals whom he felt were pro-*Nyayo* and who would never betray him. Although '*Nyayo*' was first used to indicate that Moi would follow in Kenyatta's footsteps, later, he developed what was referred to as the *Nyayo* philosophy of peace, love and unity. During his rule, the word *Nyayo* became synonymous with Moi, and many of his pet projects were named *Nyayo*, for example the *Nyayo* Pioneer Car, *Nyayo* Tea Zones, *Nyayo* Milk, *Nyayo* Wards, *Nyayo* National Stadium, etc.

The erosion of trust in the civil service was exacerbated by the fact that the new 'loyalists' who filled sensitive posts were in many cases not qualified.

Morale was destroyed. A civil service in which promotions and appointments are made, not on the basis of merit, but by other criteria such as tribe, fawning obsequiousness, recommendations from the loyal confidants of the President and the like becomes a bed of worms. This is what started happening in the civil service after the coup attempt. Powerful politicians in Moi's government began interfering with the civil service, influencing appointments and compromising the professional system and its functional stability.

Just to illustrate this interference, I recall an episode that opened my eyes to just how serious this problem was. I had a junior officer known as Franklin Bett. I had enlisted Bett as my assistant because he was an intelligent and diligent young man. He was very young, having just graduated from the University of Nairobi. Bett was an exceptional, self-driven professional and he carried out assignments with little supervision.

I was thus quite surprised when, while talking with President Moi one day in his office at State House, he informed me, "Kiereini, that man in your office is not a good man."

"Which man, sir?" I asked, and he said, "Bett."

I went out of State House wondering what Bett could have done to come to Moi's attention. Bett was just a junior official, merely my personal assistant. There were many more significant, more powerful individuals in the hierarchy, yet this young man was singled out for criticism by the President himself. By telling me that Bett was a 'bad' man, Moi did not explicitly state that I should sack him, but it was obvious that he would not disapprove if I fired him. Nevertheless, I preferred to follow the rules of natural justice, not merely act on vague hints and allegations, so I decided to talk to Bett first.

When I returned to my office, I called Bett in and asked him what he had done when he went home the previous weekend, since I was aware that he had gone upcountry.

"Nothing," Bett told me. "I just went to greet my mother."

I informed him that he had come to the attention of the President, in a negative light, and then he opened up and told me what he had done.

Bett was interested in politics in his home constituency, where the MP was Isaac Salaat. Salaat was a close friend of the President. Bett, on the other hand, was a staunch supporter of Salaat's rival in the constituency, and during that weekend, he had expressed his anti-Salaat sentiments in public and Salaat had heard about it. It seemed that Bett was already influential in the constituency's politics despite his youth, and Salaat decided to clip his wings. Probably Salaat realised that he could not approach me on such a ridiculous matter, therefore he had turned to his old friend Moi to handle the situation.

I advised Bett to tread carefully since he was treading on thin ice. Politicians, I told him, could destroy his career without a second thought. When I next saw the President, I explained that, not only was Bett a young, dedicated and hardworking professional, but that Bett was from the President's own ethnic group. This seemed to placate Moi, and he never referred to the matter again. Ironically, over the years, the two became close and Bett ended up serving as Moi's State House Comptroller. At the time of writing this account, Bett had served as an Orange Democratic Movement (ODM) MP and a Cabinet Minister in President Kibaki's coalition government.

Interference by politicians intensified and discipline was, in many cases, abandoned. Many people began operating under the patronage of untouchable insiders and godfathers. Professionalism and merit disappeared and there were no longer any consequences to fear if an officer neglected his office or took undue advantage of his position of trust. A well-connected officer could be promoted at any time despite the fact that he was totally unsuitable or even engaged in illegal activities.

This preposterous system did not please me at all. I was continually frustrated in the course of my duties and I found that Moi had undergone a metamorphosis. Whereas previously we had always been straightforward with each other, he was now holding his cards close to his chest. He was doing this with everyone, not only with me; nevertheless, I found it extremely irritating. I had worked in the colonial government and then in Kenyatta's government and we in the civil service had always been guided by professional standards. These values had continued intact in the first years of Moi's rule, and all through that period I had been confident that eventually I would retire at the age of 55, satisfied that I had acted efficiently, competently and professionally. However, after the coup attempt, I began to doubt my expectations would carry through.

As Head of Civil Service, it was my duty to ensure that everyone pulled their weight and carried out their work as per regulations. There was one officer who was not performing as expected, and I felt it was necessary to discipline him. However, this officer had let it be known that he had direct connections to the President. When I asked the PS to ensure the officer was reprimanded, the PS looked me in the eye and asked, "Sir, if I get into trouble will you protect me?"

This was a shocking revelation. Like a blow, it suddenly hit me just how bad things had become. If a person with the powerful status of a PS was asking me for protection in case he stepped on the wrong toes, then the entire civil service was going to the dogs. I was flabbergasted and did not know what to tell him. If he were sacked, I would be the one handing over the letter of dismissal. I was in an uncomfortable and infuriating dilemma, unable to think clearly ahead. Throughout my career, I had never been in such an impasse before.

I approached the President and requested permission to retire. We had known each other for quite some time and I was convinced I was his personal friend so I frankly informed him that I felt the time had come for me to move on to other things. I had been his neighbour at Kabarnet Gardens for many years before we moved to our current home in Karen and I believed he would be able to understand my position. However, he flatly turned down my request, and, in order to mollify me, remarked that he would always be there to assist me, in case I ever had a problem. He said he still needed me in his government, and the matter ended there. Thus, I had no alternative but to continue with work as usual. I was neither happy nor comfortable in the civil service during that stressful period, and this dissatisfaction was further exacerbated by an event that occurred in 1983.

Moi had gone to open the Nyanza Agricultural Show in Kisii and in the opening addresses to the public, the Minister for Agriculture, Elijah Mwangale, made a puzzling and somewhat startling statement. Mwangale said that the government had discovered the existence of a *msaliti* (a traitor) within its ranks. He went on to state that the traitor's objective was to undermine the government of President Moi and eventually topple it. Mwangale, one of the most powerful minister's in Moi's government, did not reveal who the traitor was, or the source of his information.

The announcement was bewildering. It came out of the blue, so we thought, and the fact that a minister would make such a statement at such a venue was quite extraordinary. Treason was a security issue and, therefore, should have been handled by the Ministry of Internal Security and its intelligence department or by the Cabinet, certainly not by the Minister for Agriculture at a public meeting.

These broad hints of sedition were discussed everywhere, including in Parliament and in the media, and for a while, no one was able to name the traitor. It was almost as though he was a phantom, or a figment of someone's psychotic imagination. However, a short while later, allegations were made by Mwangale again, this time in Parliament and he stated that the person in question was Charles Njonjo who, at the time, was the Minister for Justice and Constitutional Affairs.

Moi had been told many things about Njonjo, about me and about the Kikuyu, so this was not a total surprise. There were various non-Kikuyu and other people in the armed forces who went to Moi alleging that Njonjo and Ben Gethi had formed a plan to take over the government. According to these stories, Njonjo was going to succeed Moi and Ben Gethi would use the GSU to ensure his success.

The theory behind all this was that the Kikuyu had supposedly been cleverly using the Luo in the 1982 coup attempt. It was felt that it would have been impossible for the Luo to engineer the 1982 coup on their own and that the Luo were merely used to exonerate the cunning Kikuyu who were actually behind it. As soon as the coup succeeded and before the rebels had a chance to consolidate their forces, there was to be a counter-coup by Njonjo and Gethi, to put the Kikuyu back in power.

A number of officers in the army believed in this theory and went to Moi with the claim, but I am sincerely convinced this was never the case. There was absolutely no truth in this allegation, at all.

One must remember that Njonjo, all through Kenyatta's time, was a powerful man. He was close to Kenyatta and close to Moi. He had always given Moi his support, for example, in the issue about "imagining the death of the President", in 1977 and 1978. Some people had even hinted about the possibility of an understanding between the two of them. It was said that after Moi completed a term as President, Njonjo would take over.

However, I personally do not think there ever was such an understanding. I did not know of any such agreement and I sincerely doubt it existed. At that time, as per the stipulation in the Constitution, the term of office for a president was continuous, and it was not limited to two terms. After all, Moi was younger than Njonjo. Frankly, I do not know if Njonjo ever had dreams of becoming President.

Therefore, with such examples of Njonjo's exactitude about the law, and his strong support of Moi, I thought it was ridiculous to suspect him of subversion.

In fact, I was shocked and regarded the allegations as outrageous and absurd. Njonjo was my close friend and a good friend of the President's. Such assertions against his character sounded far-fetched and implausible. Once again, I was taken aback at how the atmosphere in government had changed since the coup attempt. This appeared to be no more than vulgar and sickening political manipulation and gross propaganda in order to create an environment of fear and distrust throughout the nation. It was clear that no one, no matter how high his position, was now untouchable or secure from criticism or innuendo.

This issue of treason generated intense fervour, and many politicians distanced themselves from Njonjo. KANU branch leaders once again went to extremes in vilifying Njonjo and pledging their fawning loyalty to the President and the party, but Njonjo remained mum. He made no effort to go public and tell his side of the story. I believe he was shocked by the disgusting accusations, and by the overwhelming horde of persons now hysterically baying for his blood in order to 'prove' their devotion to Moi.

It was a strange situation to be in. I was in touch with Njonjo all the time and I was also Moi's Chief Secretary. Both of them seemed to have confidence in me and at no time did President Moi ever say anything against Njonjo in my presence.

When it became clear that the outrageous matter would not disappear, Njonjo immediately wrote two letters of resignation from his posts, both as MP and Cabinet Minister. He delivered the letters to me in town around 6 pm. One was addressed to the Speaker, containing his resignation as an MP, and the other to 'His Excellency', resigning as a Minister. He told me that he had decided to step aside since it seemed he had no alternative. He had been pushed into a corner and the President had abandoned him.

I understood and sympathised, but there was little I could do to help my old friend. It was entirely a political matter and I was in no position to do anything about it.

Later that evening, I went home and tried to phone President Moi to let him know about Njonjo's resignation, but no one picked up the phone. I tried several times and when I finally spoke to the President shortly after 8 pm, and told him about the letters, he asked me, "Jerry, didn't you listen to the 8 o'clock news?"

I replied that I had not.

Moi then said that it had not been necessary for Njonjo to resign. He had appointed a Commission of Inquiry to look into these allegations and thus Njonjo would not have been able to continue as an MP or as a Minister, anyway.

I was amazed! It was difficult to find words after that.

Those who were aware of the previously warm relationship between Moi and Njonjo were stunned by the unfolding events. The two had been bosom friends, and Njonjo's support and reinforcement had been crucial in Moi's succession to Kenyatta. There were those who said that were it not for Njonjo, the so-called 'Kiambu Mafia' would have never permitted Moi to ascend to the presidency and the 'Change the Constitution' matter was only one such incident. Yet here was Njonjo, insulted, humiliated, intimidated by nauseating allegations and undergoing investigation for betraying Moi.

There was considerable speculation about what led to this incident. I recall there was the Muungano choir that entertained people during presidential meetings, which actually composed a song about the *msaliti* (traitor). They used to sing this song when the ministers and VIPs were sitting on the dais. The conductor was quite dramatic and while he was conducting, he would point at the dais. This caused many people to wonder if he was pointing at some particular individual, someone who was the *msaliti*. I am not fully certain about this speculation, nonetheless, whatever the truth was, Njonjo found himself alone and indicted.

The Njonjo Commission of Inquiry consisting of Justices Cecil Miller, Effie Owuor and Chunilal B. Madan was mandated to inquire into allegations that Njonjo conducted himself in a manner prejudicial to the security of the state, the position and image of the President and Government of Kenya. The commission was asked to inquire into allegations that Njonjo was a party to a conspiracy or conspiracies to overthrow the Moi government in the 1 August 1982 abortive coup "or concealment of such conspiracy or conspiracies".

The commission was also supposed to look into allegations that Njonjo was party to the convening of the Presbyterian Church of East African prayer meeting which took place at Rungiri on 12 June "and its conversion into an irregular political gathering". During the prayer meeting, speeches were made by both clergy and laymen, which, to many observers, amounted to a political endorsement of Njonjo, over whose head a cloud of suspicion had gathered. It received immense media coverage.

People were fascinated and spellbound by the case and were baffled and stunned when the final judgement, by the Miller Commission, found Njonjo guilty of treason. However, soon after, at a public meeting at Nyayo Stadium where the President referred to the matter, Moi inexplicably announced, "But I pardon him."

That was the end of that sad circus.

Njonjo never again ran for any elective political office. He disappeared from the political scene and the public limelight for over 20 years and, even when he once more started gingerly dabbling in politics, he remained a minor player and adopted the posture of an older, civic-minded commentator. Some people regard this second entry into politics as a challenge to Mwai Kibaki.

What is peculiar and curious is that Moi and Njonjo fell out so acrimoniously, but the two still communicated. They did not converse directly, however, and I became the reluctant messenger. Both were my friends, therefore, if they wanted to communicate on some matter, one of them would send me to the other and I would return with an answer. I considered this an amusing and quaint form of interaction, but it also increased my conviction that Njonjo had been framed and that Moi had never been completely convinced of the allegations against his former friend.

Today, Njonjo and Moi have reconciled and we all remain good friends. There is the public side of things and the personal side of things. The political aspect of life disregards personal relationships and, if disagreements become too obvious, friendships break. However, if there was any idea of enmity in the mind of either Moi or Njonjo, it never was apparent. This was the case even during the inquiry. They did not meet, but if they wanted to communicate, they did so.

In my own opinion, Njonjo was and is a good man. He was by far the best Attorney General the country has ever had, and he had an excellent understanding of his duties. Although some people blame him for drafting Section 2A of the Constitution, which made Kenya a one-party state, it should be remembered that when the Bill went to the Cabinet and thereafter to Parliament, it was passed unanimously. Blaming Njonjo for Section 2A is merely shooting the messenger. I feel that no Attorney General in Kenya's history, so far, has measured up to Njonjo's stature. I personally witnessed his professional, skilled approach to issues while I worked with him during my time as the Head of Civil Service.

Another major casualty of the events that followed the 1982 coup attempt was Geoffrey Gitahi Kariuki. 'GG,' as he was known, was the Minister of State in the Office of the President. He and Moi were close and were often together at various functions. He was one of the influential Kikuyu Ministers in Moi's Cabinet, however, for inexplicable reasons, Moi sacked GG and the KANU Disciplinary Committee subsequently announced that he had been expelled (from the party) in 1983.

Chapter 13

Bowing out of Service

My last years in the civil service were frustrating. Politicians and political influence increasingly crept into the running of the government and, as time went by, they gained a stranglehold on the administration.

At one time, a politician went to President Moi and told him that I had refused to promote his relative, who was a district officer, to district commissioner. Some people had been pressurising me to promote the man, but I stood firm and refused to do so. The individual in question simply did not qualify, and I believed in promotion strictly on merit. When Moi called and asked me about it, I told him that the man was not suitable for the job. Moi agreed with me and the person did not get the promotion. However, when I finally retired in 1984, he was immediately promoted to DC. He is my friend, nowadays, and we meet often, but my conscience at the time could not allow me to promote him.

Some of my saddest moments as Head of Civil Service were when I was forced to dismiss people who, in my opinion, had done nothing wrong. At the instigation of some politicians with vested interests, the President would instruct me to fire, for example, a Permanent Secretary. The dismissal was most likely not based on questionable performance but due to personal differences or because the politician wanted a relative, friend or fellow tribesman appointed to the post.

In the beginning, the President would call me and tell me to fire an officer, but after I had considered the reason for the sacking, I would ask the President, "Sir, can I come over and talk to you about it?"

The President would acquiesce, and I would argue the victim's case. Sometimes he would listen to me, sometimes he would not. In cases where I had been instructed to dismiss a PS, for example, I would tell President Moi about the officer's strong points and his ability to serve. If he had to relinquish the post, I would suggest another posting for him, such as heading a parastatal or a state corporation. I tried my best to save many good officers from being dropped in this manner. However, after the coup attempt and when politicians started literally running the civil service from the sidelines, I became dreadfully disillusioned. At some point, the President stopped consulting me on important decisions such as dismissals and public appointments. I heard of them through announcements on the radio.

I respected Moi and I believe he also respected my advice and suggestions. He may, occasionally, have had better information than I had. However, somehow, a time came that the President changed his mind about my advice. In fact, someone directly told him that I was diluting his authority.

Previously, when the President would call me on the phone detailing the reasons a particular officer was not suitable, I would be able to ask for a chance to discuss the matter. Later, however, he would interject and change the subject, asking, "Can you come for lunch?" That happened many times when he was in Nairobi, and he did it in a friendly way.

Sometimes the President would call me over the phone and tell me, "*Jerry, andika barua, huyo mtu aende!*" ("Write a letter, that person should go!") and I would draft the note and wait for the announcement on the 1 o'clock news. It was distressing.

Once the Commissioner of Lands, James Njenga, came to see me about a disturbing trend. Some well-connected individuals from the Rift Valley had been coming to his office with notes from the President. The notes instructed Njenga to allocate plots in various towns and settlements, to the bearers. Njenga was alarmed. In some cases, two or more people would bring notes indicating that he should allocate them the same plot. Such notes were presidential instructions and Njenga had no choice but to carry them out.

In other cases, the plots that Commissioner Njenga was being instructed to allocate were public utilities and he did so against his will.

I sympathised with Njenga. During the early years of Kenyatta's rule, the Commissioner of Lands was a European called Jimmy O'Loughlin. When any person approached the commissioner to ask for an irregular land allocation, pretending that he was sent to the commissioner by Mzee, the commissioner did not hesitate to go to Kenyatta and inform him that the allocation was irregular. Kenyatta would actually listen to him and revoke the deal.

Kenyatta was such an imposing personality that few people would dare approach him in order to let him know that something he had approved was wrong or that he had not followed the correct procedures. However,

O'Loughlin managed it and he saved a lot of prime public land in the process. He was a principled man who spoke his mind.

When this type of thing happened to Njenga, I told him that I would see the President about it. Consequently, I went to State House and had a long discussion with Moi. I informed the President that he had been deceived into approving the allocations. The plots that he had given out, I told him, were public utilities for facilities such as playing grounds, public parks and toilets. If such allocations continued, soon there would be no playing grounds for the country's children. There would be no spaces for building schools and hospitals.

I explained that even during land consolidation, every settlement area had vacant spaces, which were called 'green spaces'. Now, I informed the President, all these people were taking all such plots and this meant that soon most of the towns in the Rift Valley and some parts of Nairobi would be turned into 'concrete jungles'. It would be an environmental disaster, I told him.

The President understood and instructed me to tell Njenga to cancel all the allocations. I was overjoyed, and Njenga happily cancelled hundreds of allocations and as can be imagined, we did not make any friends among the plot allottees.

I remember one particular individual whose plot allocation was cancelled. The man, Reverend Roy Apton, was an American. His church, the Pentecostal Church of Nairobi, had been allocated a prime plot along Rhapta Road in Westlands, Nairobi. President Moi used to attend services in his church (in another location) on occasion. When the allocation was cancelled, the pastor confronted Njenga and protested. Njenga in turn, told him that he had acted on my instructions.

Subsequently the pastor came to my office and demanded to know why I had cancelled the allocation. I found his attitude incredibly arrogant but merely told him I had carried out my duty since the plot allocation was irregular and he should not have got the plot in the first place.

"I will report you to President Moi," he told me.

His threatening attitude began to irritate me.

"Listen," I informed him curtly, "Moi is my President and Kenya's President. If you wish to report this matter, report it to the American President. Now get out of my office!"

I was pleased that the allocations were cancelled. People were taking over public plots with no care for the future of the communities in those areas and they had the audacity to hoodwink the President over the matter.

Unfortunately, once Njenga and I retired from the civil service, all such plots were once again allocated. Sadly, this was a common feature of the final years of Moi's rule and today we are still dealing with the consequences of this policy.

When I drive into town, I generally take a route through Rhapta Road, and I am disappointed when I see multi-storeyed buildings coming up on the public plot that had been allocated to the American pastor. The parks and vacant places for development of public facilities in Nairobi are now nearly all gone.

Another example of this lax and thoughtless attitude concerned the decision to buy planes for Kenya Airways. At one time, Kenya Airways, the national carrier, intended to modernise its fleet. New planes were to be bought, and it was up to the Cabinet to decide which ones were appropriate. The best passenger planes at the time were made by Boeing and Airbus. A consultant team was selected to assess which company was the best buy for the money. The team did not actually come to a conclusion, but stated the comparative facts, which made it obvious that the American-made Boeing was preferable.

This occurred at the end of my term as Head of Civil Service. A larger section of the people concerned in the evaluation and decision-making seemed to favour Boeing but a firm decision was not made on the first attempt. At that point, I retired and, as though I had been an obstacle in the way, a quick decision was made to select Airbus, a new performer in the market, which had not stood the test of time. The President was persuaded to go for their aircraft and he agreed. This proved to me that the politicians were now fully in control.

Another project that was passed capriciously and with total disregard for common sense was the Turkwell Gorge electricity-generating project. The project, which was to construct a power generating station on the river Turkwell, was meant to boost Kenya's power supply and to stem the overdependence on imported power from Uganda. Again, a team was selected to study the viability of the project and they recommended that it be abandoned since there was very little water in the river to make any impact on the improvement of the country's power grid. I advised the President on the findings, but due to political pressure, the project went ahead. Today, it still makes the list of one of the biggest 'white elephants' ever spawned by the Kenya Government.

Then there was the 8-4-4 system of education and its implementation. Professor Collin B. Mackay from Canada had been commissioned to study the Kenyan education system and come up with a method of improving it. At the time, the system was that students attended primary school for seven years before proceeding on to four years of secondary school. After that, they would sit their 'O' level exams and then study for two more years graduating in 'A' level examinations before joining university. The system was thus referred to as the 7-4-2 system. Prof. Mackay recommended the 8-4-4 system, where the 'A' levels would be scrapped and, after eight years in primary school and four in secondary school, students would study for four years in the university.

Prof. Joseph Mungai, who was the Vice Chancellor of the University of Nairobi, was asked to draw up a report for implementing the programme. He came up with an excellent paper and we were all impressed with his suggestions. He recommended that the system be implemented slowly and carefully, one year at a time. Primary schools would need to construct more classrooms and new syllabuses would have to be drawn up. Teachers had to be trained and books had to be written. This would ensure a smooth transition and the change had to be undertaken systematically and not haphazardly.

However, most of us were amazed when Moi decided that the system should be implemented immediately. I was taken aback, as were Basic Education Minister Jonathan Ng'eno and his Higher Education colleague, Joseph Kamotho. There would not be enough classrooms. Teachers had not been trained to handle Class 8 students and there was neither syllabus nor books published to cater for the new arrangement.

The system was implemented with ensuing bedlam, confusion and turmoil. Perhaps Moi felt the need to assert his authority as President, and this was one of the avenues he chose. The concept of evaluating and improving the education system was definitely worthwhile, but the method of implementation left a great deal to be desired. However, this was the way things were done at the time, and many of us in the civil service felt redundant, which, I suppose, is what we had become.

In 1984, Kenya was facing starvation. We asked for aid from the United States, and the American government granted us a substantial quantity of maize to feed our people. The maize was free, but the proviso was that the Kenya Government would pay the cost of freight. We expected this to go smoothly, but there were difficulties caused by some of our people in the government.

These people had got into the habit of acquiring government contracts for themselves or for their friends. They knew that acquiring a freight contract for the maize would be lucrative and attempted to manipulate the conditions so that they would be awarded the contract.

We discovered these manoeuvres and stopped them from participating in the tender. Later, we also learned that the price of shipping the maize was too costly for the Kenya Government. When I briefed the President on these factors, he instructed me to halt the transportation contract.

The tragedy of the situation was that hungry Kenyans never got the maize at all. The American government became aware of the intended graft and withdrew the offer of the maize. Those who were supposed to serve Kenyans, instead did them a great disservice.

Once again, I approached President Moi and requested to be allowed to retire. I was uneasy with the illogical and arbitrary events that were taking place, and I was sure retirement was the right thing for me.

Gethi had faced detention and Njonjo's political career was over. Both were especially close friends, and both had had the confidence of Moi before their humiliating fall from grace. I had no pretensions – I was well aware that I might be next in line to face the axe. I had served the nation as best as I could and I felt that I owed it to myself to retire with my dignity intact instead of risking the humiliation of being kicked out of service. However excellent my record as a civil servant might be, the circumstances surrounding my departure would most definitely influence the opinions of people and of history, in judging my legacy. Once again, Moi refused.

I was increasingly frustrated. As Head of Civil Service, I felt that I was no longer in control of my docket. The chain of command had broken down, there was increasing political interference, all sorts of capricious decisions were taken and I was not accustomed to kowtowing to politicians.

To make matters worse, one day in 1984, a section in Hillary Ng'weno's *Weekly Review*, which was the leading political weekly at the time, contained an exceptionally stinging article criticising me. It questioned my relevance in office and contained considerable innuendo. It gave my date of birth and other details, implicitly insinuating that my time to retire had come.

I went to the President, showed him the magazine and complained bitterly about the article. "This is engineered to embarrass me," I told him. "You have to say something about it."

Moi informed me that he would be addressing a *baraza* (public meeting) in Nairobi's Kibera slums that afternoon. He asked me to accompany him to the meeting and said he would reprimand those who were behind the article. I was pleased because I felt that this would vindicate me. However, at the meeting, Moi discussed various issues but did not even mention the piece in the magazine. Given all that had gone on before, I should have expected this and been more cynical, but instead I was quite angry and disappointed and I felt that I could not wait any longer. I knew that when wolves smell the blood of their prey, they would keep up the pursuit until it was down. This was the way I felt.

I went to Moi for a third time and declared that I wanted to retire. After all, I was 55 years old and I myself had been sending out memos reminding civil servants that the retirement age was 55. I informed Moi that I had to set an example. To my joy, Moi finally accepted my request and gave me permission to retire, in July 1984.

The President instructed me to draft my retirement letter and said he would release the statement himself. I did as he requested and on 4 July, he called me and said that he would release the announcement that day and I should listen to the 7 o'clock news. I waited quietly at home for the news and when the announcement was read, I was overjoyed that the President had kept his word. What's more, he had not changed a single word of what I had drafted and I was grateful to him for this.

That night I slept like a baby. It was one of the happiest days in my life. I had served the government for a total of 29 years, from June 1955 to July 1984. I had been through a great deal in that period, more than many of my contemporaries in the civil service and I now felt ready to take up challenges outside the government.

In fact, I was happy I retired at that particular time. Let me explain.

Before me, there had been two Heads of Civil Service.

Duncan Ndegwa served about three years, and then went on to become Governor of the Central Bank, where he stayed for 16 years. After that, he was allowed to retire and he went in peace.

Geoffrey Kariithi succeeded Duncan and served as Head of Civil Service for 13 years and I feel he did a commendable job because it was a difficult time. After serving under Moi for about one year, he realised that he and the President were likely to have conflicts and were not going to work well together. He was quite conscious that Moi wanted another person of his own, so he did what was right and wrote a letter requesting retirement. This letter also included certain recommendations on the individuals who he thought most suitable to replace him, and had remarks and comments concerning those candidates. I am afraid I was not among those who were recommended.

However, this did not worry me. In fact, although I never mentioned it to anyone, I had known that once Kariithi retired, I was the one who would take over from him. This was because the President had continually referred matters to me, expecting me to handle them myself, as though I had already taken over. A few such things were done and I knew they upset Kariithi.

I recall Kariithi once exclaimed, "Eh! It looks as though Jeremiah has already taken over my job!" He always referred to me as Jeremiah.

At any rate, Kariithi did not receive a reply to his letter of resignation. All the people he had recommended were people that Moi could not accept. Nevertheless, Kariithi was allowed to retire gracefully, as well.

When it came to my own retirement, I was able to go just as serenely. However, after I left, there were several Heads of Civil Service and not one of them received any sort of advance notice that they were being sacked. Their abrupt removals were all announced over the radio.

This practice of announcing appointments over the radio was actually started before President Moi took over. There was a time when some people knew about their appointments in advance and a certain person from western Kenya, whose name I cannot now recall, thought he should have been appointed instead. So he and his supporters went to State House to protest. The person thought he was much more suitable for the position and had concluded that there must have been some sort of discrimination.

President Kenyatta felt very annoyed about this because he saw the protest as a challenge to his authority. From then on, most such changes were publicised without prior notice. It was felt that it was the only way to prevent protests. Some of this was rather inhumane, but under the circumstances there may not have been any other way to do it. I had a beautiful send-off, which gave me a chance to say goodbye to many of my colleagues. Nyachae, my successor, said wonderful things about me. When Moi announced my retirement, he mentioned that the country would not be losing my services because I would still be serving the nation in the capacity of Chairman of the Board of the Cooper Motor Corporation (CMC), in which the government had considerable interests.

Chapter 14

Family Life and Community Service

One of the problems in writing such memoirs is that it is often difficult to remember incidents and their sequence, unless one kept a diary of events. I never kept any diaries other than my schedule of work appointments. I was aware some people were meticulous in keeping records of day-to-day activities. Others had elaborate methods of recording everything they did.

Nevertheless, I recall many incidents quite well, from my childhood, from my years in the Civil Service, and as a businessman.

Although I have deliberately concentrated on my career in this book and avoided intruding on the privacy of my family, it would be negligent of me not to reflect a little on the central issue of those closest to me. As I stated earlier, I was first married to Esther Njeri, who was a teacher. We got married on 4 December 1954, and were blessed with four children, Douglas Kiereini, Caroline Njuhi, Rose Wambui and Mumbi.

After my first marriage ended, I thought I would not marry again. Bringing up children is a difficult task; I have never seen a more complicated undertaking. The children from my first marriage, three daughters and a son, remained with me. The youngest was four and the oldest was around 12. Frankly, it is not easy for a man to bring up children on his own. I have never forgotten the problems I went through.

Under the circumstances, I decided it would be inadvisable to remain single. I wanted my home respected and my children to have a good family to emulate.

Caroline died at the age of 15. The rest of the children have all had a good education. Douglas attended the University of Nairobi and he went on to become a valuer and banker. Currently, he runs his own school in Narok. Rose Wambui studied languages at the Sorbonne University in France and later did her Master's Degree in French at Carleton University, Ottawa, in Canada. Mumbi did her first year of studies at the University of Nairobi and then went on to do her first degree in Government at St Lawrence University in upstate New York. She later did her Master's in International Affairs and a post-graduate diploma in Public Administration at Carleton, Ottawa. At the moment, she is a public servant.

When I met Eunice Muringo, who was then the Chief Nursing Officer, I knew she was the one. I married Muringo on 13 November 1971 at "Number 10" Kabarnet Gardens. Charles Njonjo was my best man.

Here let me explain that we had nicknamed our country home "Chequers" and thus our home in town naturally became "Number 10." This was a parody on the residencies of the Prime Minister in England. "Chequers" is the country retreat and "Number 10" is the office of the Prime Minister.

Muringo and I had two children, Mburu who was born in 1973 and passed away on 13 August 2010, and Githae, who was born in 1974. Mburu and Githae studied at St Mary's School and later Mburu studied at the London School of Economics (LSE) while Githae studied Economics at Bristol. Both of them took up careers as bankers and Githae is currently in the insurance industry.

Mburu's passing on was an overwhelmingly sad loss to our family.

I now have four surviving children, Douglas, Wambui, Mumbi and Githae. I am pleased to have seven grandchildren. Douglas and his wife, Joyce have four children, Njeri, Namaisa, Gitau, and Saidimu. Wambui has one daughter, Mumbi. My youngest grandson is Gitau, the son of Mburu and Wambui, while Muringo is my youngest granddaughter.

Although the loss of Caroline and Mburu were devastating events, I am content to see my remaining children and grandchildren around me. It is pleasant to see the young ones running around without a care in the world. We have photographs of the grandchildren on our mantel piece and it is wonderful to see their cheerful faces every time I pass by.

My own children gave me a certain amount of trouble and anxious moments, just as most children do. With my grandchildren and great grandchildren, they are still too young to have done so, and I love spending time with them. Then – best of all – in the evenings, they go home to their daddies and mummies.

It is tempting to compare my childhood and the way I grew up with the conditions and circumstances of the modern world. It is all very different now. My grandchildren and great grandchildren are growing up in a unique universe. Technology, education, lifestyle and even the forms of entertainment are poles apart. The contrast of my childhood represents a stark difference.

Perhaps the main difference is that the new generation is growing up with a much wider perspective of life, whereas, in the past, children had mainly closed, parochial and limited horizons, and their values were limited to the immediate environment around them. Yet modern life has reduced the amount of quality time that families spend together.

* * *

I had lived in government houses nearly all through my career. Such houses were fully furnished with sofas, tables, beds, mattresses and all, so to a certain extent, it tended to make one rather slow to purchase furniture or one's own house. When we moved to Ruiru on the farm, we moved in without a single piece of furniture. We bought furniture and lived there for about nine years, and I made the 20-kilometre journey to Nairobi every day. However, because my wife's career as a nurse meant that she was often called on duty quite late, commuting would have been difficult.

It was actually my wife who encouraged me to make a move to purchase a house of our own in Nairobi. While we were living at Kabarnet Gardens, we would have a live, potted Christmas tree every year in December. At the end of the holiday, we would plant the tree in the garden. One day my wife and I were out looking at these four or five lovely healthy trees and she said it was a pity we would have to leave them behind when I retired. This got me thinking and eventually pushed me to the point of looking for a place of our own.

In 1977, I bought a 20-acre plot in Karen. It had an old house with a tenant, but the design of the house was truly awkward. For example, in order to get from the kitchen to the lounge, one had to pass through the bedroom! Eventually, I renovated the house to make it habitable, but first I started making plans for a new house of our own. I contacted the firm of Harban Singh Associates, which had planned and built quite a few stately homes for prominent people, and we drew up a plan of our own.

Perhaps these days it would be considered old-fashioned, but at that time, under the existing influences, the house was adjudged very stylish. It was, and still is, a lovely and elegant home. However, now that my children are adults and have moved out and onward to lives of their own, I often find it too large for us.

The construction was completed in 1980 and we moved in.

It is a wonderful place to live in and we often find ourselves doing considerable entertaining.

This was especially so when the International Council of Nurses (ICN) had one of their big meetings here in Kenya. My wife was the "Member at Large", of the Board and later she was elected President of the International Council of Nurses. The house was splendid for holding parties to entertain our international visitors. We had a great many visitors to stay with us and in that respect, we still find it very useful today.

The Karen plot actually has two boreholes, which is an anomaly in the area. The law at the time I built the house stated that boreholes in Karen should be two kilometres apart. Later, of course, due to lack of water and the unfortunate tendency of Kenyans to disregard the law, nearly everyone drilled a borehole. However, in my case, something different happened. First, I sunk one borehole to about 240 feet, so that the builders would have sufficient water for the construction and for our later domestic use.

A year or two after I completed building my house I noticed that one of my neighbours had a drilling rig in his yard. I talked to him about it, explaining that this was illegal and that it would interfere with my own water supply, but when he refused to listen, I got upset. Unfortunately, we argued about the matter and from that time onward, my neighbour refused to speak to me and became disagreeable. I tried to settle it peaceably but he continued to be stubborn and even declined to attend our neighbourhood meetings.

I went to the water department to attempt to sort out the issue but found out that they had irregularly authorised the sinking of my neighbour's borehole. I continued trying to stop the construction, but made no headway.

The next time I saw my neighbour, he came with a lawyer from Kaplan and Stratton. This time I complained bitterly.

"We are neighbours. We should be able to settle this, yet you cannot even talk to me. When I invited all the nearby home owners to discuss various issues affecting us, you refused to attend", I said. "Now you come to see me with a lawyer? Just tell me what mission you have."

My neighbour answered, "You have seen my letters of authorisation from the Ministry of Water and you have caused me to spend a great deal of money because of this. What choice do I have but to consult a lawyer?"

"What about me?" I asked. "What about all the money I spent drilling my own borehole? Now your new borehole is going to interfere with my water supply and I might not have any water at all!"

We could not reach an agreement on the issue.

However, the Ministry of Water realised that they were going to be in serious trouble because the whole dispute between my neighbour and I had been caused by the irregular authorisation of a borehole, where none should have been constructed. Therefore, they approached me and said they would sink an extra borehole for me, since there was really nothing else they could do at that stage. We finally compromised.

The ministry brought in their big rotary rig and within three days, they had sunk an even deeper borehole and sealed the casing so that it would not interfere with the aquifer, which was the source of my neighbour's water. I was quite pleased with this result and this is why I have the two boreholes.

* * *

I enjoy playing golf when I get the chance, yet during my years in government, I considered golf a waste of time. The general attitude at that time was that it was impossible to be a good golfer and simultaneously be a good worker. This misconception arose because it takes considerable time to complete a round of golf. One would be out there on the course for hours. Civil servants, even those who started playing golf years later, kept it very low key and sometimes had to lie about their whereabouts.

In those days before cell phones, some clever officers got round this problem by carrying pagers or two-way radios on the golf course. The officer would carry one radio and the other would be left with his secretary. If someone important called the office, the secretary would give an excuse.

"Oh! I'm sorry, he just stepped out of his office this very moment to pick up a document," she would say, or give some other plausible excuse to make it sound like the official was just nearby.

Then, after she hung up the phone, she would frantically try to reach her boss on the two-way radio.

"Sir, State House just called. The President would like to speak to you immediately. Please call back!"

The official would then look for the nearest available phone and call back. The President, or whoever may have phoned, would never guess that the official was on the golf course during office hours.

During colonial days, wherever there was an administrative centre, the British civil service would often set up a nine-hole golf course. Perhaps the courses were not very well maintained but they did exist and served their purpose well. Colonial officers would play in the evenings after leaving the office and did not have to waste time driving all the way to a club for an afternoon of golf.

Golf courses in Meru and Embu were destroyed by top-level African civil servants due to fanatical illusions about sports for the privileged few. There was one particular person who seemed to feel it was his mission to destroy these courses. Funny enough, his sons later became some of the best golfers in Kenya.

During our time, we were supposed to be so dedicated to our job and our duties that we had no time left over for sports or leisure. The armed forces, on the other hand, had their sports day once a week, on Wednesdays afternoon, I believe. This was part of their 'keep fit' routine.

In terms of sports, I seem to have graduated from one to the other. During my school days, I played hockey and excelled at sprinting. Once I came to Nairobi, I became a member of the Senior Civil Servants Club and, if I had a chance, I would play tennis during the day.

Here, I would like to give a little background information on the club where I spent so much of my time. Since the early days of the colony, settlers had never felt at ease with government officials who often interfered and brought a halt to their racial and other excesses. The unrestrained behaviour of some of these settlers caused great embarrassment to the government. At the Norfolk Hotel, black waiters were at one time banned from serving customers while wearing shoes. Settlers and other white guests at the hotel would take pot shots at Africans walking past the hotel, shooting above their heads and making the poor souls scatter in all directions.

Government officials, after all, were concerned with the sober administration of the colony and knew they were answerable to the British government, politicians and parliament. As a result, Government officials, while not banned from their Clubs, were treated with disdain.

As a consequence, the Civil Service Club (as it was known in those days) was originally started in 1955 to provide recreational and social facilities for senior civil servants in the colonial government. It was here they could get together and mingle and, on occasion, meet the Governor, away from the settlers and businessmen.

Although the Civil Service Club started out as 'whites only', by the 1960s there were non-European officers and we were among the first black patrons. There were still significant numbers of European members in the early years after independence, composed of those who continued working for the government or those who were retired and living in Nairobi. Quickly, however, more and more Africans joined in as the administration was localised.

The first African Chairman of the club was Bill Kimutai Martin, who was the DC for Nairobi, followed by Peter Shiyuka, the PS Ministry of Works. Later on, I became the Chairman and held the post from early 1978 to 1984, at which time I became the Patron of the Club and the Nairobi PC took over as Chairman. Sometime in the 1970s, members changed the name to the Public Service Club in order to accommodate members from parastatal organisations.

There was a time the Public Service Club was near collapse and some of us members thought we might even lose the land where it stood. This was as a result of poor management. Many members did not pay their bills and the club started running up huge debts to the extent that they were unable to buy stocks.

Geoffrey Kariithi, who was the Head of Civil Service, while I was the Permanent Secretary in the Ministry of Defence, called and asked me, "Can't you save this club? I would like you to investigate and try to rescue it."

Because of his senior position, it was not as if he was asking me to do this as a favour. He was giving me instructions; nevertheless, he found a way to tell me nicely. After all he, Duncan Ndegwa, I and a few others had been to Kagumo, Alliance and Makerere together and we shared a fairly good friendship, despite our different status.

When he asked, I told him, "Let me go find out what the problem is and I'll let you know and we can see how to approach the problem."

I did a little searching and found out that there were two problems at the source of the club's decline. Firstly, there was no decent management, and secondly, there was no discipline. There was no one who was responsible for the welfare of the club, and those who were members of the committees that were meant to keep things running, were the biggest offenders when it came to paying their bills. They were actually the worst enemies of the club!

The powerless waiters were unable to deny them services, despite the fact that they refused to pay and the situation kept deteriorating.

While I was making my investigations, I remember coming across a notorious case of a member cheating on his bar bill. One Permanent Secretary had run up an extremely large bill because he had not paid for over a year. However, he was always nice about it and constantly told the waiters that he would come and pay. Therefore, one day he asked the barman for a look at the records.

"Can you check to see how much I owe?" he asked politely. "I want to pay."

The barman was pleased. It looked like this long outstanding debt might soon be cleared. He said, "I can check the chits you have signed, sir, and see what is due."

The PS was sitting at the bar, drinking a beer and he waited until the barman sorted out the chits and then said, "So, how much money do I owe?"

There were a great many chits and the barman started working it out but the PS interrupted him.

"Look, what I want to do is to take these chits to my auditor. This debt really has to be settled."

In good faith, the barman handed over the chits and the PS took them all with him. Of course, neither he nor the chits ever returned to the club. I suppose he burned the chits, or destroyed them somehow.

This was the kind of thing that was going on at the club and I reported all the facts to Kariithi. I told him I could probably straighten out the club if he would agree to sack the committee that was supposedly running it, and let me name a committee of my own.

He gave me the go-ahead and the authority to proceed. I appointed people like Mutu wa Gethoi, Eddie Wainaina, John Mubia Wairago, John Mwakitawa, Dr James Njoroge Itotia and others as my selected team and we started changing some of the rules and closing some of the loopholes.

One of the first changes we made was to institute a 'deposit' system. Members would have to put in a deposit to have an account with the club and something like a passbook was initiated, which showed the balance in the account. Every time a member made an order, the barman would check the amount available. If there was no credit, there would be no service, a situation that would be embarrassing to the member. With this system, there was no question of getting things on credit or sending out bills.

Another thing we did in order to rebuild the club was to open up the membership to other people including individuals from parastatals and later, senior people in the private sector. I was given permission to do so, and subsequently the name of the club was changed to the Public Service Club. We had a huge *harambee* and raised enough money to build a new clubhouse, a substantial building with new facilities. It has now been expanded even further. Meanwhile the old building was rented out to a member as a school.

When I was promoted to Head of Civil Service, I, in turn, became the Patron of the Club, and I was proud of the fact that I had managed to save it.

Soon after I retired, President Moi while officially opening a road in Nakuru, an event that was broadcast live, accused the Public Service Club of "being a factory of rumour-mongering."

I felt bad when I heard the remark. I was a member of the Club and I knew just how much work we had put into it. We had even drawn up a new constitution. It was terrible to hear the Club being referred to in this manner.

I knew that someone had deliberately misinformed the President. I felt obliged to see him and clarify the matter. When I was given an appointment, I went to State House and took the club's constitution, along with me.

After some preliminary small talk, I started my defence.

"Sir, I've come to see you about this matter concerning the Public Service Club, because, as you know, I've been trying to save it. I've spent a considerable amount of my time there and I've managed to keep it on an even keel. I'm proud that civil servants and other senior people in this country have a place of their own where they can meet and discuss issues as colleagues."

I continued, "As for being the centre of rumour-mongering, implying that we are 'anti-government', I am not aware of any such thing. I know we sometimes have very open discussions about the affairs of this country. But, sir, I ..."

I hesitated and wondered if I should go further. Finally, I decided I should be completely open.

"But, sir," I said, "I know where you got this information and I know the date and the time. Before you went to open that road, you had a visitor at Nakuru State House. That visitor is not a friend of the club. In fact, he is not my particular friend either. He is the one who gave you this information. Yet he himself is not a member and he has never been a member of any club anywhere. Perhaps he didn't understand the people there, nor what was going on."

I took out the constitution I had carried with me. "Sir, when I was Chairman and Patron, we produced and approved a new constitution for the club. This is a copy. As you will note, the very first clause states that the Head of Civil Service shall be the Patron of the Club, and the Provincial Commissioner for Nairobi shall be the Chairman. They are senior people in the government and they are people who should be answerable to you. Why would they possibly head an organisation that is supposedly 'anti-government'?"

The President looked at me and said, "Jerry, you know the people in this country are really bad. Let's have a cup of tea ... let's have a cup of tea."

We had our tea and he continued, "But Jerry, you know me. You are my friend. I would not doubt you."

I knew more than that, but I left State House happy and the matter was never raised again.

However, after I retired, I had a sort of undefined feeling of unease and mixing with the club members became quite difficult. The camaraderie was no longer the same. I then moved from the Public Service Club and became a member of Nairobi Club and started playing snooker. By the way, I was extremely good at snooker, but it has now been relegated to my memories of the past.

From there I started playing golf in 1988, but only took it up seriously in the 1990s. When I joined the Breweries, I found quite a few keen golfers, and it continues to be one of my main pastimes.

* * *

Like a number of people of my age and in my situation in life, I have made great efforts to help my people at home. I have assisted in fund-raising activities and have provided as much help as I can, in developing the social amenities in the area. One of the results is J. G. Kiereini High School.

This school was originally started by some five elders, including my brother Njoroge, Mbaa wa Nyahe, Gachina Kamunyu and some others whom I cannot now recall. It was started in Kibichoi, which is in Komothai Location.

In the old Emergency village that existed there earlier, there were certain areas reserved for community services, or for public services. There was one such plot that was just under two acres. The elders started building a school there called *Wamunyugi* (of the feather) and they managed to build one classroom. This school, however, did not have a single teacher, so each time the students came, they would have to go home again. The old men were not capable of doing any teaching themselves.

The school was on the verge of closing down and the elders did not know what to do.

At that time, I was in the Ministry of Defence. Due to their acquaintance with my brother, two of the elders came to see me and told me the story about the school.

One of the old men explained, "In this area, we are the only ones without a secondary school. If you cross the river, there is a school there. In addition, if you cross the ridge over there, there is another school. But we have no way of helping our children if our school does not survive."

They also informed me that a church had already started encroaching on the plot and if things did not change, they might lose it altogether. They wanted me to do two things for them. First, they wanted the school to be registered with the Ministry of Education, and second, they wanted me to get them a teacher.

In my position in the Ministry of Defence, it was not difficult to approach the Ministry of Education. I was able to talk to the officials there and managed to get a teacher or two for the school and to get the school registered as Kibichoi Secondary School.

A short while later, one of the elders, Muiruri Ng'ang'a, who was the chairman, came to see me. He himself had never been to school at all.

He told me, "Look, although we are struggling along, we are certainly not able to administer the school. We can provide some material help, but in terms of education and technical things, we do not know what to do. We do not have any skills in management and we have no one to help us. We would like to ask you to become our chairman. Please agree. At least you know where the people are, who can help us. You can talk to them. You have been educated and you know what education means."

Peter Gachathi, who was the PS in the Ministry of Education, had appointed me as chairman to the board of Nyandarua School in Ol Kalou around that time. It was a long drive and twice I tried to resign but did not succeed. Finally, with the excuse of a neglected school in my own locality, I resigned and agreed to become the chairman of this small school, now called Kibichoi Secondary School, which was just starting up.

There was nothing much at the site other than the one classroom. Finally, we managed to get a graduate teacher and things started improving. Unfortunately, the place was so poor that I felt obligated to spend quite a bit of my own money on various needs. Little by little, we added a second classroom and then a third. The local people were willing, but they just did not have money. If I had not contributed, the school would have died.

One of the ways I encouraged them was to match every shilling that they contributed, with one of my own.

However, the school still stood on the small two-acre plot and there was a desperate need to expand. It had remained a day school because there was simply no space or money for dormitories. Then luck intervened.

President Moi was doing spontaneous trips around that time, and one day I convinced him to come and see this *harambee* school. I showed him the place and told him the story of the school and the difficulty of expansion. After that, we went round the countryside and he was impressed by the agricultural development in the area.

It should be explained that, after the Emergency, when people from the village went back to their farms, they still had plots of a quarter acre left in the area. The elders had approached the nearby plot owners and they had agreed that if they were given land elsewhere, they would allow the school to take over their little quarter acre plots.

I mentioned this fact to Moi and, since this happened to be during the time when people were being re-settled in various places, he arranged that some 150 acres of land be made available in Nakuru, for these people as well.

The District Commissioner for Kiambu was very much involved in this re-settlement process. He made up a list of the relevant plot owners, and every one of them brought in his or her title deed. As a result, they were given plots in various schemes, some in Nyandarua and some in Nakuru. In exchange for the little quarter acre plots they held, they were given plots ranging in size from three to five acres.

Through this method, we were able to obtain an extra nine acres for the expansion of the school. We managed to build a dormitory and were quite happy with the results. Unfortunately, we still had a problem with the water supply. The students had to go down to the river with jerry cans in order to get water and, naturally, such water is very dirty. I was quite worried that some of the students would get ill, or that we could even have an epidemic.

Shortly before Moi's next visit to the area, I arranged with the headmaster, Mwalimu David wa Ng'endo Ngacha, to have some girl students positioned on the slope nearby with jerry cans on their backs.

When the President and I passed by in the motorcade, I pointed out the girls and said, "You see, sir, this is where the school gets its water."

He was amazed. "Jerry, what do you mean?"

"I'm just showing you the facts, sir. There is no electricity to pump up the water, and even if power was available, there is no pump, either."

The President shook his head and exclaimed, "That is not possible!"
"This is the best they can do, sir."

Now we were travelling from Kibichoi and before we arrived in Limuru, the President had already ordered the ministry in charge of electrification, to ensure that the school received power in the next week or two. He also called Joab Omino, the PS in the Ministry of Water and Jeremiah Nyagah, the Minister, and instructed them to sink a borehole at the school during the course of the following week.

I was happy with the results, but there was still one problem to overcome. A borehole was fine, but we needed a pump to extract the water.

Sometime before this, Joab Omino, who was my good friend, had told me that there were, in fact, some pumps available. The Japanese government had supplied them to the Rural Electrification Programme (REP). I asked him to provide one of these pumps for the school, and then wrote formally to the Minister for Water to make the request.

When Jeremiah Nyagah received my letter, he called in Omino and asked him about the matter. Joab said that as far as he was concerned a pump could be sent out to the school.

"But Joab, can you read between the lines of this letter?" the Minister asked.

Omino skimmed through it and handed it back. "It seems to be in order," he said.

"But see this name here, 'Kibichoi'. This is in Githunguri constituency," the Minister persisted. "Don't you see the implication?"

I think Nyagah assumed that I was setting the stage to begin campaigns for a Member of Parliament seat in the near future. However, Joab was unable to understand what he was being asked. Perhaps he knew me too well to imagine such a thing.

"Do you know where Kiereini comes from? Don't you see the connection? Doesn't he tell you about any of this?"

Joab was quite puzzled and when he left the Minister, he came to tell me about the strange meeting. I just laughed and told him not to worry.

"If you just give the authorisation," I said, "I will sort it out with the Minister myself, in case he has any queries."

The Minister never made the query and the pump, along with a good supply of diesel, was delivered to the school. We then had water and power and, with the pump as well, there was nothing else needed. It was now merely a matter of building and developing the school.

By this time, the original five elders were no longer members of the board. After a short while, the elders must have discussed the school's history and all the problems they had endured. Without telling me, they went to the Ministry of Education and asked that Kibichoi Secondary School be re-registered as "J. G. Kiereini Secondary School".

I was embarrassed. I did not want anyone to think I was doing all this in order to make a name for myself, or for personal reasons.

When the Board was properly constituted, I told them of my objections. I said I was uncomfortable about it and that I did not want my name to appear in such a way. I had already spent a great deal of money on the institution and certainly did not want any sort of personal gain to come of it.

As a result, the Board agreed to revert to the name, "Kibichoi Secondary School", and then wrote a letter to the Ministry of Education to make the change.

I do not know how the old men heard about the letter, or exactly what action they took, but I do know that one of them was vehemently opposed to the alteration. When the Board met once more, the confrontation was almost like a war. The old men were furious.

"Do you know where this school came from?" they asked. "Do you know anything about the origin of this school? Do you know its history?"

The Board were amazed at the ferocity of the elders.

"Do you know the trouble we have gone through, and why we chose this name?" the elders demanded. "No! It will not change. We did it, and we did not ask Kiereini's permission to do so, or to register it in his name. We just did it because he deserved it!"

One of the Board members objected. "You know, this is not his school. He is not the owner."

"That doesn't matter. It will not change!"

It seemed that many of the Board members were not aware of the background of the school and the seriousness with which the local people treasured the growth and accomplishment of establishing such an educational institution. At any rate, the ministry was informed of the objection and in turn told the Board that they could not change it. I then gave up and the name remained.

Originally, the school was co-educational but there were many problems with the administration. Having teenage boys and girls together in one school was a major headache. The difficulties that we encountered were almost unimaginable. As a result, we requested the Minister to allow us to change it to an 'all boys' school.

We ensured that the girls went to good schools and there was not a single girl who lost her place during this move. Actually, I believe they were probably happier without the interference of boys. From what I have read, girls on their own do much better academically, for whatever reason.

* * *

Such fundraising endeavours in my home area and elsewhere were some of my normal activities. *Harambees* became a way of life for people like me. I have been invited to countless places for *harambees* and I have invited others many times.

There is never any obligation to donate to a *harambee*. One cannot be pressurised to assist. Nevertheless, I feel that if one is able to help, yet does not contribute, it may result in a dissatisfied feeling of guilt.

In some cases, *harambee* money was misused in the past, and misuse of donations became increasingly worse over the years. In the end, a considerable amount of money did not go into the projects for which it was intended. It went into other people's pockets or was used purely for pleasure. It was a terrible failing on the part of those who were in charge, and was difficult to oversee.

Someone once suggested to me that there might be somewhat more *harambees* for schools and clinics in Central Province, than elsewhere, but I have to say that this goes back to individual or community choices.

For example, I have been told that if one organises a fundraiser for a school or a clinic in Tanzania, there will not be much interest. However if one invites people to a pre-wedding party, there will be a wonderful response and everyone will give gifts and money. I think it is just a question of how people look at life that changes all these factors.

One can compare that to the Kikuyu Independent Schools in Central Province. These were neither government nor missionary schools, yet people came from all over Kenya to attend schools like Kiamwangi and Githunguri Teachers Training College. It seemed that, at the time, only Central had the public spirit of developing their own people in that way. It was not a matter of having excessive amounts of money. It was where they wanted their money spent, where their priorities were placed.

After Independence, Kenyatta started popularising the *harambee* spirit, but it was always the people's affair, not the government's. Neither Kenyatta nor the government was too bothered. It was President Kenyatta who said that, although the government was ready to help, it was up to an individual to develop himself or herself.

Traditionally, the phrase '*harambee*' was not known. If the Kikuyu people wanted to dig a farm or erect a home, the village would join together in *ngwatio* (cooperative work) to build a house or cultivate a farm and they would do this in turns, for each other without pay. *Ngwatio* means community participation in major household chores or projects such as tilling big parcels of land, harvesting or house building. A person would invite his or her friends and they would do the work with speed. In turn, the other members of the *ngwatio* group would invite their friends if they had a difficult task to perform.

It was certainly a form of *harambee*, and it was their way of life.

In fact, if one looks back at the traditions in most communities, it is very often the same. Labour was done communally. In some places, however, this spirit and energy was not brought forward into building clinics, schools and the like.

There was one time when a few of the older people in my area decided to build a church nearer to their homes. They said they were too feeble to walk to the only church in the locality, so they wanted one nearer to their neighbourhood. They were getting old, they did not have any money to hire labour, and so they had to do the earthworks themselves. I found it hard to imagine, because of their age.

One of them was quite dramatic about it.

"If we do not get enough help to push along the construction of the church, we will die before it is finished!" he told me.

Two of these old men were my brothers so I felt sympathetic and became committed to their assistance. We tried to get funds from wherever we could, and eventually managed to finish the building long before they passed away.

Then there was another community church in which I became involved. We were building an administrative block and part of it was given over to a small computer-training unit meant for youth, mostly girls, who could not afford to go to the more expensive training institutions. They invited me to be their guest of honour at the fundraising.

As a final example, the road through my home area was much neglected so I arranged with Arthur Magugu, who was the Minister for Roads, to have it done. It was a beautiful tarmac road when it was completed and although it has now developed a few potholes due to lack of maintenance, it is still reasonably passable.

However, I am now trying to get away from these community projects. I have retired, after all. In that respect, it is pleasant to see that Corporate Social Responsibility (CSR) has become important to many companies. This is taking over some of that public spirit. It is really wonderful to see how enthusiastically these departments, usually full of dedicated young men and women, work to make an impact. East African Breweries Limited commits one per cent of its profit to CSR.

Volunteer service has almost always been a positive force throughout Kenya. Quite a few agencies in the corporate sector are involved but this spirit has often been stifled when some public contributions are squandered and do not achieve the purpose for which they were intended.

Over the years, I would say, in general, the honesty and integrity of the people has waned. The morality of the nation has declined. This is not a mere idle allegation, it is the truth. Kenya cannot deny that national morality has gone down and leadership has failed. We are still functioning, but I feel unhappy about what I see.

Take for example the Constituency Development Fund (CDF). One would expect that this would ease the burden of the people, but instead the politicians are destroying the whole idea through their egotistical selfishness. It seems that once an MP is given the money for his constituency, he decides it is his to do with as he likes, placing his personal interests above everything else.

Yet this does not mean we should all try to go to Parliament to rectify the situation. Everyone has his own calling. I have never wanted to get involved in politics. I have always felt that if there is any assistance I can give to the people, I can do so without resorting to Parliament.

In fact, I have seen some examples and had some experiences that have taught me that, unless one was extremely lucky, the chances of having a successful life and happy family were much less if one took up a serious career in politics. I look around at a number of people who were with me in the civil service and then went into politics. Very few have accomplished much of anything for society. Some were murdered, and some were unceremoniously removed from their positions. Some no longer fit into society, anywhere.

I feel I have a better chance of a happier life and the ability to serve honestly without personal gain, outside Parliament. In fact, even before independence, I never once thought of politics.

Although the people in Githunguri have tried to persuade me many times to join politics, I have always refused. President Moi himself tried to persuade me and I told him that I was prepared to serve my country in any other capacity, but not in the political field.

People can attach any reason they like to my refusal, but the truth is that I simply did not want to be part of that type of life.

Chapter 15

The World of Business

During my years in the civil service, my main objective was always service to the nation. Our generation of civil servants was brought up to be respected by society and my main concern was to do my job and to do it well. However, little by little, over the years, I have tried to make my family more secure, to enable us to live under better circumstances. In this ambition, I was never driven by greed and I believe one can live a good life without resorting to cheating.

I originally owned four acres of land, which I had inherited from my father. However, since I had a reasonable income from the civil service, I retained the title of the piece of land but allowed my brother to cultivate it.

Although I have already given details on my land purchases in an earlier chapter, I will repeat them here in more detail.

In the 1950s, during Land Consolidation and Adjudication, I bought a six-acre farm and planted four acres of it with coffee. At one time, I had thought about putting up a house on this little farm, and had even contacted an architect to design something for me. I thought I could live in this house and easily commute to work, but before I did so, I bought another piece of land with a house already on it.

With the help of a loan from Land Bank, in 1964, I purchased a 25-acre farm in Ruiru of which 20 acres were under coffee. It had a nice little two-bedroom farmhouse, so I felt there was no need of building another, and I lived there for nearly nine years.

Perhaps my most profitable investment was the purchase of my 850-acre farm, Maakiou Estate, which I bought from a Greek family. Three quarters of this farm is in Kiambu and the rest is inside Nairobi District boundaries. I bought it in 1974 for 5 million shillings, out of which I paid half a million shillings as deposit. The balance was paid for by a bank loan from the National Bank of Kenya. Although the price of coffee was low when I bought it, it slowly started rising and by 1975, the price was double what it had been. Then came the coffee boom and prices went wild in 1975 and 1976. The prices moved from 250 shillings a tonne, to 800. I had no need to touch Chepkube coffee[1] because I had enough coffee on my own farm.

---

1   Chepkube was the name used to refer to the coffee boom of the mid to late 1970s, when Uganda's coffee could only be sold through Kenya.

In fact, we had to guard our coffee, especially when we transported it to KPCU mills in Nairobi, because people would steal it right off the lorry. It was like gold.

Because of the huge increase in coffee prices, I was able to pay off my entire loan, which had been originally scheduled for a five-year repayment period, in less than two years. I had no other loans at the time and I believe this farm is my best investment to date. I have 300 acres under coffee and the rest is for dairy cattle.

All through my years in the civil service, these pieces of land were the only investments I held. Following the Civil Service Remuneration and Terms of Service Commission report, commonly known as the Ndegwa Commission report, civil servants were allowed to engage in business as long as it did not present a conflict of interest with their jobs.

Thereafter, about 20 senior civil servants and private investors got together and formed 'Heri Limited' with the help of a bank loan. By setting up this investment company, we were able to purchase shares without hesitation, because we were not involved in either the running of the businesses or the decisions made by the management.

Heri Limited was set up for one specific purpose, to purchase shares in DT Dobie Motors. At the time, Col. David Dobie had put 5 per cent of the shares on the market and we took up the offer. Quite some time later, we increased our holdings to 45 per cent. Julius Gecau, who was then employed by Kenya Power and Lighting, looked after our interests in the company. However, D.T. Dobie continued to manage Dobie Motors and we had no influence in any decisions taken.

I left government service in 1984 but due to the fact that I had accumulated nearly one year of leave, my official retirement date was 31 May 1985. I then moved on to become the Chairman of Cooper Motor Corporation (CMC), in which the government held shares. During my stint as Chairman, I started buying shares in CMC for myself, because they were rather inexpensive at the time. CMC did not do badly in terms of returns, but it was certainly nothing exceptional.

When I started with CMC, I was the Executive Chairman. However, the Managing Director, Jack Benzimra, kept making decisions that I queried because I felt that, in some instances, they were simply not wise. Whenever I asked him why he was not involving me, as Chairman, over such issues, he had a tendency to remind me that he was older and more experienced, since he had been in the motor industry all his life. He said that he had an important stake in the company and he would never do anything to harm the management, but he seemed to forget that I was his boss. I felt that we could have moved forward faster as a commercial enterprise because the management was too lethargic.

As I wondered how to handle the situation, I registered a nominee company called Kingsway Nominees. Every time I had some money to spare, I would give it to my broker to buy shares and I made sure that I had a larger holding than Benzimra. I let it be known that Kingsway was my investment arm. My nominees in this respect were Douglas Njiiri Karago and Nanalal Sheth. Although the nominees have changed, I still have the company as an investment arm.

In 2012, some of the activities that took place in CMC while I was Chairman came under criticism (see annex).

* * *

I was the Chairman of East African Breweries Limited (EABL) for some years. The top 10 shareholders in East African Breweries Limited hold the majority, and the Diageo family of companies alone holds over half. Other large shareholders are National Social Security Fund, Barclays Bank, Stanbic, and Kenya Reinsurance. This does not leave much for the rest of us to share. In fact, the remainder is split between 23,000 investors.

Diageo invests in alcoholic drinks, but mainly in spirits. They are an international company with headquarters in the United Kingdom.

Many times, I have been asked the difference between EABL and Kenya Breweries. EABL is the holding company that owns Kenya Breweries as a subsidiary. In addition, it owns Uganda Breweries, Central Glass, and Kenya Maltings. In all these subsidiaries, it owns 100 per cent. It also owns UDV, a Dutch Spirits company, jointly with Diageo. EABL has 46 per cent and Diageo has the rest.

Perhaps my most challenging period was during the beer wars with South African Breweries (SAB). This was a most unpleasant experience.

South African Breweries had conducted its own research and a feasibility study of the Kenyan market, which showed that, at the time, about 24 per cent of the market was not fully served. This was one of the main reasons they came into the Kenyan market but unfortunately, their research was somewhat off the mark.

South Africa is one of the African countries that are far ahead of Kenya in this regard. The scale of their operations is quite substantial and, in the opinions of many businessmen, the nation is a world economy. It is possible, that if it had not been for the restrictions barring international trade when the country was under apartheid, that country would have been even further ahead, perhaps on the level of Canada. Once the restrictions were removed, South Africa was able to move up again, quite quickly.

Prior to this challenge, East African Breweries Limited was quite lethargic. One had to virtually fight to get employees to do things and achieve their tasks. The staff felt there was no reason to move forward. After all, they had never had a true competitor before. They were still making money and, even when they were told they could make more, they never saw a reason to put in more effort.

At any rate, SAB came in and was fully prepared to beat EABL in the market. They had studied many factors before they came and built their factory in Thika. They employed their own people and enlisted the support of some politicians who were their mentors.

Suddenly, EABL woke up to the fact that they could go down. They realised that they had competition and that they could actually lose the market. The board and the whole management had to consider measures necessary to counteract the opposition and SAB's aggressive marketing. To do so, we had to change our method of management and had to employ consultants to assist us. We met in many places to plan new approaches and tactics and the word 'strategy' became very important in our new management style.

During the time they were in the market, the best that SAB could do was about 7 per cent of the total beer market and their scheme was often just to intimidate EABL. They would say that they had 9 or 10 per cent of the market in order to dampen our morale. Despite introducing new brands such as their 'Castle' flagship, their beers did not make significant in-roads in the Kenya market. As a result, unfortunately, they found themselves going down very fast.

Finally, they realised that our brands, particularly Tusker, were just too strong. To minimise their losses, Johannesburg told them that they would have to pull out.

We both agreed to call a truce and find a formula that would be mutually beneficial. However, SAB and EABL were both hit financially because of spending so much money on marketing. During the whole venture, SAB may have lost as much as 100 million dollars.

EABL survived the losses because of the effort they put in, something they had never done before. The management learned that they could never be 'too good' and that challenges should never be ignored. Now they have moved forward, using the same methods that SAB had used, to improve their sales. Overall, it was a tough time and I was sad to lose a few friends, due to the fierce competition.

At the beginning of these beer wars, Njenga Karume was one of our biggest and oldest distributors. Through Kiambu General Transport and Nararashi Kenya Distributors, he supplied more than half of Nairobi and all of Kiambu. These were very important areas.

Due to various decisions made by EABL, he took the company to court and accused it of breach of the agreement. He had a letter from the previous Chairman of EABL, Brian Hobson, stating that his contract could only be terminated with appropriate notice and that notice could reasonably be as much as 10 years. Njenga took EABL to court on the basis of the contents of Hobson's letter and won the first round.

We were not satisfied with the judgment because we had given him notice according to his most recent agreement, which was 90 days only.

EABL were doubtful whether or not we should appeal. I received a two-page letter from our lawyer at Kaplan and Stratton explaining that, should we attempt the appeal, we would lose. However, I overruled the lawyers. I disagreed with this assessment and said that if we were to lose, we should lose in the appeal. Therefore, we decided to go to another firm, Mutula Kilonzo Advocates, and we won the appeal. We were awarded costs, but we actually lost much more.

While the case was going on, I received many calls. People were concerned that Njenga and I, who had been friends for many years, were now fighting. Before the first case, I sent one or two friends to Njenga to offer a compromise, or some ex-gratia payment, but this was not acceptable.

* * *

Although I am not an expert on investments, people tend to come to me for financial advice. My reply is, consult those who are in the know. One must make a careful assessment of the facts, examine the balance sheets over a period of years in order to get the history of the company's performance and evaluate any possible risks.

A study of the combination of these factors will give one a better conception of future performance. However, professionals know that there is never a guarantee of earning profits.

Risk management is a critical science and investment is always a gamble. One must consider the type of business and the economic situation at the time. There is no clear rule on investment because everything is dynamic and many conditions have to be taken as variables. Try to look into the future to see what the facts will mean two to three years down the line.

I have read a number of books discussing the ideal way of making investments. However, the general consensus is that each case has its own merits and that no one theory will fit all scenarios. Under such variables, my own practice is to consult those whose business it is to be knowledgeable in these fields, such as financial managers and investment managers.

My first investment in the private sector was in Unga Group, which previously went under the name Mercat Group. I believe the word 'mercat' means 'market' in the Scottish language. Philip Ndegwa informed me that someone wished to sell their shares and thus they were available for purchase. I then used up my 25 per cent lump sum commuted pension, which I had earned upon retirement, to purchase these shares.

Another fascinating aspect of business today is that women in management are doing better than ever before. There are more and more who have the opportunity to get involved and stand on their own. This is not a sudden development; they have grown into this role as their access to education improved.

During my own time in school, there was no secondary school for girls until Alliance Girls High School was started in the late 1940s. Now such schools are everywhere. There are many women who proceed on to university studies, then get jobs and sometimes do better than the boys. They are catching up quickly.

* * *

It is sometimes said that Kenya's laws are over-protective and that there is too much bureaucracy for potential investors. It is true that there are some places where one can get licences faster. The difference in some other countries is that they have what is called a 'one-stop shop' where one can get a licence, investment approval and all the things that are required, in one place. This makes the system easier, faster and definitely more attractive.

Initially, it was important that strict licensing regulations be adopted in Kenya, so that only genuine investors were allowed to compete. However, changes have taken place. Regulations have improved and we are no more protective than many other countries. Yet, in any situation, there is always room for improvement. We can still enhance the system to attract investors, especially by making sure all procedures are carried out in the correct manner.

For example, in tourism there are many opportunities to improve the business, to develop and expand our attractions to include new sites. Our tourists could be treated better, and given more exhaustive information on the country. One wonders if we properly use the money given to the Kenya Tourist Board. We need to market ourselves better and smarter and give a great deal more information on our potential as a site for investment and as a holiday destination.

I have a number of other concerns. For example, it is necessary to make the process of application easier and make any existing bureaucracy as straightforward as possible in order to attract financiers. Various steps can be undertaken to make the investment climate more attractive to foreign investors. One of these is to simplify the application and approval of licences while making information readily available, so that investors can see what they are coming into. In fact, from what I see as the general trend, the time is quickly coming when the question of protecting the indigenous investor will cease to be a priority. We will be expected to compete on a level playing field.

To a limited extent, there may be some political interference in the bureaucracy, but I believe it is negligible. There may be a delay in some instances, because a bribe was not paid. This is unfortunate, but it is not a practice peculiar to Kenya. It is, in fact, much worse in some other countries. Nevertheless, we should always be critical, even over-critical, in order to bring such matters forth. Those who are honest should be open and bring these incidents to the attention of the authorities.

Another issue that needs to be examined is queues. There should never be a line waiting for government services. A long queue is a sign that there is something wrong. Senior men in the ministries should investigate and ensure they do not occur. This is a sign of inefficiency and that procedures are not being followed properly. A line of people waiting for service means there is either gross inefficiency or some sort of dishonesty. Technology should be adopted more quickly, especially in government, to address this issue and the mind-set of the civil service must change.

For example, there used to be queues at EABL and this was because many suppliers came personally for their cheques. Instead of the staff mailing the cheques when they were ready, the suppliers had to stand in line to collect their payments. Occasionally a cheque might be hidden or there would be spurious excuses. Through innovation, EABL was able to eliminate these queues.

In addition, when I have an appointment in a government office I cannot understand why I should wait. If I am told to come at a particular time, why should I wait? Personally, I know that if I have a visitor at a particular time, I cannot possibly give anyone else that same block of time. One should never double book. It is bad management and reflects badly on the officer who keeps one waiting. One must manage one's time and manage it well. This applies to files as well. Why do files pile up? Why do people take files home? Anyone coming to my office will never find more than the files for that particular day. While I was in the civil service, and even now, I never worked at night and I never took work home. My principle is that, whatever can wait until tomorrow, can wait. Nevertheless, whatever must be done today must be done.

* * *

Any company that neglects developing a policy on the environment is lagging behind. The environment is vital. EABL is very much involved in sound environmental practices. Although this awareness is a fairly recent phenomenon, it is taken extremely seriously.

The Breweries has an environmental programme worth over a billion shillings. All effluent is processed and cleaned before it goes into the sewers. In addition, EABL have planted a forest in the valley near the factory. The National Environmental Management Authority (NEMA) is very happy with what has been accomplished and a representative from the Ministry of the Environment has launched a number of activities. Breweries are also involved in tree planting and Mau Forest rehabilitation. All such activities are done through the EABL Foundation, which is a whole department of its own.

There is also the Corporate Social Responsibility (CSR) programme, something that started recently as well, which is an important component of Breweries policies. Previously this aspect was not well-defined and perhaps it was not regarded as crucial, but today it is a significant part of EABL's guiding principles.

The activities of the Foundation include, for example, educational scholarships, construction of ablution blocks to supply water, tree planting, energy efficiency and recycling and also the promotion of responsible drinking in regard to alcoholic products.

* * *

One of the strongest forces changing the world of finance today is the phenomenon of globalisation. This is a wide subject that has many facets and, in a small way, Kenya is already involved.

If one looks at our most basic commodities, for example, handicrafts, Kenya is already marketing products to the world, although this is on a rudimentary level.

Concerning the larger, more sophisticated market, we are also trading with the world. This had never happened before. Suddenly our people have a much broader understanding of world trade than they have ever had and we have people involved in international businesses. There are many such examples. Prominent Kenyan business executives have invested heavily in a number of Kenyan companies and multinationals. They have extensive interests in property management, insurance, courier services, advertising, manufacturing, investment funds, in the media and others.

Furthermore, in addition to such enterprises, there are also joint ventures between Kenyan and international organisations.

Some activists say that this rapid rise is due to the fact that many more people were able to take up businesses. This may be true, but one must also keep in mind that it takes years of experience to accumulate knowledge, discipline and insight to invest and manage an international business. Such skills are not widespread in any population.

As for Kenya, we have greater numbers of Africans getting involved in business, both locally and internationally, than many other countries, which started at about the same time we did.

EABL is already in Tanzania and Uganda and will soon find itself a strong business force in South Sudan, the DRC and Rwanda. Businessmen are forward looking and once legal measures are taken to open the movement of business, trade and employment, the horizon will widen.

Within the East African Community, Tanzania and Uganda are hesitant to have free movement of labour. They fear that if employment is opened up, Kenyans will take up many of the top jobs in those countries, at the expense of their local people. Nevertheless, none of us can go far alone.

If Kenya and Tanzania are compared, it must be admitted that Kenyans have done more to train their own people. We are faster in such matters and our concept of education and the work ethic is different as well. Unfortunately, Tanzania made a false step with the introduction of socialism and *Ujamaa*, which were espoused by the first president. There is still a psychological hangover from that period. For example, if one looks at the Tanzanian stock exchange, it is a minor market, open only two or three days a week.

Although there are other languages in use, all Tanzanians speak one language, Kiswahili. Although this is certainly a great advantage within the East African region, internationally, Kiswahili is not widely spoken and thus it becomes a weakness. In Kenya, on the other hand, many people speak English, and English is the primary means of global interaction.

Nevertheless, the Breweries still has room for improvement. One has to remember that the Breweries did not start out as an African venture. It was started by Europeans and it was under European control until it was listed as a public company when others were able to buy into it. For a long while after that, a large portion was owned by local shareholders, but at the moment, the majority shareholding in EABL is by foreigners.

Once a company is listed, unless restrictions are made through the Capital Markets Authority (CMA) and the Monopolies Department, there is not much one can do to control the shareholding. Diageo holds 50.03 per cent; however, they did not go out of their way to acquire this amount. They did not even want to get to this stage. It was more the result of a combination of factors.

First, when Breweries were going to re-start in Tanzania, it purchased a half-built brewery in Moshi and needed money to complete it in order to enter the Tanzania market once again. The regulators allowed it to declare a rights issue, in order to make such funds available.

Then, around the same time, there was a stockbroker who had an argument with the Breweries. He claimed that he had returned his empty bottles but had not been paid his deposit. He quoted figures, but his did not agree with the figures at Breweries. When he was asked to produce additional proof, he was unable to do so. He was advised to go to court but for some reason he did not take up the opportunity.

Instead, since he was a stockbroker, he decided he was going to fight the Breweries in a more devious manner and me, in particular, because I was the one making the decisions.

Meanwhile, the rights issue came along and we clearly said we would decide the price, as is allowed by the CMA, by taking price of shares for five days in a week to see how the shares behaved and then take the average price for those five days. We did this and the price came to fifty-three shillings per share.

Before we completed the documentation and the rest of the requirements, the stockbroker sold five hundred shares at forty-nine shillings and he took that as evidence that we had deliberately over-priced the shares in the rights issue so that Africans would be unable to buy any. He went to the Press, created a fuss and sent messages on the internet. He discouraged many people from buying shares and it was quite effective.

Now Diageo had underwritten the rights issue and they were under obligation to take up any rights that were not taken up by the owners. This obligation landed them with 50.3 per cent.

As I said, they had no plans to take this up. In fact, they were unhappy about the action because they had not put funds aside for such a huge expense. They bought the shares merely because they were required to do so. Although they needed to have authority from the CMA and the government, in order to own more than the certain percentage which is allowed for foreign companies, they were granted special permission because of the circumstances.

All the same, EABL is a good model of a local and international company. Unilever (formerly East African Industries) and British American Tobacco (BAT) are others that are performing well, but they have never been local.

The Breweries was founded in Kenya as a local company. We were quite proud of this, as became evident when South African Breweries entered the market and attempted to compete with us. Kenyans took a stand to support us. In addition, the morale of our staff was high. They were happy and very proud to belong to EABL and put in considerable effort to help us be successful.

The main contribution the Breweries makes to this country is in the form of taxation. Remittances in tax vary from year to year, but payments range in billions of shillings.

I am extremely proud of my contribution at the Breweries. I was there for twenty-four years. One of the things I was most pleased with was the fact that we were able to produce leaders who went into other areas of the industry. Gerald Mahinda, who was the Managing Director, was posted to run Diageo business in the whole of South African region. Breweries have produced many such leaders at lower and upper levels, and recruitment was done globally.

Chapter 16

Reflections

Once I retired, I found myself with huge heaps of documents that I simply did not know what to do with. Although my secretary warned me that I might one day require these papers or wish to refer to them, I wanted to make a clean break so I burned nearly everything I felt I would no longer require or was of no use to me as a private individual. Unfortunately, when I was in the process of writing my memoirs, I wished I had these records as reference material, because they would have served as excellent reminders of the little day-to-day events and occasions that occupied me.

I enjoy reflecting on the various events of my life that are most important to me. Just the other day, I started thinking about my personal motivation. Perhaps, it is the grace of God that motivates me from day to day, but this is difficult to determine.

What started me thinking was a trip out to my farm that I made with my son, Mburu, shortly before he became ill. He was clever and thoughtful and we often had long, pleasant conversations.

Mburu was a strong and energetic sportsman and athlete, with a passion for rugby and football. He loved the outdoors and had a wonderful sense of humour, often self-deprecating. He was always committed to excellence, whether at work or in play. Unfortunately, during the last few years of his life, he developed Motor Neurone Disease (MND) and his health, always so robust, slowly deteriorated.

In one of our trips to the farm, he asked me, "Dad, why is it so difficult for you to break the monotony of your life? You always wake up early every morning. You drive out, you go to the office and you stay there nearly the whole day until 5 o'clock, unless you are going to play golf. Then you drive home like everyone else. Yet you often tell us that you do not have a salary. Are you afraid you will become a pauper if you stay at home? Why not just pay an occasional visit to the office and then you could take it easy the rest of the time?"

At first, I just did not know what to say to him so I thought it over.

Finally, I said, "I think this routine gives me the spirit to continue living and I hope I can do this for quite a while longer. Because there are people my age who cannot do anything, who are sick, or who do not even know where they are. I just feel like I need this routine and challenge to keep going."

This is true. I have a little office in town and every time I go there, or do anything else, I try to make a contribution to life, or to whatever happens around me. I feel I still have much to offer to others and, given my age, I consider that my input, based on the experiences of a lifetime could be useful.

There are investments I look after in my office and I remain quite busy. I use a computer to keep myself up to date on what is happening, and although I do not often use the internet, I can receive and answer emails on my own. The typing skills I learned at the Indian High Commission still serve me well. I have good basic computer knowledge and there are always people ready to help me if I need to know more.

When it comes to my personal contribution, I look to my strengths, or to the unique abilities I feel I have. These are somewhat difficult to define, but I have learned, over my years at work, that I can be of immense help to people through these qualities.

My main talent is that I have the ability to organise other people. I have never been one to do things all by myself. I have always been there to guide and to advise, to help people plan and to ensure that whatever plan is adopted, it will be successful. It is more than merely delegating work, and I hope that my particular talent in this regard has helped people to develop their own strengths and move on.

* * *

It often seems to me that everyone is concerned with wealth and the accumulation of material goods. Yet I feel these are not really necessary to experiencing true happiness and satisfaction.

For example, my childhood would, by today's standards, be considered very deprived. Nevertheless, the fact is that I do not feel that I grew up poor at all. I grew up among the society and the community around me and we all had the same standards. I did not feel the lack of shoes, for example, because no one else had them. When we were naked, we were all naked.

I never felt that I lacked anything, and what I had was enough. I was happy.

Later, as a young man, when I was wondering, "What do I really want out of life?" or "Why does one go to school?" I found my answer one day, in a small report in a newspaper.

There was an article about a person who had served a certain company for 25 years, and when he retired, he was given a bicycle as a retirement gift. There was a photo accompanying the article, which showed the retiree posing with the bike.

This made me think about my priorities. I decided I would be happy by giving service. I would like to work, wherever it might be, for at least 25 years and get a bicycle or something similar, some gift of appreciation.

At the time, I never really thought about anything beyond working for 25 years. I did not think about whether I would have money or anything like that. In those early days, while I was teaching and later as a young civil servant, I did not know what I would become. I did not know whether I would go beyond the status of a clerk.

Later, I became more ambitious. Opportunities arose and the banks were lending money. The expectations of society changed and the drive for wealth came in slow stages. When Europeans started selling their farms, bank loans became available and people of my generation took advantage of the fact. It was on a 'willing seller, willing buyer' basis and I recall that Kenneth Matiba, Duncan Ndegwa, Sam Waruhiu, several others and I went in enthusiastically.

Because of the way I invested, my progress was quite different from many others and slowly and gradually, I began to build up with the help of bank loans.

However, for many others, this gradual process seemed to be too slow. As the years went by, the idealism of service seemed to lose its attraction for some civil servants. A number of those who were in places and positions where decisions were made to import or export, or decisions on the use of government facilities, made money irregularly while they were civil servants.

Our society seems to thrive on rumours, and I am sure there are also stories about me. I do not know exactly what people think of me having been in the Ministry of Defence as a Permanent Secretary or in the Office of the President in charge of internal security. All I can say is that I never misused my position. In fact, it is difficult to comprehend how irregular tendering can occur, given the many regulations that govern the process. It seems impossible, but the human mind is ingenious when seeking its own benefit.

Misuse of office may have happened in a small way before, but if so, the Minister would have had to ensure that the civil servants under him cooperated. Now it is everywhere. Interference with regulations opens the door to all types of abuses. Those who act in this manner know well that one day they may have to face the consequences.

Most civil servants who retired earlier were never wealthy people. They retired with pensions, which were not really much, but they never complained. People were more service-oriented. Service to the nation and to the people was regarded as more important than the salaries or anything else. For example, a teacher would be called *'Mwalimu'* and given respect for the rest of his life, and this had nothing at all to do with how much property or wealth he had accumulated.

The guardians of the public purse became the thieves who preyed on them. It is sad to look back on these events and realise that such people are still walking free, unpunished.

* * *

One of the interesting dynamics that occur when we grow old is that our attitude towards others changes. This happens to everyone, I suppose.

In the past, I never found myself limited in any way. In the civil service, we were a large group of roughly the same age, the same class and shared a similar educational background. These days however, I sometimes find it difficult to relate. When I go to places, I never know what kind of people I will meet. Even in my own club, there is only a certain small group I can mix with. The others are much, much younger than I am and I find that when we are together, they seem to be uncomfortable and I discover that I am uncomfortable as well. We cannot share a discussion. I suppose this is more due to age than anything else ... a natural, yet surprising process.

I do not know quite where to place myself. If ever there was a call for wealthy people to parade, I certainly feel I would not be able to go. Conversely, if a call was made for poor people to parade, I could not join them either. I do not feel I belong in either circle, but people think I am wealthy and that is where the problem lies. Yet if the opposite of poverty is wealth, then class me as wealthy, but I will still be doubtful of the truth.

Even so, being able to afford some of the things one wants, is quite nice. One of the assets I have is a beautiful, beige five-seater Mercedes 450 SLC sports car, which I bought in 1978 for Kshs 680,000. It has a dual exhaust and is built very low to the ground, which gives it great handling and balance.

A few friends of mine also purchased such cars. We bought these after the days of the coffee boom. Because of this boom in the seventies, we developed odd ideas about status and money. We would not allow people who had cars with a single exhaust to sit with those of us who had dual exhaust systems, at clubs and social events. I have to laugh at it now.

There was also a man who did all his banking after hours, for fear he would meet 'poor people' in the banking hall. Once, when my friends and I were all socialising at the club, he pulled out his bank statement and showed it to a young girl sitting near him. In one of those odd moments of silence that sometimes occur in a noisy crowded place, he loudly asked her, "How does it feel to be sitting next to a millionaire?"

We all found it hysterical.

* * *

I nearly thought that Kenya was going to break up during the crisis over the 2007 election between the Orange Democratic Movement (ODM) and the Party of National Unity (PNU). I did not know how we would solve the situation and did not even imagine a coalition was possible. However, Kenya has a very peculiar way of going so far, up to the brink of disaster, and then turning away.

Tribal clashes are not new. They took place after the 1992 elections and reappeared during other elections. There were no arrests and the clashes were allowed to go on in order to get rid of the Kikuyu vote in the Rift Valley. In 2008, however, it was on a larger scale.

We should not have been caught unprepared when these clashes broke out. Disagreements and aggression were apparent earlier on, yet nothing was done to prevent the escalation of violence. Strangely, the retaliation that followed came as a surprise to those who had started the mayhem. It is hard to believe that no one foresaw this retaliation.

Yet the nation survived.

I would like to make a few observations concerning the running of the government. Some of the current conditions are a shock to me. For example, these days, when minutes of every Cabinet meeting are leaked to the media, I see failure somewhere along the line of authority. Such breaches of secrecy never happened in our time. Ministers take an oath to serve the President and keep state secrets, and are not mandated to leak the details of Cabinet meetings to anyone. Nowadays, it is sad to see that the trust of collective responsibility is broken and ignored and the media reveals the ugly details of quarrelling Cabinet members. It is not supposed to be like that.

This problem arose after President Mwai Kibaki and Prime Minister Raila Odinga decided to form the coalition government. The legislation for the new setup after the 2007 elections debacle was hurried and not well thought out. It was not a serious coalition and it was just cobbled together for political expediency in a time of crisis. Creating the post of Prime Minister was a temporary solution to a difficult situation.

* * *

Everyone has their own ideas of what might be best for Kenya and how we can improve our society and government.

Our first constitution, particularly before it was amended so many times, was perhaps the best that this country could have. If there were sections of that constitution that were obsolete, it would have been far better to look at it as a living document, and amend or add whatever we thought was missing or remove what we thought was inadvisable, as an evolving document rather than just saying it is 'bad'.

As for public morality, discipline and ethics in the public service that I used to know, we were guided by discipline and principles and there were sanctions for those who did not follow those principles or policies. For such a structure to function, it must be respected from the top to the lowest level. If that ethical behaviour is lacking in the public service it affects the whole spectrum of life in the country.

I think the government and many people have discussed this aspect and I believe that was why John Githongo was appointed head of the Department of Ethics.

Whether Githongo was the right or wrong person to occupy the position is not possible for me to know, but the idea of having such a post was a great idea and a person in such a position must be a man or woman of the highest integrity. The system cannot be one-sided – it has to be holistic. Everyone must understand that if they do not follow certain norms, there will be sanctions. Unfortunately, that does not happen anymore. It simply has not materialised.

We were used to such a system during those days when we were training and working in the early civil service. We had a set of rules to follow and someone ensured that we followed them. Whether it was money, or policy, or behaviour, we were expected to follow certain standards and guidelines.

As a matter of practice, minor, seemingly insignificant matters were carefully assessed. We were meticulous, even in trivial issues, in order to avoid giving the impression of compromising ourselves.

In the communities of the past, a culture was followed. For example, if they met on a path, a young person would always give way to an older person. That custom of respect is no longer followed. Discipline of that sort no longer exists. Moreover, it is not only the youth who neglect ethics and culture.

I am at a loss to explain how or why it has happened. I think it requires some sociologist or psychologist to analyse this enormous change.

The first thing that must be understood, to restore a sense of moral values, is that no privileged classes should exist, whoever and wherever they are. There cannot be any single person, whether he is the son of a president or the son of the head of breweries, who is immune from the law.

I think this impunity, this loss of ethics in society, is a disaster for our country. Impunity removes responsibility and accountability from people altogether. For example, in the old days there were primitive ways of controlling people's behaviour through superstition and brutality. Crime and deviance were restrained through fear and curses. Such things may have worked for an unsophisticated and simple society, but these days, no matter how loudly a preacher may talk about evil or devils, people know that nothing will come to haunt them.

Naturally, these methods are inapplicable in the modern day and age, but we can still get the same effect by just and swift punishment through the judicial system. That is to say, if anyone breaks the law, he ought to be punished, without regard to his position or class, taken to court and judged according to the laws.

However, for such a system to work, the courts must be principled, the police must be ethical; everyone involved must be honest and trustworthy. One rotten institution will destroy the whole process.

It is odd that neither Christianity nor Islam seems to have helped us out of this dilemma. Religion itself cannot recreate human beings. People no longer just take things on faith. These days if one tells people that God will be angry and punish them, they will ask "which god?" The God of the Muslims, Catholics, Anglicans, or some other evangelical church? People start analysing situations and come to their own conclusions. Religion *per se* cannot help our current situation.

When I see the kinds of sects and preachers we have these days it makes me ask myself what happened and when and how. Someone who has never gone to church suddenly starts his or her own religion. There are many such preachers who start in a small way and when they see that religion makes money for them, they expand and become commercial. I do not know – maybe God will come and smite all these people. Although I am not religious, I myself would never behave in such an underhanded way. Why do these people do such things – collecting money from the poor and gullible? They get rich and have no shame.

I do not think it is possible to regain integrity easily. It will be a difficult task because society has gone too far to the other side. We have been without public morality and without guiding principles for a long while.

I believe it is possible to change, in fact, we will need to change – we can no longer go on looking at the injustice happening around us and just wonder what we can do about it. Somebody has to believe in something, move forward, and influence other people to evolve a system of guiding principles of morality. There must be a way of reminding people that we have to go back to the basics. We must face this challenge and find victory for the future of Kenya.

ANNEX: Public Statement Issued on 14 May 2012
Setting the record straight on issues at CMC Holdings Ltd.
By Jeremiah Gitau Kiereini

I have served this country in many senior positions; both in the public sector as Chief Secretary, Head of Civil Service and Secretary to the Cabinet, and in the private sector as Director and Chairman of many companies, including East African Breweries Limited, CMC Holdings Ltd and many more.

In a lifetime of dedicated service to the country and the business community, my conduct has always been beyond reproach and following considerable media reports regarding events at CMC Holdings Limited ("the Company" or "CMC"), I now feel compelled to clarify some of the issues raised as follows:

1. *I was at all material times a non-Executive Chairman of the Company. In such capacity, and as is the usual practice, I did not deal with the day-to-day details of accounts and management responsibilities. That was the exclusive preserve of the Chief Executive Officer (CEO) and the management of the Company. I did not at any time own any shares in the Company although a family Company, Kingsway Family Holdings Limited, presently owns 12.5% of the shares of the Company. It's also instructive to note that I am not a Director of the Company, having resigned voluntarily in March 2011. I value and cherish the long and mutually rewarding relationship, which I have had with CMC since 1984.*

2. *I have at all times cooperated, submitted and voluntarily given all material facts truthfully to each and every inquiry or investigation concerning the Company. I appeared before the forensic investigation teams from PricewaterhouseCoopers ("PWC") and Webber Wentzel and duly provided them with all such information as I had pertaining to the Company. My lawyers, duly instructed, also appeared before the ad hoc Committee appointed by the Capital Markets Authority ("CMA") and made representations on my behalf.*

3. *I am, however, dismayed that despite the adverse media reports touching on my integrity, not a single journalist or media house*

has ever sought my comment and/or clarification either directly or through my legal counsel before publishing the highly scandalous allegations. I am therefore constrained to issue this public statement to set the record straight.

4. The former CEO of the Company, Mr Martin Forster, who served the Company for 33 years made a public statement on 28 March 2012 regarding his involvement and assessment of the issues and he exonerated me fully and unconditionally from any dishonesty or wrong doing. Coming from the CEO with whom I worked for many years, this is an important vindication of my integrity and reputation.

5. The explanation and information disclosed to me over the operation of a scheme where commissions from manufacturers (Land-Rover Jaguar and Nissan UD) were retained in a foreign account named Corival (1996) was that the entity was a subsidiary of CMC Holdings and my understanding was that the arrangement was in the best interests of CMC and its employees. It is wrong for any report, be it the PWC Report or the Webber Wentzel Report or any other, to characterise commissions payable by manufacturers as "over invoicing". CMC was, and is entitled to commission payments as standard practice by vehicle manufacturers worldwide. My understanding at all material times was that the Company was receiving commissions, in the ordinary course of business and applying the same as the management deemed to be in the best interests of the Company, its business and employees.

6. The establishment of the Corival bank account was done by Mr. Paul Benzimra, a son of the then CEO, Mr. Jack Benzimra and a Mr. Stanley Lewis.

7. There is absolutely no truth in the allegation that I was party to the establishment of the Fairvalley Trust. I was informed of the existence of this trust by Mr. Jack Benzimra when he was CEO because it had already been established before I joined CMC.

8. As I came to learn subsequently, the Fairvalley Trust received funds from the Corival bank account in good faith basically to optimise CMC interests. It is instructive to note that Mr. Benzimra, Mr. Martin Forster and myself were at various times Directors of CMC, and in that capacity, kept the Trust ongoing securely at all times. If this were not the case, nobody would have known there was such money

and members of CMC management would eventually have lost it, if that had been any part of our plan or intention! I am disappointed that my efforts to preserve and secure Company funds have been misconstrued deliberately and maliciously with a view to tarnishing my reputation and subjecting me to public ridicule.

9. The incumbent Directors, Chairman of the Board and the CEO of the Company bear a similar responsibility and it is my hope and belief that the Trust is still an ongoing viable asset managed to the benefit of past, present and future employees of CMC as per the instrument establishing it.

10. The use of Corival funds to lend money to CMC is true and was based on prudent and strategic considerations. CMC Holdings had borrowed funds from the African Development Bank ("ADB") to finance a new building in Kampala in an effort to keep up with business expansion locally. After about a year, it was realised that the foreign currency loan from ADB was increasingly too expensive in relation to local currency revenues. Thus, the Corival foreign currency account was used to pay off ADB and the funds re-paid to the Corival account by the local unit at a much lower interest rate. I am not aware of any "business model" where the Company borrowed money in order to lend it.

11. On the accusation that the Board appointed a Company Secretary who was not qualified, my understanding was that the position was held by Mr. Shashi Shah, who also served as Finance Director but was qualified as Company Secretary as required by law. Mr. A. I. Musotsi was designated as a 'Minutes Clerk' who merely took minutes and never signed any official document, or minutes as Company Secretary.

12. On the issue of any statutory disclosure on my part, I do not understand how a non-executive member of the Board would communicate with CMA to inform them of non-compliance with the Corporate Governance Guidelines. I believe that such is the duty of the CEO. I also believe that if there was any non-compliance, the external auditors of the company would have brought the matter to the attention of the Board. Let me explain that at all times, every year, we had external auditors who gave us a clean report and never questioned or qualified any of the reports or accounts of the

Company. In the context of the foregoing, one has to appreciate the role of a non-executive Chairman of any Board of Directors. In such position, I was not involved, and neither was I expected to be involved, in the day-to-day running of the Company. The CEO and his management team had been hired to do that and it was not my role to micro-manage them. I appeared in CMC offices only when I had to chair Board meetings, usually once a quarter. For anybody to now allege publicly and sensationally, without a shred of evidence, that I "stole", "looted", "stashed" and "hid" Company funds is the height of irresponsible and unprofessional journalistic practice. I have been defamed in the grossest way possible and my reputation and standing violated irresponsibly but I have retained my calm and composure because as the adage goes, the truth will always come out and prevail.

13. I aver publicly and in utmost good faith, that at all times when I served at CMC (as indeed in all other places at senior public and private positions in my long career), I have always acted responsibly, applied myself diligently and exercised all necessary caution and honesty to preserve the dignity and effective service that has given me a fulfilling life. I fully intend to continue on this path and no amount of mudslinging or vindictive manipulations will deter me from my life-long resolve to render such service as I can to my country and fellow citizens.

14. Finally, it is inaccurate, malicious and a violation of my basic human rights to speculate adversely on my suitability to serve on the board of any company, public or private. My ultimate vindication is my record of diligent and honourable service in both the public and private sectors. That record speaks for itself and will not be tainted by unproven, unsubstantiated and malicious allegations made against me.

15. Similarly, unfounded and malicious allegations driven by speculative and self-serving motives have been made about my family company's shareholding in CMC. We are and shall continue to be committed and steadfast shareholders of the Company regardless of the unfortunate goings-on fuelled by partisan interests, which have no regard for the business interests of the Company. I urge all the parties concerned to put the interests of the Company first and to chart a new course beneficial to the Company, its shareholders and employees.

I therefore reject and condemn in the strongest terms possible the sustained smear campaign against me and my reputation. A lot of the falsehoods, half-truths and defamatory allegations peddled in the media in the recent past concerning me and my role in the Company could have been avoided if any effort had been made to give me a hearing and to convey my side of the story. I am a firm believer in truth, fairness and justice and I do not think it is too much to expect the same from others.

Jeremiah Gitau Kiereini (EBS, EGH)

Index

A
Aggrey, Dr Arthur Kwei 38, 40
Amalemba, Musa 86
Anyona, George 201
Apton, Reverend Roy 212
Arafat, Yasser 1
Askwith, Thomas G. 91, 93
Ayodo, Samuel Onyango 42
Ayubu, Mwangi 29

B
Ball, S. J. 38
Baring, Sir Evelyn 56, 64, 91-92, 102
Barlow, Rev. 28
Base, David 97
Beauttah, James 34
Benzimra, Jack 236-37, 255
Bett, Franklin 203-04
Bockett, Alan 137, 154
Boit, Sila 125
Bottomley, Arthur 83
Breckenridge, Caroline 93
Breckenridge, Major J. B. W. 88, 93, 95-96
Brockway, Fenner 83
Brown, Peter 134
Bull, Mr. A. F. 27

C
Carnoy, Martin 38
Carothers, Dr J. C. 92
Cauri, John Kamau 68, 77-80
Collins, Mr. 97
Cowan, John 88-89
Coward, J. D. 141
Cumber, John 109, 116
Curtis, Arnold 55

D
Dada, General Idi Amin 167-68, 170-72
Davies, H. O. 65
Desai J. M. 83
Dobie, Col. David 236
Doe, Samuel Kanyon 197
Dolimore, Mr. 41
Douglas, Kiereini 219

E
Elkins, Caroline 97, 105, 109
Ellerton, Jeff 156
Erskine, General Sir George 75-6

F
Forster, Mr. Martin 255
Francis, Carey 37, 39-40, 42-3, 45-46, 83

G
Gachathi, Peter 78, 228
Gachukia, Harrison 40
Gakuo, Dr Njuguna 67
Gathigira, Henry Kiama 40
Gavaghan, Terence 89, 97-100, 109
Gethi, Ben 160, 193-95, 198-99, 200-02, 206, 215
Gethoi, Mutu wa 198, 225
Gichoya 131
Gichuru, James 39, 57, 141, 147, 161-62
Gikaru, Eliud 29
Gikera 4
Gikonyo, Betty vi
Gikonyo, Muchohi 47
Gioko, Njega wa 113-14
Gitau (grand-son) v, 219
Gitau, Joan 42, 50

Githae, Kiereini xi, 219
Githongo, John 251
Griffiths, James 57

H
Halsey, William (Bill) 98
Hamduni 52
Hinga, Bernard 160
Hinga, Waiyaki wa 169
Hodge, Donald 116
Hoyt, Elizabeth 53

I
Itote, Waruhiu (aka General China) 74
Itotia, Dr James Njoroge 225

J
Jones, Griffiths 156
Jones, Prof. Thomas Jesse 38
Josiah, Ezekiel 122, 126
Josiah, Sam 125

K
Kaggia, Bildad vi, 63-4
Kahangara, Chief Luka 74-5
Kamau, Waira 59-63, 65-6, 86, 156, 163-64
Kamba, John 68, 77, 83
Kamotho, John Joseph 214
Kang'ethe, Joseph 34
Kanyotu, James 193, 198, 201
Kapila, Achroo 65
Karago, Douglas Njiiri 68-9, 77-8, 80, 126, 154, 237
Karanja, Josephat Njuguna 29, 36, 52
Karengo, Wahome xi
Kariithi, Geoffrey 29, 126, 162, 179, 183-85, 216-17, 224-25
Kariithi, Geoffrey Karekia 122

Kariuki, Geoffrey Gitahi (also GG Kariuki) vi, 54, 179, 209
Kariuki, J. M. vi, 90
Kariuki, Joseph 50
Kariuki, Peter Mwagiru 191-93, 199
Karumba, Kung'u 64
Karume, Njenga vi, 159, 178, 239
Keen, John 41
Kenyatta, Margaret 42
Kenyatta, Mzee Jomo xi, xv, 56-60, 64-5, 69, 90, 92-3, 111, 125, 132-35, 141-47, 150, 153, 156-58, 161-64, 166-69, 176-85, 194, 202, 204, 206, 208, 211, 217, 232
Khan, Genghis 49
Kiama, Stanley Gathigira 28
Kiano, Dr Julius Gikonyo 117, 182
Kibaki, Mwai 51, 119, 136, 182, 195, 204, 209, 251
Kibathi, Wilson Gitangu 85
Kibe, Joe 129
Kibuga, Munene 131
Kiereini, Douglas 126, 137, 218-19
Kiereini, Eunice Muringo v, xi, 219
Kiereini, John Kirika 29
Kiereini, Mumbi xi, 126, 137, 218-19
Kiereini, Steven (nephew) 29
Kihara, Paul 177
Kihuria, John Njonjo xi
Kimani, Edward Kariuki wa 159-60
Kimathi, Field Marshall Dedan Waciuri 74, 104, 163
Kimuri, Gitau wa 36
King, Martin Luther (Junior) 1
King'ori, Loise Gakenia xi
Kioni, Stephen 54
Kipkorir, Benjamin Edgar vi
Kirika, Nahashon (step-brother) 3, 21
Koinange, Joe 29, 184, 198

Koinange, Mbiyu 60, 161, 178
Koinange, Senior Chief 60, 92, 112
Kubai, Fred 47, 59, 63-4
Kung'u, Senior Chief Waruhiu wa 64

L
Lall, Chaman 65
Leakey, Canon 92-3
Leakey, L. S. B. 92
Lewis, Mr. Stanley 255
Likimani, Muthoni vi
Lloyd, Frank 109, 130
Lockhart, Rev. Richard Arthur 29, 46

M
MacDonald, Governor 142
Macharia, Mwangi 48
Macharia, Rawson 65
Machere, Steven 130
Mackay, Prof. Collins B. 213-14
Mackenzie, Bruce 123
Madan, Chunilal B. 208
Magugu, Arthur 233
Mahihu, Eliud 151
Mahinda, Gerald 245
Maina, Charles 172
Makanga, Bernard 130
Malechela, John 52
Malinda, John 125, 151
Malmqvist, Emma xi
Marai, David Mugo 29, 36, 43
Marai, Gakure wa 1-3, 13-14
Marai, Mugo 13-14, 29, 36,
Marshall, Thurgood 65
Martin, Bill 41
Martin, Mr. Bill Kimutai 224
Masika, Neville D. xi
Mathaai, Prof. Wangari vi
Mathenge, Isaiah Mwai 85, 106
Mathenge, Stanley 74

Mathews, John St. 116
Mathu, Eliud 39
Mati, Fred 179
Matiba, Kenneth Njindo 137, 248
Maudling, Richard 83
Mbogo, Archie 151
Mbotela, James 27
Mbotela, Leonard Mambo 196
Mbotela, Walter 59
Mboya, Thomas Joseph 57, 82-83, 106, 139, 175
Mburu, Kiereini v, 219, 246
McGill, Father 46
McGuiness, Mr. 95, 97
Michuki, John Njoroge 119, 125, 177-78
Miller, Cecil 208
Mitchell, Sir Philip Euen 47, 56, 58
Mohammed, General Mahmood 196-97
Moi, Daniel arap vi, 54, 119, 134, 142, 153, 158, 162, 170, 173, 175-77, 179, 181-83, 185-89, 193, 195, 197-98, 201-212, 214-17, 226, 229, 234
Mugabe, Robert Gabriel 147
Mugambi, Joe 54
Mugo, Jeremiah 3, 18, 70
Mugo, Micere xi
Mugo, Mukwa- 42
Mugo, Ngugi wa 23
Muhoho, Peter 27
Muigai, Githu xiii
Mulinge, Jackson 167-69, 192-93
Muliro, Joseph 129
Muliro, Masinde 142
Mungai, Prof. Joseph vi, 214
Munyiri, Chief Kombo 113-14
Murgor, Charles 157-59
Musau, Harrison 195
Musembi, Joseph 125
Musotsi, Mr. A.I. 257

Index

Muthoni, Isabella 42
Mutiga, Moses 125, 135
Muturi, Harun 160-61
Mviti, Godfrey 29
Mwakitawa, John 225
Mwande, Aloys 26
Mwangale, Elijah Wasike 205-06
Mwendwa, Kitili 137, 168

N
Namaisa 220
Namu, David 199
Ndegwa 70
Ndegwa, Duncan vi, 29, 134, 137, 151, 155-59, 177-78, 183, 216, 224, 236, 248
Ndegwa, Philip 240
Nderi, Ignatius Iriga 65, 160
Ndolo, Major General J. M. 166-170, 174
Nesbit, James 41
Neville Judge 135
Ngacha, Mwalimu David wa Ng'endo 229
Ngala, Ronald 77, 82, 133, 141-42
Ngei, Paul Joseph 64
Ng'eno, Jonathan 214
Nguri, Jotham 130
Ng'weno, Hillary 215
Njanja (step-mother) 3, 12
Njenga, James 211-13
Njeri 220
Njeri, Elizabeth (Beth) 3, 9, 18
Njeri, Esther 79-80, 85, 126, 218
Njeru 193
Njinu, Bernard Kiarie 201
Njonjo, Charles Mugane 156-61, 173, 179, 181, 185-86, 195, 200, 206, 207-09, 216, 219

Njoroge, Zakayo 3, 7, 10, 12-15, 18-20, 31, 227
Njuguna, Gitau wa 2
Njuhi (mother) 2, 10
Njuhi, Caroline 219
Ntimama, William ole 122
Nugi, Joe Mwega xi
Nyachae, Simeon vi, 129, 185, 217
Nyagah, Jeremiah 230
Nyahe, David 68-69
Nyamu, Habel 151
Nyerere, Julius Kambarage 172-73

O
Obote, Milton 167, 172
Obuon, Joseph Ogidi 191, 199
Ochuka, Hezekiah 191, 196-97, 199
Odinga, Jaramogi Oginga vi, 137, 139, 142, 145
Odinga, Raila Amolo vi, 201, 251
Oduor-Otieno, Dr Martin vi
Ohanga, B.A. 86
Ojal, J. M. 39
Okero, Omolo 52
Okondo, Peter Habenga 190
Okumu, Pancras Oteyo 191, 196-97, 199
Okwiri, Isaac 122
O'Loughlin, Jimmy 211
Omino, Joab 230
Oneko, Achieng' 64
Oranga, Peter 125
Orengo, James Aggrey Bob 201
Otieno, Wambui vii
Ottaway, V. A. 27
Owuor, Effie 208
Oyugi, Hezekiah 201

P
Panjabi, Mr. 68
Pant, Apa 67, 73

Patel, D. L. 68
Pinto, Pio Gama 83, 106
Potter, Henry 58, 64
Pritt, Denis 65, 69

R
Rainor, Bill 135
Ruriga, Chief Njagi 130

S
Saidimu 220
Sam 20
Sandys, (Colonial Secretary) Duncan 136
Sawe, General John 193
Schilling, Donald 38
Shah, Shashi 256
Shako, Juxton 122, 126
Sheth, Nanalal 237
Shiyuka, Peter 119, 125, 224
Singh, Harban (Associates) 220
Singh, Jaswant 65
Somerhough, Anthony 65
Souza, Fitz de 65, 142
Swynnerton, Roger 110-12, 117, 119

T
Templer, Sir Gerald 91
Thande, Kariuki 162
Thangwa, Kuria Mungai wa 69

Thiong'o, Ngugi wa vi
Thuku, Harry 9, 34, 169
Tipis, Justus K ole 134
Towett, Taita 134
Tshombe, Moise 125, 134

W
Wabera, Daudi 125, 136
Wainaina, Eddie 225
Wairago, John Mubia 225
Waiyaki, Mugo 43
Wambui (daughter-in-law) v, 219
Wambui (step-sister) 3
Wambui, Rose 126, 137, 218-19
Wamwere, Koigi wa 201
Wango'mbe, Chief Nderi 65
Wanjama 78
Wanjigi, Maina 30
Wanyutu, Waweru 86
Waruhiu, George 178
Waruhiu, Sam 248
Waweru, Chief Magugu 86
Whyatt, Sir John 109
Wicks, Sir James 179
Wilson, Bob 122-23, 129
Wilson, Dick 98, 109
Woodley, Alderman 47